The Meaning of Everything

The Story of the Oxford English Dictionary

Sir James Murray, academic cap firmly in place as a symbol both of his authority and his dedication to lexical scholarship, at his desk in the gloom of his Scriptorium, with tens of thousands of quotation slips jammed into the wooden pigeon-holes that covered every vertical surface of the building.

The Meaning of Everything

The Story of the Oxford English Dictionary

Simon Winchester

OXFORD
UNIVERSITY PRESS

OXFORD

UNIVERSITY PRESS

Great Clarendon Street, Oxford OX2 6DP

Oxford University Press is a department of the University of Oxford.
It furthers the University's objective of excellence in research, scholarship,
and education by publishing worldwide in

Oxford New York

Auckland Bangkok Buenos Aires Cape Town Chennai
Dar es Salaam Delhi Hong Kong Istanbul Karachi Kolkata
Kuala Lumpur Madrid Melbourne Mexico City Mumbai Nairobi
São Paulo Shanghai Taipei Tokyo Toronto

Oxford is a registered trade mark of Oxford University Press
in the UK and in certain other countries

Published in the United States
by Oxford University Press Inc., New York

© Simon Winchester 2003

Database right Oxford University Press (maker)

First published by Oxford University Press 2003

British Library Cataloguing in Publication Data

Data available

Library of Congress Cataloging in Publication Data

Data available

ISBN 0-19-860702-4

1 3 5 7 9 10 8 6 4 2

Typeset in Pondicherry, India, by
Alliance Interactive Technology
Printed in the United States of America

In memory of Jenny McMorris
A great friend to the OED
And of us all.

Also by Simon Winchester

Contents

Acknowledgements

The idea that I should write this book came first from Alysoun Owen, an editor at Oxford University Press who had once read *The Surgeon of Crowthorne* and put it to me that since in that story I had written what was essentially a footnote to history, would I now care to try writing the history itself? It seemed a splendid idea, and it would have made for a pleasing symmetry to deliver the manuscript to Alysoun in due course—but for the fact that she took off on maternity leave shortly after I had begun work on the book. She was succeeded by the admirably competent Rebecca Collins, to whom I am extremely grateful; but since this book was in essence Alysoun's idea, I owe her a very great deal for first getting me involved in what turned out to be the most enjoyable of tasks.

Enjoyable and stimulating though the work may have been, its complexities would have tried me sorely had not Elizabeth Knowles—an old OUP friend with whom I have been in touch ever since she advised me on early drafts of the W. C. Minor story—agreed to help with the telling of this tale also. She advised me both on the book's overall tone and structure, and on the finer details relating to lexicography and etymology. Philip Durkin, an expert on etymology and a philologist at the *OED*, was most helpful in navigating the minefields of Chapter 1, and worked with Elizabeth on such vexing matters as the supposed origins of words like *periwinkle*, *skirt*, and *ketchup*.

It is to Peter Gilliver, a senior lexicographer at the *OED*, that I owe perhaps the greatest debt. Peter's eternal enthusiasm for the

Dictionary and its makers, and his fascination with the eccentricities of its making, should by rights have led him to write this book himself. But his current continuing work on the *OED*'s third edition is an all-absorbing task, and that Peter felt able to step aside from these private ambitions to help me—by illuminating the unlit nooks and crannies of the story, and by digging out stories of age-old lexicographical conundrums that made the telling of this story such fun—is something for which I will always be grateful.

Martin Maw, the OUP Archivist, was helpful and hospitable in equal measure. No request, whether for a long-forgotten picture or a long-lost quotation slip, ever managed to fox him, and he responded to my Ypres-like barrage of queries and demands with endlessly good cheer. It is to his former colleague Jenny McMorris that this book is dedicated: we all miss her greatly, but few more so than Martin, and I hope that he will infer from the dedication my gratitude to the OUP archives team more generally, even though, of course, we all wish to memorialize Jenny in person.

Madeline Kripke kindly copied many rare papers and documents from her immense collection of dictionaryalia, and offered much sage advice.

I am grateful to Robert Faber at the *Oxford Dictionary of National Biography* for asking contributors involved in preparing *OED*-related essays to let me see, in advance, some of what they had written; this was a favour that proved to be a very great help.

Sarah Barrett copy-edited the manuscript from her Somerset home, and did so with speed, finesse, and great charm; and Carolyn Garwes prepared the index.

My London agent Bill Hamilton, of A. M. Heath, dealt with the very particular publishing idiosyncrasies of so venerable a firm as OUP; and Peter Matson, of my New York agent Sterling Lord Literistic, was unfailingly helpful and supportive over such fascinating complications as made it across the Atlantic. Also in New

York I am especially grateful to my long-time friend Casper Grathwohl of OUP for his wise counsel during the editing and publishing process.

As so often, I owe a great deal to my son Rupert Winchester, who worked tirelessly at the OUP archives, and at the London Library, through all stages of the making of this book. He is the stuff of which any father would be most proud.

I wrote this book in a little barn on my farm in Massachusetts during what turned out to be one of the wildest, coldest, and darkest of New England winters in living memory. But I was kept warm and content through it all by my partner Elaine, and it is a tribute to her determination, support, and comforting kindness that this book was finished, on time, with both of us looking happily back at a winter exceedingly well spent.

S.B.A.W.
Sandisfield
June 2003

List of Illustrations

The Meaning of Everything

The Story of the Oxford English Dictionary

Prologue

T he culminating celebrations of what was to be called 'the greatest enterprise of its kind in history' took place in 1928—and on Wednesday 6 June of that year, the date when this majestic phrase was first spoken, in England it was Derby Day.

A great horse race on a sunny afternoon tends always to bring out the best in people, and it is probably fair to say that the concern of most in England that summer's day was not so much with historical enterprises, however great or small they might have been, but rather more prosaically with whether to 'have a flutter'—whether to back the Epsom favourite, that morning a horse called Fairway, or whether to risk a tanner, a shilling, or half a crown on a rank outsider called Felstead, on whom the bookies were offering tempting odds of 40 to one.

The prosaic concerns of the people suggest the placid temper of the time. With Europe and the world beyond generally at peace and with a fair measure of prosperity all around, a good number of those living in the British Isles, where this story both begins and ends, do appear to have been in an appropriately summery and congenial mood that day. And the weather certainly helped: the forecasters in London recorded this first Wednesday in June as having been, after an early cool dew-crispness, both nicely sunny and shirtsleeve warm, the islands basking beneath an anticyclone anchored benevolently over the Western Approaches.

All England, it is probably fair to say, languished that day in the careless blue-skies rapture of early summer, with little but pleasure—the 148th running of the Derby foremost among them—on the nation's horizons. True, there were a few small smudges of cloud to spoil the idyll. There was an outbreak of smallpox in Wandsworth, and it seemed, rather ominously, to be spreading. A Romanian woman was arrested on the Old Kent Road for trying to evade paying duty on a consignment of watches and artificial silk handbags. And in central London, a needle-woman and a dispatch clerk—neither a trade that would be formally recognized today—were found dead in Hyde Park, with neck wounds suggesting that at least one of the pair had succumbed to what the newspapers darkly referred to as *felo de se*, the archaic legal phrase then much used by the polite for the indelicate crime of suicide.

But these trifling domestic disturbances aside, about the most surprising news of that June morning revealed that only two transatlantic telephone calls had thus far been placed from the entire city of Manchester during the first six months of the year. Not that interest in North American matters was by any means slight: many in England were captivated that summer by the news of Miss Amelia Earhart, a lady from Kansas who was waiting none too patiently at an aerodrome in Halifax, Nova Scotia, for a doggedly persistent bank of fog to clear away. When it finally did so, she was flown in a small aircraft across the ocean to an airfield near Cardiff in south Wales, a 3,000-mile journey that propelled her to fame as the first woman *aviatrix*—the word was brand new, having first appeared in a newspaper only nine months before—

ever to make a crossing of the Atlantic. (If she had admirers in Manchester it may well have turned out—history does not record—that some of them telephoned the news of her arrival to friends far away, thereby reversing the city's curious and brief reputation for isolationism.)

If these were rather carefree and prosperous times, for very many they were also cultured and learned times besides. Since the story that follows concerns the crafting of a monumental intellectual enterprise, it is perhaps worth recalling just how very well educated people in fact were in those days—or at least to recall how very well educated the educated classes were, for this (like it or not) is a tale of a leisured undertaking that is necessarily and intimately involved with the complexities of British social stratification. The project whose completion was celebrated on this Derby Day was one that had taken much time and much learning—and many will say that it was undertaken, and completed, and duly celebrated, mainly because people, or people of a certain kind in the Britain of the day, were quite simply possessed of much time and much learning, and in far greater abundance than many like people possess it today.

Items from the newspapers of the time hint at the almost incidental, quite casual cleverness of the cleverest of the reading public. An illustration of the kind of thing appears that day in the 'Telegrams in Brief' section of *The Times*, in which it reports, without explanation or adornment, that:

> *Further hostilities are reported between the Zaranik tribe and the forces of the Zaidi Imam Yahya of Sana'. The Zaranik attacked a Zaidi detachment at Mansuria, near Hodeida, and have been plundering caravans trading with Sana'.*

No further details are offered to suggest where all this fighting was (Yemen, one imagines), nor of the identities of the parties to the feud. The newspaper's editor presumes that readers, quite simply, had sufficient education to know.

And by and large, newspaper editors in London were probably right in making assumptions like these. The English establishment of the day may be rightly derided at this remove as having been class-ridden and imperialist, bombastic and blimpish, racist and insouciant—but it was marked undeniably also by a sweeping erudition and confidence, and it was peopled by men and women who felt they were able to know all, to understand much, and in consequence to radiate the wisdom of deep learning. It is worth pointing this out simply because it was such people—such remarkable, polymathic, cultured, fascinated, wise, and leisured people—who were primarily involved in the creation of the mighty endeavour that the following account celebrates.

On that idyllic and blissfully warm Derby Day evening, two magnificent social events were due to be staged, at the beating heart of the nation's social life. Up in London—it was always Up, except for those who lived in Oxford, who regarded going everywhere else as Going Down—Prince George's older brother, Edward, the very Prince of Wales who would in time become king and then abandon his throne for his love of a Baltimore divorcée—would preside that evening over one of them, the year's official Derby Ball held at the Mayfair Hotel.

This was a very grand dance indeed—a party that would attract only the great and the good, the nation's A list, men and women from the very finest of the county families all kitted out in the fullest of full fig, with all available medals and miniatures and sashes and Orders to be worn with flash and abandon, and with the unassailable wealth of the landed classes on shameless show. The Earl of Derby's great race (which, it turned out, the rank outsider Felstead did indeed win, to the amusement of the attending King and Queen, to the bookies' great chagrin, to some punters' great joy, and to the humiliation of a crestfallen *Times* racing correspondent, who had predicted quite otherwise) was the grandest fête staged each year for those able to afford what was still called 'the sport of kings': those who attended the ball that followed the race whirled like stately dervishes until three, when dawn came up in all its brief midsummer eagerness.

But it was the other event of that Wednesday that more particularly concerns this story. It was a dinner, and it was as formal in its own way as the ball in Mayfair, except that it took place not among the fashionable *demi-monde* of the West End but in the more cerebrally active neighbourhood of the City of London. Specifically, it began at eight o'clock sharp, in Philip Hardwick's grand faux-Palladian palace just by St Paul's Cathedral, and known as the Goldsmiths' Hall.

On this very site those who worked in and with gold—for centuries known as members of the Worshipful Company of Goldsmiths, the fifth most senior of the twelve original livery companies of London—had practised the mysteries of their craft since the fourteenth century. The hall was then employed, as it still is today, as the London Office of Assay, where precious metals are measured for their purity and value. Its grandest room is the Livery Hall, which seats 200 among pillars and portraits and beneath a vast array of chandeliers and tracery. And it was there, on 6 June 1928, that the company's Prime Warden, the renowned crystallographer Professor Sir William Jackson Pope, formally staged the celebration that both begins and ends this story.

It was a dinner for 150—all of them men, one feels slightly shamed to note today—each one of whom was monumentally distinguished in achievement and standing. If the Derby Ball attracted the nation's richest and most glittering, then the Goldsmiths' Hall that evening attracted the nation's brightest and most wise—a stellar gathering of intellect, rarely either assembled or able to be assembled since.

There were two bishops, three vice-chancellors, a dozen peers of the realm (including the Earls of Birkenhead, Elgin, Harrowby, and Crawford & Balcarres, the Viscount Devonport, the Lords Aldenham, Blanesburgh, Cecil, Percy, Queenborough, Wargrave, and Warrington of Clyffe), 27 knights of the realm (among them Sir Ernest Rutherford, splitter of atoms; Sir Arthur Quiller-Couch, Cornishman and editor—under the pseudonym 'Q'—of the then best-known of poetry anthologies; Sir Henry Newbolt, whose imperially minded, patriotically inspired poetry was known to every jingoist in the land; Sir Gerald Lenox-Conyngham, inventor, Triangulator and Surveyor of India, and first-ever Cambridge Reader in Geodesy; Sir Owen Seaman, the noted satirist, *Punch* editor and parodist who also 'set great store by social activities, shot and swam well and had been Captain of Clare boats'; and Sir Charles Oman, who, despite being 'in no sense a thinker', held the Chichele Chair in History at Oxford, was a world-renowned numismatist, and wrote screeds of fascinations about Domesday Book).

As if these ennobled and honoured figures were not sufficient, there were also twenty professors (one of them, listed simply as J. R. Tolkien, would go on—with an additional initial R—to worldwide fame as the fantasist inventor of Hobbits and Gollum and the Lord of the Rings), any number of generals and colonels and half-colonels, as well as printers, headmasters, college presidents and deans and wardens in monstrous abundance. There were also eight of the capital's leading journalists. Those newspapermen on one side of the central table found themselves sitting sandwiched between Sir Archibald Garrod, the nation's leading authority on diseases of the joints, and a Great War historian (and biographer of Wellington) named C. R. M. F. Cruttwell. On the far side, their colleagues were book-ended by Brigadier-General Sir Harold Hartley, CBE, MC, FRS, a chemical engineer who in 1928 predicted that the world's population in 2000 would be three billion (it turned out in fact to become twice that), and by one F. S. Boas, an expert on Elizabethan manuscripts. One supposes the newspapermen probably talked mostly among themselves.

The diners were well looked after by the Goldsmiths: they feasted on caviar and smoked salmon, clear turtle soup, saddle of lamb or quail, Muscat salad, York ham, asparagus, chilled fruit mousse, and Italian biscuits. The wine list was fairly impressive too: the men began with a Vino de Pasto sherry, then took a 1917 Pommery & Greno champagne and a 1900 Grafenberg-Auslese hock, then a very much more popular wine than now; they next drank a 1907 Chateau Margaux with their lamb (or a Grand Musigny of 1911 if they preferred the quail); and they finished with either Fine Old East India Madeira or, carefully decanted by the Livery Hall footmen, an 1896 Crofts port.

And it was with one of these two latter ancient and fortified wines that the diners were to raise their glasses for the toasts—for indeed, it was the toasts, rather than the dinner, for which they were all attending.

There were four of them. The first two were formalities only—toastmasters appeared from behind the arras to propose that the Church and His Majesty the King be offered the salutations of the assembled, and in short order thereafter similar good wishes were offered to Her Majesty the Queen, the Prince of Wales (by then presumably dancing his Derby evening away a mile away at the Mayfair Hotel), and the other members of the royal family. It was then announced that, royalty having been suitably recognized, those who wished might now smoke.

And then, as glasses were clinked, cigars were lit and lucifers put away, chairs pushed back from the long tables, and a hush was demanded, so from the centre of the high table rose the slightly less than commanding figure of the celebration dinner's most celebrated guest, the Right Honourable Stanley Baldwin, PC, MP, the nation's three-term Conservative Prime Minister.

Perhaps no political leader or statesman in British history could have been better suited to the task that lay at hand. Baldwin, the calm, taciturn, steady, unadventurous, pipe-smoking son of a Worcestershire ironmaster, a figure of elaborated ordinariness—and a cousin of Rudyard Kipling—was both extraordinarily well-read (though his history degree from Cambridge was modest) and inextinguishably proud of being a sturdily provincial Englishman. 'I speak', he once wrote, 'not as the man in the street, but as the man in the field-path, a much simpler person, steeped in tradition and impervious to new ideas.'

A colleague assessed Baldwin rather more acutely, in writing specifically of how this then 61-year-old politician saw his role as the nation's elected leader.

> *Above all he must be patriotic; a lover of his fellow-countrymen, of his country's history, of its institutions, its ancient monarchy, its great parliamentary traditions, its fairness, its tolerance.*
>
> *All these things were innate in his own disposition. But he steeped himself in them, as the part which it was his duty to play as Prime Minister, and they became more deeply ingrained in consequence.*

It was thus in part Stanley Baldwin the actor—a man whose radio-ideal voice was said to be 'delightfully modulated' and who was known for taking the greatest of care in selecting the words he spoke—who rose before his quietening audience. He was to deliver a speech which, if by no means the most important of his long career, must surely have been one of the most pleasurable, both to utter and to hear.

He was there for no less a task than to propose a formal Toast of Gratitude and Admiration to the Editors and Staff of what was to be formally and unforgettably called *The Oxford English Dictionary*—for the twelve mighty tombstone-sized volumes were now, and after 70 long years of terrible labour, fully and finally complete. The first two sets had been made and formally presented: one had gone to King George V, the other to the American President, Calvin Coolidge. Downing Street had been obliged to purchase its own official set for Mr Baldwin—and rarely, he later said, did a day go by when he did not consult it.

In 15,490 pages of single-spaced printed text, and at long, long last, all 414,825 words that the then Editor-in-Chief, Professor Sir William Craigie—this Derby Day newly knighted, and newly blessed with an honorary degree (which Oxford had bestowed on him the day before) and now positively beaming with pride from his place to the Prime Minister's left—all the words which Sir William and his colleagues had amassed and catalogued and listed and annotated and which were thus far in their sum reckoned to make up all that was then known of the English language, had now been fully and properly defined, their preferred and variant and obsolete spellings all listed, their etymologies all recorded, their pronunciations suggested, required, or demanded.

There were in addition no fewer than 1,827,306 illustrative quotations listed—selected from five million offered by thousands of volunteer readers and literary woolgatherers—that showed just how and when the uses and senses and meanings of all of these words had begun and evolved and then, in the nature of the English language, had steadily and ineluctably reshaped and reworked themselves. These were essential: the millions of words from these quotations offer up countless examples of exactly how the language worked over the centuries of its employment, and by their use they mark the *OED* out as the finest dictionary ever made in any language, and made, as it happens, of the language that is the most important in the world, and probably will be for all time.

And the work that was unveiled during that glittering Goldsmiths' summer evening was not simply magnificent in its unrelenting scholarship: it was almost unbelievably big—fat, heavy, shelf-bendingly huge—as a monument to the labour of those who fashioned it. A total of 227,779,589 letters and numbers, occupying fully 178 miles of type, had over the 70 years just now ended been corralled into place between the thick blue or red morocco covers of the first editions of this unanswerably monumental book.

Dr Craigie and his staff—and the memories of many who had not lived to see their project finished, not the least of these being the great James Murray and Henry Bradley, whose names will deservedly be rather more intimately connected than is Craigie's with the making of the Dictionary—were all there to bask in their rightly earned glory, and to accept the gratitude of a grateful nation. And Mr Baldwin, more fully aware than most of the special significance of his task, rose to the occasion with an eloquence quite suited to the moment. It was a long speech—though read today, so many decades after its delivery, it seems fresh and interesting and not at all tedious—and there is much to savour in it. Most of all, its closing paragraphs.

> *Lord Oxford once said that if he were cast on a desert island, and could only choose one author for company, he would have the forty volumes of Balzac.*
>
> *I choose the Dictionary every time. Like Ezekiel in the valley of dry bones, I should pray for the four winds to breathe upon those words, that they might emerge and stand upon their feet an exceeding great army. Our histories, our novels, our poems, our plays—they are all in this one book. I could live with your Dictionary, Dr Craigie. I choose it, and I think that my choice would*

be justified. It is a work of endless fascination. It is true that I have not read it—perhaps I never shall—but that does not mean that I do not often go to it.

Let me remind you of those words which Dr Johnson used in his famous Preface about translators in his time, and which I think are apt today: 'If the changes that we fear be thus irresistible … it remains that we retard what we cannot repel; that we palliate what we cannot cure. Life may be lengthened by care, though death cannot be ultimately defeated; tongues, like Governments, have a natural tendency to degeneration; we have long preserved our constitution; let us make some struggle for our language.'

It is in that great spirit of devotion to our language as the great and noble instrument of our national life and literature that the editors and the staff of the Oxford Dictionary have laboured. They have laboured so well that, so far from lowering the standard with which the work began, they have sought to raise it as the work advanced. They have given us of their best. There can be no worldly recompense—except that every man and woman in this country whose gratitude and respect is worth having, will rise up and call you blessed for this great work. The Oxford English Dictionary *is the greatest enterprise of its kind in history.*

And all that was most suitably and appositely said by the Prime Minister on what the newspapers reported the following morning had been, for a thousand other reasons too, one of the happiest of Derby Days of all time. It was the conclusion of a story that properly began on a chill and foggy winter's evening almost 71 years before: the story that is told in the pages that follow.

Picture Acknowledgements

The publisher wishes to thank the following who have kindly given permission to reproduce illustrations. Page numbers in parenthesis show the placement of the illustrations in the text. All items belonging to OUP are reprinted with the permission of the Secretary to the Delegates of the Press.

Murray in the Scriptorium (frontispiece) by courtesy of the National Portrait Gallery, London; Richard Chenevix Trench (48) Hulton Archive; Herbert Coleridge (51) OUP; Frederick Furnivall (60) Hulton Archive; Frederick Furnivall with rowing eight (62) Hulton Archive; Scriptorium at Mill Hill (106) OUP; Appeal to Readers (108) OUP; Slips for 'mechanical' (113–14) OUP; Benjamin Jowett (122) by courtesy of the National Portrait Gallery, London; A proofed page from the first fascicle (125) OUP; James C. Gilbert (126) OUP; Henry Hucks Gibbs (130) by courtesy of John Murray; The first fascicle (139) OUP; Henry Bradley (151) OUP; Scriptorium at Banbury Road (165) OUP; Inside the Old Ashmolean (177) OUP; Fitzedward Hall (191) by courtesy of John Murray; W. C. Minor (195) by courtesy of John A. Minor; Charles Onions (203) OUP; William Craigie (204) OUP; J. R. R. Tolkien (207) Haywood Magee / Hulton Archive; James Murray with daughters *c*.1915 (228) OUP; Ten-volume set of the *OED* (232) OUP; Robert Burchfield (245) OUP.

Picture research by Sandra Assersohn.
Thanks also to Rupert Winchester, Martin Maw, OUP Archivist, and Peter Gilliver, Associate Editor for the *OED*.

I

Taking the Measure of It All

The English Dictionary, like the English Constitution, is the creation of no one man, and of no one age; it is a growth that has slowly developed itself adown the ages; its beginnings lie far back in times almost pre-historic. And these beginnings themselves, although the English Dictionary of today is lineally developed from them, were neither Dictionaries, nor even English.

(James Murray, 'The Evolution of English Lexicography', 1900)

1. The Making

The English language—so vast, so sprawling, so wonderfully unwieldy, so subtle, and now in its never-ending fullness so undeniably magnificent—is in its essence the language of invasion. It was always bound to be so: geology and oceanography saw to it that the British Isles, since long before their populated time, were indeed almost always islands, and the ancestors of all who ever lived there first arrived by sea from beyond, bringing with them their customs, their looks—and their languages.

Of the gigantic amassment of words that make up the stock of the English language—the 414,825 that were discerned and discovered and catalogued in time for publication in 1928 of the first edition of the great Dictionary that is the subject of this story, the hundreds of thousands that had already been listed in Webster's wildly successful American dictionary, together with the scores of thousands that have been found or created in the decades since—the huge majority were conceived or otherwise made whole through the good offices of outsiders, visitors, or invaders.

Of those settlers about whose language we know something, the Celts—who came from gloomy forests and swamps in the upper valleys of the Danube—are generally counted as the first. They swarmed westwards across Europe some time during the Bronze Age; about 500 years before the birth of Christ they settled themselves, among other places, on the cliff-protected fortress of the rainy and foggy islands that lay off the continent's north-western shores. Those that settled in the generally more climatically benign southern half of the islands called themselves Britons—a name from which in time was to come the British Isles, and, indeed, Britain.

Here they created for themselves some kind of home and civilization, and they spoke languages that have left precious little trace on modern English, but which are preserved as the basis of such Welsh, Cornish, Scots Gaelic, and Irish as is still spoken today. There are a very few words—*brock*, for badger being one, *combe*, meaning a deep valley, and which appears in some English village names and in contemporary Welsh, another, *torr*, a mountain peak—which seem to have survived, at least among those who speak preciously or somewhat pedantically today. Some Celtic place names—*London*, *Dover*, and *Kent*, the rivers *Thames*, *Exe*, and *Wye*—exist today as well. Late in their history the Celts borrowed—probably; there is still debate among etymologists—a small number of words, such as *assen* for ass and maybe the word *cross*, from visiting Christian missionaries. But generally their linguistic role in the speech and writings of future English generations was fairly minimal; shortly after the beginning of the Christian era any idea that Celtic British might have a long-term linguistic influence was brushed aside: thousands of well-armoured and tactically adept legionnaires swept ashore and, before the language had the chance properly to take hold, promptly placed all south Britain under the colonial suzerainty of Rome.

The Romans remained in Britain for the next 400 years. By the time they left in AD 409, to attend (in vain) to the fate of their fast-crumbling Western Empire in Europe (Rome would be sacked by the Huns a year later, and the Empire would die after only seventy more), Britain had been under their military and cultural influence for very nearly the same amount of time as separates us today from the Renaissance. The Romans did leave something of an imperial linguistic legacy: by the time the next flotilla of invaders reached the shingle beaches of what is now East Anglia, a language had already taken root in the southern isles of the British archipelago that was a mixture, on the one hand, of the early Celtic dialects (or British, as some might call it) and, on the other, of that language which many English schoolchildren would recognize all too glumly as that still used today in texts like Caesar's *Civil War, Book Two*.

The Latin-based hybrid tongue of the Roman-Britons that, had it remained unsullied by what happened next, might well one day have stood alone as the language of the islands, then dominated. In all but the most remote mountain valleys of Wales and Cumberland, and in those still more isolated Scottish glens where the much-feared and wildly painted Picts held sway, a form of language that would have been understood both by the subject natives and by the governors and legates who directed them and the soldiers who policed them was widely spoken. Had the events of the fifth and sixth centuries never taken place, Britain's linguistic evolution might have been much the same as that which was

3

suffered or enjoyed by the similarly Roman-colonized peoples of Spain or France.

But in fact it was all to turn out very differently—and that was because, in the middle of the fifth century, the longboats of a score of entirely new and unanticipated invaders and settlers slid up from the east onto the beaches of southern and eastern England, where there are now such counties as Yorkshire, Norfolk, Essex, Kent, and Hampshire. The flimsy craft that had made it across the heaving grey waters of the North Sea had all set out from the ragged, north-jutting Baltic peninsula of what is now known as Denmark. The invaders themselves had an easy time of it; the Romans had gone, and the remaining Celts were in no position to mount much of a defence. They were in consequence to be swiftly dominated by the newcomers, invaders who were linguistically of Germanic stock—Teutons. But though the invaders arrived at more or less the same time, they were not all the same people. Some, to an extent indicated by where their longboats had been launched, were Frisians, other were Jutes, still other Saxons, and—most importantly for the naming of both the English nation and the language that resulted—some of them were called Angles.

We know something of their arrival. Hengist and Horsa, for instance, were—according to legend—two Jutish brothers who landed at Ebbsfleet on the muddy Isle of Thanet in the mid-fifth century, established with their compatriots a series of settlements in Kent, Hampshire, and the Isle of Wight, and set about decades' worth of slaying every Celt they encountered. The Saxons did much the same, landing in 477 in East Anglia and spreading themselves south and westward, pushing the Celts relentlessly westward to Wales and Cornwall and the Scottish borderland. And the Angles, who arrived from Denmark at a series of landing places just to the north of the River Humber

4

in 547, established a kingdom in what is now Northumberland. The Venerable Bede, writing in Latin from his monastery on Tyneside two centuries later, captured something of the ferment of the time:

> *In a short time, swarms of the aforesaid nations came over the island, and they began to increase so much that they became terrible to the natives themselves who had invited them. Then, having on a sudden entered into league with the Picts, whom they had by this time begun to expel by force of arms, they began to turn their weapons against their confederates ...*

The consequence may have been bloodshed and turmoil, and the slaughter may have lasted for a very long and wretched time; but it left the makings of the first building blocks of what was to become today's English language. It also left a small number of names that are distinctly recognizable today. For example, the Teutons called the Celts *wealas*—foreigners—and it is from this word that we get the modern name *Wales*. The Celts first called their new oppressors *Saxons*, then *Angles*: King Aethelbert was known as *rex Anglorum*, the country became known as *Anglia*, and the words *Engle*, *Englisc*,[1] and *Englaland* all slowly crept into common currency, until by the eleventh century the nation in the making was formally known as *England*.

Not that the people were by then speaking or writing anything that would be very easily recognizable as English. Their language used to be known as Anglo-Saxon; nowadays, in an effort to promote the notion of English as an ever-evolving language, it is more generally called Old English. It was written—at least in its earliest incarnation—in runes, the writing system of intersecting straight lines that had been imported by the invaders. (Three of the runic letters—those corresponding to present-day B, H,

---

1 The -*sc* sound was pronounced as -*sh*.

and R—look almost identical to the current capital letters. The rest are easily decipherable, but unlike anything written today.) The more sophisticated writers of Old English (such as those in Northumbria) used a system that is now called *futhorc*, the acronym (much like the word *alphabet*) for the first six letters of their 31-letter alphabet (with *-th*—known as the *thorn*—being elided into a single symbol).

The vocabulary of Old English—with its total lexicon amounting to perhaps 50,000 words—depended to some degree on borrowings from the available languages that were already being spoken in the British Isles. These were items that came either from the vanquished Celts—a tiny number of their British words (*crag* and *dun* and the aforementioned *brock*, *combe*, and *torr* among them) still surviving today—or some couple of hundred words coming from the Latin of the departing conquerors (although in most cases these words appear to have been borrowed on the continent before the Anglo-Saxons came to Britain). A fair number of these words—*cyse*, *catte*, *weall*, and *straet*, meaning *cheese*, *cat*, *wall*, and *street* in Old English respectively—still exist, albeit in modified form, in today's modern word stock. But for the most part, Old English was a tongue that grew out of its own resources, and these resources reflected in large measure the Germanic origins of the new settlers.

Not a few romantics in modern times have touted the notion of the Teutonically inspired Old English as being the purest form of English ever written and spoken. Dickens, Hardy, and Gerard Manley Hopkins were enthusiastic backers of this idea; in more recent times George Orwell was a great supporter too, and publicly yearned for English to be purged of all its Latin, French, Greek, and Norse loans, and to be centred around and dominated by the short, simpler words that were of an undeniable 'Anglicity'—what some call the 'common words' of the English language. He keenly wanted English, as the sixteenth-century humanist John Cheke had once written, to be 'written cleane and pure, unmixt and unmangled with borrowings of other tunges'.

The Dorset dialect poet William Barnes, much taught at my own Dorchester boarding school, went rather further by creating his own vocabulary of new words, all of them rooted firmly in his beloved Anglo-Saxon. A small number of these—his preference for using *faith-heat* for enthusiasm, *word-strain* for accent, and *wheelsaddle* for bicycle—achieved some success and are to be found in occasional popular use. But given the multiplicity of loanwords on offer, many of them exceedingly pretty to look at and to say, his success in going retro was not quite what he would have liked.

The grammar of England's post-Roman times—of which we know something from studies of great epic poems like *Beowulf,* or the story of the shepherd-turned-poet Caedmon, as told by the Venerable Bede, or the famous *Colloquy* written by the eleventh-century Abbot of Eynsham, Ælfric—has a relict Teutonic feel about it. The order of words in a sentence, the inflections at the ends of words signalling the task they perform, both present a language steadily evolving into something very different from Latin, something that approaches the modern idiom but which has much remaining in common with the manner of speech in the north Germany of the time: '… then arose he for shame from the feast,' Ælfric writes, 'when he this answer received.'

The vocabulary, though, is much more familiar to our modern ears. A raft of pronouns and prepositions—*us, for, to, him, in, he*— are there in Old English, to languish unchanged for more than 1,000 further years (not, however, that their meanings were always identical to the sense the words possess today). A number of verbs have the same or a quite similar look and sound: *singan* for sing, *stod* for stood, *ondswarede* for answered. *Ingang* and *utgang* are not dissimilar to the Eingang and Ausgang one might see today in Frankfurt railway station.

And in *Beowulf* a large number of all words in the text are complex combination words, known today as kennings. One such is *beadoleoma*, which means sword, but which translates literally as a combination that will be well known to fans of *Star Wars*, 'battle light'. There are in addition some 50 words in Old English which signify the sea—most of these are kennings, and they include handsome and poetic combinations such as *hwaelweg* (whaleway), *drencflod* (drowning-flood), and *streamgewinn* (waters-strife). None survives today, more's the pity. Nor do either *waegflota* or *waeghengest*—wave-floater or wave-steed—by which the Old English meant what we today call *a ship*.

The reign of Old English was to end in the twelfth century; but before it did so, two more linguistic invasions took place, enriching yet further—with words from Latin and from Norse—the steadily swelling vocabulary of the islands.

New Latin words entered the lists between the eleventh and twelfth centuries, largely as a result of the proselytizing work of Christian missionaries (all of them Latin-speaking) who, some long while earlier, had flooded across the British Isles, eager to save souls. They claimed to be bringing 'the Word'; to a remarkable and unforgettable extent, but somewhat at a variance from what they intended, so they did.

Religious words, not surprisingly, make up a goodly proportion of the list. Although a trinity of key words that attest to the very heart of belief—*God, heaven, sin*—are actually of Germanic origin, Latin-originated words first recorded either in the eleventh century or some while later—many coming into Middle English through French—and dealing with churchly mechanicals, are there in abundance: *abbot, alb, anchorite, angel, antichrist, canticle, chalice, cloister, font, idol, martyr, pope, priest, prophet, psalm, relic.*

But God was not all: visitors from the Continent over several centuries brought with them the names of plants, fruits, and trees hitherto entirely unfamiliar to the islands: *cedar, cucumber, fig, ginger, laurel, lentil, lovage, radish*; and they told of exotic animals quite unknown to the Teutonically-influenced Britons—*elephant, leopard, scorpion, tiger*. The fact that *dirge, marshmallow, periwinkle,* and *sock* also quite probably entered the islands at around this time and probably from the same ultimate source might seem at first blush slightly more perplexing, except that the visitors probably sang in a dull monotone, knew more than a little of the local botany, and wore soft foot-coverings to protect them against the raw English winters—and moreover had names for them all.

New Norse words were introduced in a far less congenial fashion. The Vikings began raiding and pillaging England in the eighth century; the Danes did much the same a century later, first ruling all of north-east England under terms of a treaty to which they submitted the weakling English, then in 991 going further and seizing the English throne, running all England's affairs for the next 25 years. Along with making mayhem in, or a fiefdom out of, England, both sets of northern adventurers introduced into English hundreds of their own words—many that turned out to be of the most profound importance and yet, in terms of their exoticism and interest, among the most prosaic in the tongue.

Both, same, seem, get, give, they, them, and *their* all stem from these northern, ice-bound people too. *Skirt, sky, scathe, skill,* and *skin* employ a well-known two-letter Scandinavian beginning. And we can somehow understand that the gloomy antecedents of Ibsen would have given to English the likes of *awkward, birth, dirt, fog* (perhaps), *gap, ill, mire, muggy, ransack, reindeer, root, rotten, rugged, scant, scowl,* and *wrong*. There is rather less obvious connection with *cake, sprint, steak,* and *wand*—though these jollier words did indeed come from the

9

Norsemen too. As did *Thursday*—or rather, it was modified by them, since an earlier version of the day that honoured Thor did in fact appear in Old English itself.

But for all this, Old English was first and foremost a home-grown language—by far its greatest component being the Teutonic stock of words gifted by the Jutlanders and Frisians and Angles who began to drift into the population in the wake of Hengist and Horsa. The total accumulation of Latin and Norse loanwords (and a triflingly small number of probable French lendings, too—among them words like *prisen, castel,* and *prud,* which equate to today's *prison, castle,* and *proud*) amount to no more than three per cent of Old English's word stock; Germanic words account for almost all the rest. And though we glibly say that the language as written and spoken 1,000 years ago is recognizable to the modern ear—it is certainly more so than the Celtic of the very early British—the numbers suggest otherwise: something like nine out of every ten of the Old English words have since fallen into disuse. It was really not until Old English began to transmute itself into Middle English that we start to see and hear and read something that is a simulacrum of what we see and hear and read today.

It was the invasion of the Norman French that changed everything. The defeat of King Harold at the Battle of Hastings in 1066 resulted in the installation of a dynasty of French kings on the throne in London (the first, the Hastings victor William I, actually spending very little time in England), and for the next 300 years the French held sway over almost all areas of English power, governance, and culture. Norman French became the language of England's administration and of the country's politer forms of intercourse. Old English came briefly to be despised, regarded haughtily as the language of the peasant and the pleb.

And yet, though much changed, Old English did in fact survive. It survived in a way that the British of the Celts did not manage to survive the Germanic invasion six centuries before. After a century-and-a-half of linguistic mystery when no one is certain quite what happened to the language, Old English lived on, transmuted itself into what is now called Middle English, adopted thousands of new loanwords from the French and became stronger by doing so (doubling its word stock in no time at all, to the 100,000 or so words of the twelfth-century lexicon), and finally emerged, fully established, to be displayed to greatest advantage for all time in the writings of that most impressive of the early figures of English literature, Geoffrey Chaucer.

Since this chapter aimed principally to explain (or remind those who know) about the origins of the English vocabulary, and about the means that have been sought to catalogue and enumerate its complicated immensity, it is unhappily (because it is so fascinating) of little relevance to write much about Chaucer's literary achievement, or about the sheer beauty and staggering accomplishment of his poetry and prose. He tells us how the English men and women of the fourteenth century spoke to one another; he tells us how they cursed and complained and questioned and told each other jokes; he ranges in his interests from the highest-flown kind of rhetoric to the most banal of domestic chit-chat. It is the quantity, the breadth, and the assortment of his writings that elevate him above all others of his time; and more's the pity that we cannot linger here to revel in his legacy.

Chaucer's vocabulary, reflective of all that was said and written around him, shows clearly the great measure of change that by his time had come upon the language. In the 858 lines in his *Prologue* to the *Canterbury Tales*, for example, there are almost

500 French (or rather, Norman French) loanwords. Historical studies suggest that by 1365, some 300 new French words were being incorporated into English every year. But it must be stressed that it was not that French was being spoken; the English language, reviving itself from its mysterious dark age, was including and assimilating new French-originated words, speakers and writers using them as replacements for words that had vanished during the time when spoken and written French did dominate the nation's language.

And so we find, for instance, words (from the Norman French—and in many cases, of course, ultimately from the Latin or the Greek) of administration and law—*accuse, adultery, chamberlain, crime, decree, duke* (though not *lord, lady, knight,* or *earl,* which are all home-grown Old English, displaying Orwell's favoured Anglicity), *inheritance, larceny, libel, messenger, pardon, parliament, reign, revenue, sue, treasurer, trespass, verdict, warrant,* and *warden.* There are religious words, inevitably—*cardinal, choir, saint, virgin*; there are French words for foodstuffs—*beef, pork, sausage, sugar, tart*; for fashion—*broidery, brooch, chemise, petticoat, satin, taffeta*; for science—*gender, geometry, medicine, plague, pulse, stomach, surgery*; and for the home—*blanket, closet, pantry, porch, scullery, wardrobe.* There are, besides, a slew of phrases still familiar in Modern English: *have mercy on, take leave, learn by heart,* and *on the point of,* for example,[2] all have their origins in this wonderfully energetic period in English linguistic history.

---

2   The phrase *to look up,* as in *to look something up in a dictionary,* does not, however, come about in this way, though it sounds as though it might. It did not appear until 1692, when an Oxford historian named Anthony Wood wrote the phrase in a book called *Life, from 1632 to 1672, written by Himself.*

And then came William Caxton, and with him the very beginnings of Modern English. It was in 1474 that, having learned the techniques of printing from the master craftsmen of Cologne, this 50-year-old Kentish businessman set himself up in Bruges and created, on a wooden press of his own making, the first ever book to be printed in English, *The Recuyell of the Historyes of Troye* (which, in addition, he had translated from the French—*recuyell* meaning, essentially, compilation). The reception of this 700-page work convinced him: he had no doubt at all now that the new technology which he had mastered in Europe, if taken back home to England, would have an incalculable effect both on society at large and on the nature of the language that people would read from his printed books and papers and pamphlets, and which in turn they would come to speak.

And so two years later he came to London, and established his own print shop and publishing house beside Westminster Abbey. From the hands of Caxton and his apprentices came some 103 printed works[3]—one edition of Chaucer's *Boethius* and two of the *Canterbury Tales* among them. Moreover, the books that he made were (as Caxton was not shy of advertising) available to almost all, for the simple reason that they cost almost nothing to produce. Compared to the laborious and costly hand-copying of manuscripts, the books and pamphlets that were now being turned off his creaking wooden presses were inexpensive in the extreme. 'If it plese ony man ... to bye ...', announced one of Caxton's printed flyers, '... late hym come to Westmonester ... and he shal have them good chepe.' What more eloquent declaration could there ever be of the lasting benefits of printing?

With the advent of printing, as exemplified by Caxton's house,

3 Caxton's first London book was *The Dictes or Sayengis of the Philosophres*, translated from the French (by Earl Rivers, a well-known gallant famous for his duel with a figure known as the Bastard of Burgundy) and published in 1477.

came a greater awareness of the multifarious dialects in which English was then both spoken and written, and the beginnings of a feeling that there should be a standard written form of the language. A famous story relates to Caxton's own puzzlement over the word 'eggs'—should he use the northern form, *egges*, or the southern version, *eyren*? It took many years before questions like this were fully answered—a question over the use of apostrophes, for example, never being fully answered to this day.

Any remaining hopes, nurtured as they were by a small corps of romantics, that the language might still be shorn of all its non-Germanic words and returned to the purity of its ancestry were to be dashed during the two centuries that followed the Caxton revolution—the Renaissance. With the furious development of science, arts, exploration, and travel, the language became ever more steadily enriched—unkinder souls might say polluted—by an almost uncountable mass of newly imported words from abroad. The size of the lexicon had doubled in the years after the Norman invasion; in the Renaissance it doubled again, such that by the beginning of the seventeenth century there were reckoned to be at the very least 200,000 knowable words waiting to be used.

The conventional sources—Latin, Greek, Italian, Spanish, Portuguese, and French—supplied many of them; but now, with the wanderings of the fleets and their inquisitive occupants producing words from all over, the English vocabulary was enhanced not merely by the usual suspects but by words from India and Turkey, Arabia and Malaya, Japan and the native peoples of North America, and 50 other countries besides.

Some of the more romantically inclined writers of the day

despised the trend—John Cheke, for example, was still vainly wishing for a return to his 'clean and pure tunge'. On the other hand some modernists, like the author and diplomat Sir Thomas Elyot, positively craved foreign words, as though they were plagued by some curious lexico-xenophilic sickness. Elyot was on intimate terms with King Henry VIII (the monarch loaned him books from the royal library, to help with a Latin–English dictionary he was then compiling), and was said to be a brilliantly skilled translator, widely travelled, and a hugely competent linguist. He wished above all to have his native English 'augmented' and 'enriched' with new words from around the world, to describe and define all the wondrous new objects and ideas that the Renaissance was bringing in its wake. And by and large, he got his way. The purists, never a formidable army at the best of times, were during the Renaissance being routed. English in the sixteenth century was getting larger and larger, and by doing so was fast strengthening itself for its unanticipated role as the coming language of the world. Analyses suggest that between 1590 and 1610 around 6,000 new words were being added to the lexicon every year—more than at any time in history (save possibly, we feel intuitively, for today).

There are far too many words newly introduced in the Renaissance to be listed here, in a short book which is simply the story of one dictionary, and is by no stretch of the imagination a dictionary itself. But sometimes the loveliness of the assemblages are just too beguiling to pass up: so it is pleasing to note that during the 200 years following Caxton, English welcomed from abroad such words as *anonymous, atmosphere, catastrophe, criterion, delirium, enthusiasm, fact, idiosyncrasy, inclemency, lunar, malignant, necessitate, parasite, pneumonia, sculptor, skeleton, soda, vicinity,* and *virus* (all from either Latin or Greek); *battery, bayonet, chocolate, confront, docility, grotesque, moustache, passport, tomato,* and *volunteer* (from or through the good

15

offices of the French); *balcony, cupola, ditto, granite, grotto, macaroni, piazza, sonata, sonnet, stanza,* and *violin* from Italian; *anchovy, armada, armadillo, cannibal, mulatto, Negro, sombrero,* and *yam* from or via either Spanish or Portuguese; and a gallimaufry of delights from some 50 other contributing tongues, including *amok, paddy,* and *sago* (from Malay), *caravan*[4] and *turban* (Persian), *kiosk, sherbet,* and *yoghurt* (Turkish), *raccoon* and *wampum* (Algonquian), *cruise, frolic,* and *yacht* (Dutch), *knapsack* (Low German), as well as *guru* from Hindi, *ketchup* from Cantonese, *sofa* from Arabic, *shogun* from Japanese, *sheikh* from Arabic, and *trousers* from the Gaelic spoken by the Irish.

Shakespeare—as vital a purveyor of what would go on to become Modern English as William Caxton had been two centuries before him, and as were the various great English bibles produced shortly after him—was the first to employ a great many of these words. By doing so he offered actors the chance to enrich the language of those who came to see his plays. In *Othello,* for example, the Moor entreats the Duke of Venice to offer his wife Desdemona 'Due reference of place and exhibition, With such accomodation and besort as levels with her breeding', and thereby offers the first known usage (*Othello* was published in 1604) of the word *accommodation*[5]. Likewise, when Antonio and Bassanio's friends are chatting in the opening scene of *The Merchant of Venice,* Solanio gives us the first use of the word *laughable*—'they'll not show their teeth in way of smile Though Nestor swear the jest be laughable'. *Laugh* itself is a word from the widely approved Old English; in 1596 Shakespeare added the Norman French

---

4   The word *caravan*—meaning a travelling company—is of course connected to the name of the inns—the *caravanserais*—in which the travellers stayed. The distance between two caravanserais—a day's travel, in other words—is known by the Turkish loanword *menzil.*

5   *Besort,* now obsolete, meant 'suitable company'. Shakespeare uses it again, as a verb, in *King Lear,* but afterwards it seems to lapse. Incidentally, the earliest print of the play spells *accomodation* with a single 'm', the bane of many a bee.

suffix -*able*, and lo! the combination still exists happily today, four centuries later.

(It has to be said that Shakespeare did advance the cause of a number of words—like *besort*—that never made it, or which staggered along lamely for only a short while. Among those he used, but he almost alone, were *soilure*, *tortive*, and *vastidity*, which mean, as one might expect, staining, twisted, and big. In these cases, and a score of others, his clever Latinate constructions fared rather less well than the simpler old synonyms from northern Europe. But he also gives modern readers such hyphenations as *baby-eyes*, *pell-mell*, and *ill-tuned*, and dozens of insults that employ the word *knave*—of which *whoreson beetle-headed flap-ear'd knave* (from *The Taming of the Shrew*) has become a minor classic.)

And since Shakespeare—and since William Hazlitt and Jane Austen, since Wordsworth and Thackeray, the Naipauls and the Amises, and the fantasy worlds of the hobbits and Harry Potter, and since science and sport and conquest and defeat—the language that we call Modern English has just grown and grown, almost exponentially. Words from every corner of the globalized world cascade in ceaselessly, daily topping up a language that is self-evidently living, breathing, changing, evolving as no other language ever has, nor is ever likely to.

A glance at any map will suggest hundreds upon hundreds of constructions and imports that we now know to be more a part of today's English than they ever were of the native tongues where they were first born. *Glasnost* and *perestroika*, for example, are firmly ensconced in the English vocabulary now, despite their being utterly unfamiliar outside their native Russia before 1989. *Anorak*, from Greenland, is a word which, when introduced, described a foul-weather garment; it has since become used (though only in Britain) as a term of disapprobation, describing someone seen as rather too interested in a subject most reasonable people would think of as wholly boring. *Sauna, dachshund, ombudsman, waltz, cobra, bwana, ouzo, agitprop, samovar, kraal, boondock, boomerang, colleen, manga, kava, tattoo, poncho, pecan, puma, piranha*—the list of foreign borrowings introduced over the past two centuries is near-endless. The 200,000 words that could be counted in the lexicon at the close of the Renaissance have in the centuries since tripled, at the very least, and the rate of expansion of the planet's most versatile and flexible vocabulary seems in no danger of slowing.

2. The Measuring

And yet, and yet. Until the very beginning of the seventeenth century, a time when the English language could quite probably number fully a quarter of a million words and phrases and those individual items of vocabulary that are known as lexemes among its riches, there was not a single book in existence that attempted to list even a small fraction of them, nor was there any book that would make the slightest attempt to offer up an inventory.

No one, it turned out, had ever bothered. No one had ever thought of making a list of all the words and noting down what they seemed to mean—even though from today's perspective, from a world that seems obsessed with a need to count and codify and define and make categories for everything, there seems no rational reason why this might have been so. That no one cared enough about the lexicon to make a list of what it held seems barely credible. It was as though the language that had been developing over the centuries had created itself invisibly, had somehow crept silently over the minds and manners of all those who spoke and read and listened to it, and never in such a demonstrative or showy way as to make any speaker or listener or reader aware that it actually was an entity, that it was something that could and should be measured, enumerated, catalogued, described. English seemed to most of its users to be somehow like the air—something that had always been there, to be as taken for granted as the very atmosphere itself, inchoate and indefinable, and thus somehow not amenable to proper measurement or systematic knowledge. It was a thing simply to be felt, breathed, and uttered—and never something so base as ever to be studied, annotated, or counted.

To those of us who reach for a dictionary or a thesaurus at the first moment of literary puzzlement, the lack of any such book must have been an inconvenience, to say the least. And yet it was an inconvenience suffered in silence by the best of them, and for a very long time. William Shakespeare, for example, had no access to a dictionary during most of his writing career—certainly from 1580, when he first began, it was a quarter of a century before any volume might appear in which he could look something up. We have already seen how frequently and flamboyantly Shakespeare contributed words to the language (*dislocate*, *dwindle*, and *submerged* are three more to add to those above); but to do so he had, essentially, either to find such words in other writings, note down words or expressions that he heard in conversation, or else invent or conjure words out of the thin air.

That is not to say there were no reference books available at all. In the late sixteenth century bookstore tables were weighed down with all manner of missals, biographies, histories of the sciences and of art, prayer books, Bibles, romances, atlases, and accounts of exotic travel. Shakespeare would have had access to all these, and more. He is known (from a careful statistical examination of his word usages) to have used as a crib a *Thesaurus* edited by the Bishop of Winchester, one Thomas Cooper,[6] and probably

6 The tiresome making of this book once exasperated the 'utterly profligate' Mrs Cooper so much that she tossed the entire manuscript into the fire—prompting her imperturbable husband simply to sigh wearily and begin compiling his book all over again.

also a volume called *The Arte of Rhetorique* by Thomas Wilson. But that is all: neither Shakespeare, nor any of the other great writing minds of the day—Francis Bacon, Edmund Spenser, Christopher Marlowe, John Donne, Ben Jonson—had access to what all of us today would be certain that he would have wanted: the lexical convenience that went by the name that was invented in 1538, *a dictionary*.

The 1538 creation was not, however, for the purposes of most English writers, of any real convenience at all. It was a book that had been edited by Sir Thomas Elyot—already famed as an enthusiast for all words foreign—and it was, like all such volumes before, a translating dictionary, in this particular case offering words in Latin, with their English equivalents, and vice versa. It offered no sense of the meaning of the words—just their equivalence in another tongue. No one had by then come up with the idea of what we now know a dictionary to be: a list of English words in (most probably) an alphabetical order, with the meanings and perhaps the various senses of each listed, and perhaps some guidance as to the spelling, pronunciation, and origin of each word as well.

A man named John Withals took a hesitating few steps towards the ideal, producing twenty years after Elyot a Latin–English vocabulary book in which the words were organized into categories. He collected together words that had something to do with *skie*, for example, or *four-footed beastes, partes of housinge, instruments of musicke*, and *the names of Byrdes, Byrdes of the Water, Byrdes about the house as cockes, hennes etc; of Bees, Flies and Others*. The usefulness of such a book is now self-evident: rather than merely offering a means of translating one word into another language, Withals's small volume classified them, and by doing so reminded readers of, let us say, the names of birds, nudging them towards improving their knowledge. Can't remember the name of a bird between *shrike* and *tern*? In Withals there is *swallow* and *swift*—and at a stroke his book becomes, if little else, an aide-mémoire. He called it *A Shorte Dictionary for Yonge Beginners*: it became a standard school textbook and was wildly popular, remaining in print for more than 70 years, at least until 1634.

The longevity of Mr Withals's book hints at the growing popularity of this entirely new trend in seventeenth-century publishing. There was evidently a pressing need for a change towards volumes that had utility *in English alone*, and not merely as vehicles for the use of another language. It was a need that was occasionally voiced publicly, as on stage in *The Duchess of Malfi*, when John Webster had the Duchess's brother Ferdinand exclaim, after puzzling over the word *lycanthropia*,[7] 'I need a dictionary to't!' On a more scholarly level the drumbeat of need was signalled too: as when the newly appointed headmaster of the Merchant Taylors' School, Richard Mulcaster, declared: 'it would be a thing verie praiseworthy ... if som one learned and as laborious a man, wold gather all the wordes which we vse in our English tung ... into one dictionarie.' Mulcaster promised that he would gather up and deliver one, but never did; nor did his fellow grammarian William Bullokar. Nor did anyone else.

Until finally, in 1604, *som one learned* did go out gathering, and eventually produced what the entire literary universe was apparently baying for. This historically important (but otherwise generally unremembered) figure was a schoolmaster from Oakham in Rutland called Robert Cawdrey, and he offered—by courtesy of his publisher, 'Edward Weaver, of the great north door of St. Paul's'—a slender octavo book of 120 printed pages entitled *A Table Alphabeticall, conteyning and teaching the true writing and understanding of hard usuall English words, borrowed from the Hebrew, Greek, Latin or*

---

7   A psychiatric condition in which the sufferer imagines himself to be turning into a wolf.

French, &c. The book had gathered up 3,000 of these 'hard words', and had been particularly edited, Cawdrey stated on his title page with all the magnificent carelessness of the times, 'for the benefit and helpe of Ladies, Gentlewomen, or any other unskillful person'.

The book was by today's standards more a synonymicon than a true dictionary—it offered very brief (often one-word) glosses, rather than true definitions. So *abbreuiat* was 'to shorten, or make short' and an *abettor* was simply 'a counsellor'. Moreover, the words with which Cawdrey had chosen to enlighten England's 'Gentlewomen and unskillful persons' were the improbably contrived portmanteau words—the so-called inkhorn terms—with which the loftiest members of London high society liked to pepper their salon conversations in the hope of sounding more erudite and cultured than perhaps they actually were. He lists for their assistance words like *bubulcitate, sacerdotall, archgrammacian*, and *attemptate*—all of them extravagances now mercifully gone the way of the doublet, the ruff, and the periwig. Just as his readers would likely have no interest in serge, black bread, or objects carved in deal, so Robert Cawdrey has no interest in the commonplace words of the time—and so his *Table Alphabeticall*, while its publication marked a pivotal moment in lexical history, was in fact a work of very limited utility, and barely comparable with what would come in its wake.

But for all its shortcomings, Cawdrey's was the first *monolingual* English dictionary ever made, and in its wake—because of the need expressed by Mulcaster and Bullokar and Webster—came a huge number of others,[8] as though a floodgate had suddenly been cranked open. In the early days of the century most of these, too, dealt with difficult words, as though their easier kinsmen

---

8 One of them was made by John Bullokar, said perhaps to have been the 'chyld' of the grammarian William Bullokar, though no one seems certain.

A

Table Alphabeticall, con-
teyning and teaching the true
vvriting, and vnderſtanding of hard
vſuall Engliſh wordes, borrowed from
the Hebrew, Greeke, Latine,
or French. &c.

With the interpretation thereof by
plaine Engliſh words, gathered for the benefit &
helpe of Ladies, Gentlewomen, or any other
vnskilfull perſons.

Whereby they may the more eaſilie
and better vnderſtand many hard Engliſh
wordes, vvhich they ſhall heare or read in
Scriptures, Sermons, or elſwhere, and alſo
be made able to vſe the ſame aptly
themſelues.

Legere, et non intelligere, neglegere eſt.
As good not read, as not to vnderſtand.

AT LONDON,
Printed by I. R. for Edmund Wea-
uer, & are to be ſold at his ſhop at the great
North doore of Paules Church.
1 6 04.

The beginning of it all: the first true English-only dictionary, published '*for*
the benefit of Ladies...or other unskilfull persons'—by the Coventry schoolmaster
Robert Cawdrey, in 1604.

somehow did not require explication. One of these, however, Thomas Blount's famous *Glossographia* of 1656, does begin to get to grips with the fantastic complexity of ordinary English, as the author made clear in his 'Note to the Reader':

> *Nay, to that pass we are now arrived, that in London many of the Tradesmen have new Dialects; The Cook asks you what Dishes you will have in your Bill of Fare; whether Ollas, Bisques, Hachies, Omelets, Bouillons, Grilliades, Ioncades, Fricasses; with a Haugoust, Ragoust etc. The Vintner will furnish you with Montefiascone, Alicante, Vornaccia, Ribolla, Tent, etc. Others with Sherbert, Agro di Cedro, Coffa, Chocolate, etc. The Taylor is ready to make you a Rochet, Mandillion, Gippon, Justacor, Capouch, Roqueton or a Cloke of Drap de Bery, etc. The Shoomaker will make you Boots, Whole Chase, demi-Chase, or Bottines, etc. The Haberdasher is ready to furnish you with a Vigone, Codeck or Castor, etc. The Seamstress with a Crabbet, Toylet etc. By this new World of Words, I found we were slipt into that condition which Seneca complains of in his lifetime; when men's minds begin to endure themselves to dislike, whatever is usual is disdained: They affect novelty in speech, they recal orewarn and uncouth words; And some there are that think it is a grace, if their speech hover, in thereby hold the hearer in suspence, etc.*

Perhaps today we are uncertain how to eat *Ioncades* (a junket) or have forgotten that a *Mandillion* is a kind of overcoat and a *Castor* is a hat fashioned from beaver fur. But these were not hard words, of the kind Cawdrey sought to explain—these were the jargon of trade and fine living, and in publishing them Blount tells us somewhat more about the language of the day than did most of his counterparts. Moreover, he offers citations for some words—and he makes an observation that, we now know, underpins the entire story of the book that this account celebrates: he realizes that he is indeed a lexicographer, and that the task of such a specialist is one that 'would find no end, since our English tongue daily changes habit'.

For that reason alone, Thomas Blount, barrister of Worcestershire, Catholic to the core, wealthy and leisured and a linguist of considerable talent, deserves to be remembered: not as the father of modern dictionaries maybe, but as the lexicographer who saw the light—who realized the ceaseless magnitude of the task (if it were ever to be undertaken) of gathering together all of the thousands upon thousands of ever-changing words with which generations of invaders and wanderers had littered and seasoned the peculiarly English means of saying things. To remark that English lexicography is like herding cats, as the saying has it, is only the half of it.

But the word-herders then began in earnest, however difficult the task. After Blount there was Milton's nephew John Phillips, who put out another 11,000-item 'long hard word' dictionary two years later. He had countless fights with Blount (mainly over allegations of plagiarism, to which all dictionary editors—who are bound to use earlier dictionaries to make sure they've left nothing out of their own—are prey); and in 1706 (ten years after his death) his work was expanded into a 38,000-word monster, a volume which counts as one of the first true lexicons to break out of merely listing inkhorn words for the benefit of society dandies. John Kersey, who edited the new sixth edition of Phillips, called it *The New World of Words: or a Universal English Dictionary containing*—and after listing, once again, the inclusion of hard words from a variety of languages, added, splendidly, that these would be found together with a brief explication of all terms that relate to the Arts and Sciences, either Liberal or Mechanical, viz.

> *Grammar, Rhetorick, Logic, Theology, Law, Metaphysicks, Ethicks, Natural Philosophy, Law, Natural History, Physick, Surgery, Anatomy, Chymistry, Pharmacy, Botanicks, Arithmetick, Geometry, Astronomy, Astrology, Cosmography, Hydrography,*

Navigation, Architecture, Fortification, Dialling, Surveying, Gauging, Opticks, Catoptricks, Dioptricks, Perspective, Musick, Mechanicks, Statics, Chiromancy, Physiognomy, Heraldry, Merchandise, Maritime and Military Affairs, Agriculture, Gardening, Handicrafts, Jewelling, Painting, Carving, Engraving, Confectionery, Cookery, Horsemanship, Hawking, Hunting, Fowling, Fishing etc.

The mould had now been broken. Over the coming half-century there were to be dozens of new dictionaries published, as a craze for consumable lexicography swept across England like a hurricane. The names of those who made them have long since vanished from all worlds save those of collectors—names like Nathaniel Bailey and Francis Gouldman, B. N. Defoe, James Manlove, J. Sparrow, Thomas Dyche, Francis Junius, and Edward Cocker. Their creations grew steadily larger and larger as the size of the language became ever more fully realized; and by the middle of the eighteenth century, with dictionaries containing 50,000 or 60,000 words thundering from presses up and down the country, it was abundantly clear that the craft of the lexicographers who made them was no longer an idle occupation of the leisured dilettante, but an entirely professional calling.

The phrase 'according to Cocker', which was heard around this time, was invested with a meaning which flatters the profession to this day. It means reliably or correctly or according to established rules. It was to be the dictionary-makers' equivalent of the more widely known games players' phrase, 'according to Hoyle'. It made lexicography a respected way of life.

And then came Samuel Johnson, 'the Great Cham of Literature', and with him, the turning point. It was Tobias Smollett who coined the name—meaning, essentially, a figure of authority and autocratic self-confidence—and applied it to the bookseller's son from Lichfield in Staffordshire, the schoolteacher turned journalist and parliamentary sketch-writer and wanderer and conversationalist who would become one of the towering figures of English letters. The magisterially famous Dr Johnson created his great dictionary in 1755—in two volumes, in scores of editions, the book that all educated households possessed and took down whenever anyone asked simply for 'the dictionary', set the standard for the following century, and some still think for all time, of just what an English dictionary should be.

It is important to reiterate in this context that Johnson's work set standards for all future *English* dictionaries. For the way that English had developed, and the way that in the eighteenth century it was coming to be recognized at home, was profoundly different from the way that other languages were then being seen, and were being recognized and then collated and corralled into dictionaries elsewhere. The point is an obvious one: but it bears repeating, as it underlies—indeed, is vital in every way to—the making of the book that plays the central role in this story.

For English is not to be regarded in the same way as, say, French or Italian, and in one crucially important way. It is not a *fixed* language, the meaning of its words established, approved, and firmly set by some official committee charged with preserving its dignity and integrity. The French have had their Académie Française, a body made up of the much-feared Forty Immortals, which has done precisely this (and with an extreme punctiliousness and absolute want of humour) since 1634. The Italians have also had their Accademia della Crusca in Florence since 1582—since long before, in other words, there was even a nation called Italy. The task of both bodies was to preserve linguistic purity, to prevent the languages' ruin by permitting inelegant importations, and to guide the public on just how to write and speak. The two bodies were established, in short, to prescribe the use of the language. No

A

DICTIONARY

OF THE

ENGLISH LANGUAGE:

IN WHICH

The WORDS are deduced from their ORIGINALS,

AND

ILLUSTRATED in their DIFFERENT SIGNIFICATIONS

BY

EXAMPLES from the beſt WRITERS.

TO WHICH ARE PREFIXED,

A HISTORY of the LANGUAGE,

AND

AN ENGLISH GRAMMAR.

BY SAMUEL JOHNSON, A.M.

IN TWO VOLUMES.

VOL. I.

Cum tabulis animum cenſoris ſumet honeſti :
Audebit quaecunque parum ſplendoris habebunt,
Et ſine pondere erunt, et honore indigna ferentur,
Verba movere loco; quamvis invita receſant,
Et verſentur adhuc intra penetralia Veſtæ:
Obſcurata diu populo bonus eruet, atque
Proferet in lucem ſpecioſa vocabula rerum,
Quæ priſcis memorata Catonibus atque Cethegis,
Nunc ſitus informis premit et deſerta vetuſtas.   HOR.

LONDON,

Printed by W. STRAHAN,

For J. and P. KNAPTON; T. and T. LONGMAN; C. HITCH and L. HAWES;
A. MILLAR; and R. and J. DODSLEY.

MDCCLV.

For more than a century after its publication in 1755, Samuel Johnson's massive work was *the* dictionary, essential to the library of every educated household.

such body has ever been set up in England, nor in any English-speaking country.[9]

And though George Orwell might have longed for an Anglo-Saxon revival, though John Dryden loathed French loanwords, despite Joseph Addison's campaigns against contractions such as *mayn't* and *won't*, and although Alexander Pope pleaded for the retention of dignity and Daniel Defoe wrote of his hatred of the 'inundation' of curse-words and Jonathan Swift mounted a life-long attempt to 'fix our language forever'—no critic and advocate of immutability has ever once managed properly or even marginally to outwit the English language's capacity for foxy and relentlessly slippery flexibility.

For English is a language that simply cannot be fixed, nor can its use ever be absolutely laid down. It changes constantly; its grows with an almost exponential joy. It evolves eternally; its words alter their senses and their meanings subtly, slowly, or speedily according to fashion and need. Dictionaries that record and catalogue the language thus cannot ever be *prescriptive*; they must always be entirely *descriptive*, telling of the language as it is, not as it should be. Samuel Johnson's majestic *Dictionary of the English Language*, published first in 1755 and remaining in print for well over the century following, is a classic of this kind. It is as full a record as Johnson and the six serving men who worked with him as amanuenses for six years in cramped rooms south of Fleet Street could determine, of the entire assemblage of words that were employed by all who lived in the realm—the words used by the learned, the nobly born, the doctor, the dandy, and the

---

9 Except South Africa, which has its own 'English Academy' based in Johannesburg, charged with promoting 'the effective use of English as a dynamic language'. The French and Italians would deny the use of the word 'dynamic', urging upon their respective peoples the need for linguistic stability and an abhorrence of change.

divine and, most important of all, the words used by the common man of the street, the slum, the farm, and the field.

(There has long been a running argument over whether Johnson himself ever thought it desirable to fix the language in the aspic of his authority. The current view is that at first he did—that he initially espoused the conservative views of Swift and Addison and their like, and had half a mind to make a dictionary that laid down rules, just as an Academy might. In his Plan for the dictionary, written in 1747, he said he wished 'to preserve the purity and ascertain the meaning of our English idiom'. But halfway through the task he realized that, in dealing specifically with the endearingly unruly monster that was English, this simply was not possible. He then, perhaps reluctantly, fell in with the dictum laid down by a predecessor lexicographer, the former Surrey ploughboy and inventor named Benjamin Martin, twenty years before Johnson began his monumental work:

> *The pretence of fixing a standard to the purity and perfection of any language is utterly vain and impertinent, because no language as depending on arbitrary use and custom, can ever be permanently the same, but will always be in a mutable and fluctuating state; and what is deem'd polite and elegant in one age, may be counted uncouth and barbarous in another.*

And Johnson agreed. Whatever he had said in his Plan of 1747, he was not to repeat in his Preface of 1755. His aim in making the great dictionary was, he then admitted, not 'to form, but to register' the language. In this way a whole new way of dictionary-making, and an entirely new intellectual approach to the language, had been inaugurated.)

The approach that Johnson took was not to decide for himself what words meant, not (to reiterate the point) to *prescribe* how they should be used—but instead to let the printed record of centuries-worth of writing and literature illustrate how words had actually been used in the past, and tease from the record the variety of historic meanings, from the time each was invented and first introduced, and as their various senses shifted like silverfish over the succeeding centuries. 'When I took the first survey of my undertaking,' he wrote in his famous Preface,

> *I found our speech copious without order, and energetick without rules: wherever I turned my view, there was perplexity to be disentangled, and confusion to be regulated. Having therefore no assistance but from general grammar I applied myself to the perusal of our writers; and noting whatever might be used to ascertain or illustrate any word or phrase, accumulated in time the materials of a dictionary which, by degrees, I reduced to method.*

This was a method which Johnson perhaps honoured more in the breach than the observance. But it nonetheless set the pattern for all the best dictionaries for all time to come: no better means has ever been developed for producing as near as possible a complete record of a language.

There are essentially three sources for the words that are to be put into a new dictionary. There are those to be found in existing dictionaries (a fact which caused scores of earlier dictionary makers to cry plagiarism whenever an unusual word found in one book was then found in another published subsequently). There are words which are heard in conversation. And there are words that are to be found by a concerted trawl through the texts of literature. Johnson leant heavily on this third source—only, as it turns out, not heavily enough. For he took the unilateral decision—to save himself time and money—only to read the books that had been published since 1586, and the death of Sir Philip Sidney. *Beowulf* and the *Canterbury Tales* were not to be considered; none of the works from Caxton made it into Johnson's lists; Bede's writings were not included; nor was Domesday Book; neither were the Bibles of Wyclif and Tyndale. A mere century and a half of English literature was to provide the wellspring for his book: not a few have since expressed surprise that, despite so limited a source, so very many words made it in at all.

There were, in the end, 43,500 of them, supported by 118,000 illustrative quotations (a good number of which were amended by Johnson if he didn't like the originals). The headwords were listed alphabetically in a book that was printed in a first edition of 2,000 copies, and sold for £4 10s. 0d. a copy—a good deal of money for 1755. Realizing this, Johnson produced a second edition in 165 weekly parts, at sixpence each. This did the trick; by the end of the century every educated household had, or had access to, the great book. So firmly established did it swiftly become that any request for 'The Dictionary' would bring forth Johnson and none other. One asked for The Dictionary much as one might demand The Bible, *Hymns Ancient & Modern*, or The Prayer Book.

Examined with the steely-eyed rigour of today, there are in Johnson eccentricities in abundance. Some of his definitions are infamously political, like 'Oats: A grain which in England is generally given to horses, but which in Scotland feeds the people'. Some were reckoned libellous, as 'Excise: A hateful tax levied upon commodities, and adjudged not by the common judges of property, but wretches hired by those to whom excise is paid'. Not a few were self-effacing, like 'Lexicographer: A writer of dictionaries; a harmless drudge, that busies himself in tracing the original, and detailing the signification of words'.[10]

Others were simply frightful, entries that breached the lexicographer's guiding principle that in writing a definition, no word

---

10 He did not, however, venture anything quite so cynical as Ambrose Bierce's later definition of the word *dictionary* in his own classic work *The Devil's Dictionary: A malevolent literary device for cramping the growth of a language and making it hard and inelastic.*

may be used that is more complex or unfamiliar than the word being defined—which was very much not the case with Johnson's definition of 'Network: Any thing reticulated, or decussated, at equal distances, with interstices between the intersections'. Small wonder that Johnson collected some harsh critics—like Thomas Babington Macaulay, who was to curse him as 'a wretched etymologist', and another, who wrote that 'Any schoolmaster might have done what Johnson did. His Dictionary is merely a glossary to his own barbarisms.'

Dr Johnson was sufficiently brazen and self-confident not to have been distressed by such carping. But he must have taken some pleasure in hearing that his book attracted the prurient as well as the pedant. On being accused, by a genteel society lady, of failing to include obscenities in the book he replied, in a mixture of the caustic and the sardonic: 'Madam, I hope I have not daubed my fingers. I find, however, that you have been *looking* for them.'

As the eighteenth century gave way to the nineteenth so the number of new dictionaries multiplied, each one larger and more comprehensive and more authoritative than its predecessors. Perhaps the most notable was the formidable *American Dictionary of the English Language*, edited by the 'short, pale, smug and boastful' schoolmaster from New Hartford, Connecticut, Noah Webster.

This 'severe, correct, humourless, religious and temperate' man had already enjoyed extraordinary popularity with his earlier books—his first spelling book became the best-selling volume in the United States, exceeded only by the Bible, and in its heyday it thundered off the presses at the rate of more than 500 copies an hour. As a result the word *Websterian*—meaning 'invested with lexical authority'—rapidly entered the language, making its first appearance in print in 1790 (as it happens, a full year ahead of the

33

A

DICTIONARY

OF

THE ENGLISH LANGUAGE:

INTENDED TO EXHIBIT

I. THE ORIGIN AND THE AFFINITIES OF EVERY ENGLISH WORD, AS FAR AS THEY HAVE BEEN ASCERTAINED, WITH ITS PRIMARY SIGNIFICATION, AS NOW GENERALLY ESTABLISHED;—

II. THE ORTHOGRAPHY AND THE PRONUNCIATION OF WORDS, AS SANCTIONED BY REPUTABLE USAGE, AND WHERE THIS USAGE IS DIVIDED, AS DETERMINABLE BY A REFERENCE TO THE PRINCIPLE OF ANALOGY;—

III. ACCURATE AND DISCRIMINATING DEFINITIONS OF TECHNICAL AND SCIENTIFIC TERMS, WITH NUMEROUS AUTHORITIES AND ILLUSTRATIONS.

TO WHICH ARE PREFIXED

AN INTRODUCTORY DISSERTATION

ON

THE ORIGIN, HISTORY, AND CONNECTION OF THE

LANGUAGES OF WESTERN ASIA AND OF EUROPE;

AND

A CONCISE GRAMMAR, PHILOSOPHICAL AND PRACTICAL, OF THE ENGLISH LANGUAGE.

By NOAH WEBSTER, LL.D.

NEW YORK, 1828.

IN TWO VOLUMES.

"He that wishes to be counted among the benefactors of posterity, must add, by his own toil, to the acquisitions of his ancestors."—*Rambler.*

REPRINTED BY E. H. BARKER, ESQ. *of Thetford, Norfolk,*

FROM A COPY COMMUNICATED BY THE AUTHOR, AND CONTAINING MANY MANUSCRIPT CORRECTIONS AND ADDITIONS.

VOL. II.

LONDON:

PUBLISHED BY BLACK, YOUNG, AND YOUNG,

FOREIGN BOOKSELLERS TO THE KING,

2 TAVISTOCK STREET, COVENT GARDEN.

MDCCCXXXII.

Noah Webster created—entirely alone—his wildly popular *American Dictionary of the English Language* in 1828. For years afterwards this huge volume—defining twice as many words as Johnson—even outsold the Bible.

34

similarly freighted eponym *Johnsonian*). And when, in 1828, and after fifteen years of solitary work, Webster completed his dictionary,[11] it was almost double the size of Johnson's, with 70,000 headwords, 1,600 pages, and a preface declaring the book's solemn determination to fix and purify a language that Johnson—with his inclusion of vulgarisms and other low words—had in Webster's view dared to cheapen and to coarsen.

Despite the rivalry between the two men, between their two books, and between the two languages, the value and scale of both Johnson's and Webster's work is unchallenged. And since Webster was the larger, more comprehensive, and editorially less eccentric of the pair of books, it goes without saying that even while Johnson remained in print, Webster fast became the gold standard of the lexicographers' art, and sold almost as well in England as it did back home in America.

There was one final attempt to better even these. Charles Richardson, a schoolmaster from Clapham, published in two volumes *A New Dictionary of the English Language* in 1837—and he did so by employing what, by the developing standards of the day, was a most curious style. He almost entirely did away with definitions—but instead showed how each word had been used by illustrating usages with quotations. He decided that there had been four distinct linguistic eras in the story of English; the first ran from 1300 to the accession of Queen Elizabeth I in 1558. The second ended with the Restoration of the Monarchy in 1660. The third and shortest period closed with the reign of the first Hanoverian monarch, George I, in 1714. And the fourth period extended into the nineteenth century—more precisely, to 1818, when Richardson's

11 Webster finished his work while in Cambridge, in England—something of an irony, considering that he was a keen opponent both of Johnson and the notion that England was the fount of all authority over a new language—*American English*—that Webster, with vocal defiance, considered entirely separate.

dictionary began to appear, in parts, as contributions to the multi-volume *Encyclopaedia Metropolitana.*

Richardson endeavoured to show, for all words he included, quotations from each of the periods during which the word was known to have existed. He felt that only thus—by depicting a word's history, its *biography*—could the dictionary user have full and familiar knowledge of how best to employ the word himself. He considered definitions by and large to be irrelevantly prescriptive: far better to show how others had utilized the word than to insist on how it should be utilized in future. It was an approach—dictionary-making based on what were to be widely called 'historical principles'—that won Richardson a deserving place in the canon of lexicographers: and it was an approach that was eventually to inform, in all its essentials, the making of the greatest dictionary of them all.

3. The Mission

And yet none of these volumes was truly good enough. Not one of them—not Johnson, not Webster, not Richardson—ever did the English language justice. Nor did any of the dictionaries, so far as the growing army of nineteenth-century philologists felt, contain all the words that made up English in its entirety. To be sure, no one could be certain just how many words were in the language. But there was a feeling abroad that the total had to be very considerably more than the 80,000 or so (Webster had listed 70,000) that even these skilled lexicographers were managing to come up with.

At first this feeling was ill defined—no more than a vague unease. But in the early summer of 1842 came the beginnings of a formal acknowledgement of it. A wealthy Oxfordshire landowner and Anglo-Saxon expert named Edwin Guest—his financial condition underlining the assertion that what was to follow would be the work, initially, of men who were both learned *and leisured*—established what was to be called the Philological Society. He did so with other luminaries—most notably Thomas Arnold of Rugby School and Hensleigh Wedgwood, grandson of the potter Josiah, and one of the most notable etymologists in the land. The purpose of the Society—which exists still—was to 'investigate the Structure, the Affinity and the History of Languages'. Its first paper, which reportedly stimulated animated discussion among the members, was a classic of arcane enthusiasm: 'The dialects of the Papuan or Negrito race, scattered through the Australian and other Asiatic islands.'

Over the coming years the energies and fascinations of the Society turned steadily towards English. In the very early days a most curious parallelism developed between philology and, rather curiously it would seem today, the science of geology—with both rocks and the language thought to have a divine origin. Once Charles Lyell had published his *Principles of Geology* in 1830, though, it started to become evident and more widely accepted that the earth might not, after all, have been fashioned by God—and that being so, there was a period when the study of the language alone was thought divinely blessed, a science 'beyond the domain of matter'. Until more sensible ideas prevailed some while later, the geological metaphor was still employed to describe the nature of English—such as in this description by William Whewell, a founding member of the Philological Society and Master of Trinity College Cambridge.

> *The English language is a conglomerate of Latin words, bound together in a Saxon cement; the fragments of the Latin being partly portions introduced directly from the parent quarry, with all their sharp edges, and partly pebbles of the same material, obscured and shaped by long rolling in a Norman or some other channel.*

37

But although dictionary-making and geology long enjoyed a curious affinity, philology itself was eventually freed from what its adherents found a frankly rather weird association—an association born out of the belief that both sciences gave support to the words of Genesis and the orthodoxy of Christianity. Fifteen years after the Society's founding, though, such philosophical wonderings had rather diminished, and the Society was busily discussing such more obviously secular matters as 'Diminutives in *let*', 'On the word *inkling*', and 'On the derivation of the word *broker*' (this last discussion led by Hensleigh Wedgwood). There were papers also on the complexities of some foreign tongues—on 'The Termination of the Numeral Eleven, Twelve and the equivalent forms in Lithuanian', for example, and a spirited piece on the Tushi language, which is (or was) apparently well known in the Caucasian hill town of Tzowa, and which might be regarded today as a somewhat tricky tongue for beginners, given that the Tushi for the number 1,000 is the sonorously complex form of words *sac tqauziqa icaiqa*.

In June 1857, while the members were gamely pausing to learn Tushi counting (*cha, si, xo, ahew pxi, jetx* ...), three of their number—Herbert Coleridge, Frederick Furnivall, and the Dean of Westminster, Richard Chenevix Trench—set about discussing their principal concern about the English language. It was a worry that had begun to evolve from decades of undefined uneasiness, such that now at last it was a settled concern: that the dictionaries then currently in print were just not good enough. William Whewell had mentioned such a thought back in 1852, when he was still gripped by the idea that English had been handed down from the clouds. Five years later, and under the guidance of the holy *xo*, the ideas began swiftly to coalesce.

The Philological Society, these three men supposed, would be the body best suited to remedy the situation. And as that summer of 1857 began so they decided that their best contribution to philological inquiry would be to establish a Committee to ascertain just what words might have been left out of the English dictionaries. They would call it the Unregistered Words Committee, and its members would go out of their way to scour the literature and read newspapers and popular journals and listen to song scores and to conversation, and thereby add significantly, it was hoped, to the understanding and inventorying of the total stock of English words.

The first report of this Committee was to be announced five months later, at a meeting of the Society due to be held on Guy Fawkes Day, Thursday, 5 November 1857. There was much anticipation. Philology is by reputation a somewhat arid calling; but on that Thursday night there was a buzz of excitement from the members who filed in through the cold and foggy gloom into the London Library—a body which had long hosted the Society, in an unheated upstairs room in the premises still occupied, at the north-west corner of St James's Square.

So it was to general surprise and initial dismay that members were informed that the Report would not in fact be read that night. In its place one member of the Committee, the eminent divine Dean Trench, soon to be Archbishop of Dublin but at the time Dean of Westminster,[12] would present the first part of a paper. It was to be called 'On Some Deficiencies in our English Dictionaries'.

This was the paper that finally brought substance to what had hitherto been a half-formed presentiment. This was the document which at long last defined the problem that had long nagged at the serge-clad shoulders of a score of wordsmen. This was the

---

12 He was a brilliantly polymathic figure. He was also lame after breaking both knees— not through an excess of piety, but from stumbling down the gangplank of the Kingstown packet.

presentation that was to set in train the events that would lead, inexorably, to the making of the dictionary that all since Stanley Baldwin have considered to have—or which has long striven to have—essentially no deficiencies at all.

The audience, all men, most of them middle-aged, most of them resplendent in frock coats or in the astrakhan-collared capes and greatcoats and silk scarves and top hats that had comforted them against the cold yellow November fog, listened attentively to the grave Doctor as he enumerated the problems. There were, in essence, seven.

Obsolete words, for a start, were not fully registered in any dictionary thus far published. Secondly, families or groups of words were only capriciously included in these same dictionaries—some members of families made it in, some did not. Then again, such histories of words as were included in dictionaries rarely looked back far enough—the cited earliest appearances of many words was all too frequently given as far more recent than their actual inauguration, because the research had been performed too sloppily. Fourthly, important meanings and senses of words had all too often been passed over—once again, the research had too often been too perfunctory. Little heed had been paid to distinguishing between apparently synonymous words. Sixth, there seemed to be a superabundance of redundancy in all previous dictionaries—too many of them were bloated with unnecessary material, at the expense of what was really wanting. And finally, much of the literature which ought to have been read and scanned for illustrative quotations had not been read at all: any serious and totally authoritative dictionary had perforce to be the result of the reading and scanning and scouring of *all* literature—all journals, magazines, papers, illuminated monastic treatises, and volumes of written and printed publicly accessible works great, small, and impossibly trivial.

No, nothing that had so far been made was good enough. What was needed was a brand new dictionary. A dictionary of the English language in its totality. Not a reworking of the existing mis-formed and incomplete works; not a further attempt to make any one of the past creations somehow better or more complete; not a supplement, as the Unregistered Words Committee planned to publish. No, from a fresh start, from a tabula rasa, there should be constructed now a wholly new dictionary that would give, in essence and in fact, the meaning of *everything*.

Whatever this was, it had to be a book—an enormous book, quite probably, though not even Dean Trench was bold enough to hazard a guess as to how enormous—that did its level best to include the totality of the language. And by that was meant the discovery and the inclusion of every single word, every sense, every meaning. The book had to present a complete inventory of the language—such that anyone who wanted to look up the meaning of any word must be confident of finding it there, without a scintilla of doubt.

Moreover, the book that Dean Trench had in mind must, he said, be sure to present (unlike Richardson's) an elegantly written and carefully thought out definition, an exquisite summation of every single sense and meaning. It had to offer every variant spelling of every word ever known, as well as its preferred present-day spelling. It had to explain, in detail and as comprehensively as could be ascertained, every single word's etymology. It had to show how best every single form should be pronounced.

And it had to offer up—Dean Trench here returning to Richardson's 'historical principles'—a full-length illustrated biography of every word. The date of each word's birth had to be determined, and a register of the ways in which it grew and evolved and changed itself and its meaning over the years and decades and centuries after its first making. And this should generally all be accomplished without passing judgement on how the word was used—for, said the Dean, now warming to his theme, it had to be understood that 'a dictionary is an historical monument, the history of a nation contemplated from one point of view—and the wrong ways into which a language has wandered may be nearly as instructive as the right ones'.

The audience must have been startled, perhaps not a little overwhelmed, at the breadth and magisterial challenge of the project that Dean Trench had in mind. This was to be an inventory of *all* known English words? The meanings and senses were those to be found from the close reading of *all* of known published English literature? At first blush it seemed too mighty a project for anyone to imagine, let alone to contemplate. And yet as the Dean explained matters in more detail—and as he unveiled his principal idea for the making of something better than all that had gone before, something that he planned to call *The New English Dictionary*—so the men in their leather chairs began to nod their heads in agreement.

Yes, they began muttering to one another—this dictionary idea sounded like a scheme that was on just the titanic scale which Victorian Britain seemed these days to be taking in its stride. Was Britain not at the time unquestionably the most powerful nation on earth? Did her navies not sail unchallenged in every ocean between the Poles? Did not a quarter of the world's peoples bow down in abjectness and supplication before Her Majesty?

And was there not in addition something *muscularly Christian* about the language that was spoken? (Dean Trench was quite certain that there was.) Might it not be that making an inventory of the language, and by so doing asserting and underlining its greatness, would not just help the English language around the globe? By thus extending its usefulness and ubiquity it would not only spread English influence abroad, but spread the influence of the Church of England into the darkness of the native world as well. Victorian Britain, however absurd and jingoistic it may look through today's more critical lenses, represented an attitude suffused with near-absolute self-confidence and greatness of ambition. It existed at a time of great men, great vision, great achievement—and armed with hopes and intentions spiritual, moral, and commercial, there was almost nothing that it could not do.

Huge ships, immense palaces, bridges and roads and docks and railways of daunting scale, brave discoveries in science and medicine, scores of colonies seized, dozens of wars won and re-volts suppressed, and missionaries and teachers fanning out into the darkest crannies of the planet—there seemed nothing that the Britain of the day could not achieve. And now, to add to it all—a plan for a brand new dictionary. A brand new dictionary of what was, after all, the very language of all this greatness and moral suasion and muscularly Christian goodness, and a language that had been founded and nurtured in the Britain that was doing it—the idea seemed no more and no less than a natural successor to all of these other majestic ventures of iron and steam and fired brick. Yes, the men upstairs in the London Library said, with a growing hubbub of enthused excitement—it could be done. Moreover it should, it must, and it would be done.

To soothe any lingering doubts about the practicality of the project, Trench finally pulled the rabbit from his hat. He second-guessed his audience when he asked, rhetorically: How shall all these books, in which the meanings of all words resided, be read? This was his reply:

In that most interesting preface which Jacob Grimm[13] *has*

---

13 Of fairy-tale fame—Jakob and Wilhelm Grimm wrote sinister children's stories as well as dictionaries.

prefixed to his own and his brother's German dictionary, he makes grateful and honourable mention of no less than eighty-three volunteer coadjutors, who had undertaken to read for him one or more authors, and who had thrown into the common stock of his great work ... the results of their several toils. It is something of this common action which the Philological Society has suggested to its members. It entertained, also, from the first a hope, in which it has not been disappointed, that many besides its own members would gladly divide with them the toil and honour of such an undertaking.

An entire army would join hand in hand till it covered the breadth of the island ... this drawing a sweep-net over the whole extent of English literature, is that which we would fain see ...

And all saw that this, at a stroke, was indeed a most brilliant plan. The English-speaking peoples of the world would *themselves* be asked, begged, cajoled, pleaded with, and otherwise persuaded to join in concert, with the idea of listing the entirety of their very own language. A task which might take one man 100 lifetimes could take 100 men just one, or 1,000 men just a few years. To ask 1,000 to take part should not (the muttering, nodding, clubbably chattering philologists were saying as they filed back out into the fog) be an outlandish notion. This dictionary could well work. It might be three or four volumes in length. It might take five years, or seven, or even ten. But it could be done. Of that, at long last there now was no longer any doubt.

Moreover, by involving in the making of the lexicon the very people who spoke and read the language, the project would be *of the people*, a scheme that, quite literally, would be classically *democratic*. The book that Dean Trench had in mind was not the prescriptive invention of one man, nor even of a small number of men, nor of a committee. It would instead be a descriptive creation from all men; it would reflect the people's words and the

44

people's uses of them, and so be in yet more ways unlike any other dictionary ever made. It was a quite astonishing and revolutionary dream.

All that remained to lift this project from the idylls of drawing-room conversation and lecture-theatre dialogue to firm and effective action was a plan. As it happened, one was to come about in very short order.

A year after Dean Trench's speech, the Society passed a formal resolution to the effect that *A New English Dictionary on Historical Principles* was to be undertaken; a year later still the plan was devised, printed, and published. In the early summer of 1860 the Rules for the making of the great book—the *Canones Lexicographici*—were published too—giving instructions for attending to the minutiae that lay ahead.

The plan was for a very different book from that which was eventually to be created. The first idea was for a dictionary in three parts, with Part I containing most words, Part II holding technical words and proper names, and Part III the etymologies of all the words contained in the first two parts. But whether or not that plan was adhered to, the moment it was published, and a road-map for the journey had been officially made, so the boiler then fired; the steam-pump turned; the gearwheels meshed, and the whole laborious and pioneering process of making the dictionary to end all dictionaries was finally set in motion.

It was 12 May 1860—and though most of those involved thought their work would come to fruition within the following decade, it was in fact to be 68 years and three weeks from that starting date before the great work finally saw the light of day. The Rules were in place, the team was assembled, and now, that late spring day, the clock had finally started ticking.

2

The Construction of the
Pigeon-Holes

*I believe that the scheme is now firmly established ... and I
confidently expect ... that in about two years we shall be able
to give our first number to the world. Indeed, were it not for the
dilatoriness of many contributors, I should not hesitate to name an
earlier period.*

(Herbert Coleridge, first editor of
The New English Dictionary, 30 May 1860)

*The great fact ... is, that the Dictionary is now at last really
launched, and that some forty pages are in type, of which forty-
eight columns have reached me in proof.*

(James Murray, third editor of
The New English Dictionary, 19 May 1882)

Almost 22 years separate this pair of laconic announcements,
more than two decades dividing wish from fulfilment, man's
hopeful proposal of the plan from cool disposal of it by God or the
Fates. Those who were so eagerly hoping for the Dictionary to

appear were obliged to endure what was, by any standards, a long, long wait. The first years of the project were, in short, a most frustrating time. They were years marked by periods of hesitation and uncertainty, by outbursts of anger, threats of abandonment, frustrated argumentation, and (in one case) untimely and inconvenient death. Only in the later years, once a proper sense of organization had finally gripped the near-foundering project, were there any signs of progress and real achievement.

What in those early years was familiarly known as 'the Philological Society's Dictionary' had in essence three founding fathers—Chenevix Trench, Herbert Coleridge, and Frederick Furnivall. They were men of strikingly different backgrounds and attitudes, united only by their fondness and fascination for the language;[1] their variety of styles lent much, of both benefit and disbenefit, to the early workings of what, it fast became clear, was going to be a most formidable enterprise.

Richard Chenevix Trench came from a distinguished Irish clerical family,[2] was intellectually stellar enough to have been made a member of the Cambridge Apostles at Trinity, and was, at first, an unstinting admirer of Spanish literature. While still a youngster he seems to have been briefly infected with a heady sense of idealism: he flitted off to Spain to fight as a volunteer for the liberal insurrectionary Jose Torrijos, participating in a valiant attack on Cadiz—returning to London unscathed but apparently deeply embarrassed. It was, so far as one can tell from his admiring biographers, the only time in his life that he displayed the merest trace of foolhardiness, levity, or frivolity.

As his family expected of him, Trench promptly entered the

1 They had already spent time together as members of the Unregistered Words Committee, itself a precursor to the dictionary project.

2 The distinction only slightly dimmed over time: one descendant went on to become Provost of Eton, another (known to me) the manager of an oyster bar in Hong Kong.

In 1857 the Dean of Westminster, Richard Chenevix Trench, set in motion the making of an entirely new kind of English dictionary with a powerfully critical speech to the Philological Society, saying the existing volumes were just not good enough.

Church of England on his return home, and casting all romantic notions aside for good, duly progressed up the ecclesiastical ladder with efficiency and dispatch. He first became a deacon at Norwich Cathedral, went briefly back to Ireland to help famine victims as a curate in the parish of Cloughjordan, Co. Tipperary, then took up the post of curate in Colchester, and subsequently became perpetual curate of Curbridge, in the see of Winchester. It was during the six years that he spent here in Hampshire that he developed his reputation as a scholar, a liberal-minded reformer (becoming a fast friend of William Wilberforce, the great anti-slavery campaigner), a poet and—most significantly in this context—a philologist. He lectured widely on the nature and origins of the language, and, being a quick study, published three popular and well-regarded short books during the 1850s, *The Study of Words*, *English Past and Present*, and *A Select Glossary*.[3] After a curiously extended delay he joined the (by now fifteen-year-old) Philological Society in 1857—having been elected Dean of Westminster the year before—and for a while ran the Unregistered Words Committee for the Society from his official residence just beside Westminster Abbey.[4] He then, as already mentioned, gave the two-part

3   The Glossary 'of English Words used formerly in Senses different from their Present' makes for a charming read. We find a slightly regretful tone, as in Trench's remarks about the word *Orient*: 'This had once a beautiful use, as clear, bright, shining, which has now wholly departed from it. Thus, the "orient" pearl of our earlier poets is not "oriental" but pellucid, white, shining. Doubtless it acquired this meaning originally from the greater clearness and lightness of the east, as the quarter whence the day breaks.'

4   Trench arrived to find that his house, still known today as Dean's Yard, was— according to a grumble from his wife, Mary—filled with 'dead things' bones'. The previous Dean had been William Buckland, later to be the first professor of geology at Oxford, and an insanely eager palaeontologist. Buckland was notorious also for trying to eat specimens of every living thing, in his later years declaring mole to be the nastiest, followed by bluebottle. As if the disagreeable relics of Dean Buckland were not enough, Trench soon found that the purlieus of his Abbey in mid-Victorian times were no better than a slum—'one reeking and irreclaimable centre of filth and misery'. His work on collecting words for the new Dictionary had perforce to begin under somewhat uncongenial circumstances.

lecture on the shortcomings of existing dictionaries at the London Library in November 1857, which set in motion the plan for creating the great new replacement. Once the Society agreed on the idea, he promptly formed two committees—one on etymology, one on word history and literature—and for a while ran these, also, from Dean's Yard.

But before long the relentless press of his diocesan work proved too time-consuming, and within a few short months he told his colleagues that he could no longer continue: from henceforward, he said, work on the new book would continue under the editorship of Herbert Coleridge—and all correspondence on the matter would pass to him, at his elegant four-storey pale yellow mansion on the east side of Regent's Park, Chester Terrace. There have been many addresses associated over time with the making of the Dictionary: No. 10 Chester Terrace, London NW, is in all probability the one that most properly can lay claim to being its birthplace.

The man who was technically the book's first editor, Herbert Coleridge (though he is rarely identified as such in most of the official publications), was far from being a middle-aged divine: at the time of the founding of the Philological Society he was just twelve years old, and when Trench made his Guy Fawkes Day speech, a mere 27. He had been elected to the Society that same February, swiftly impressing all around him with his curiously precocious erudition: he won a stunning double first degree in classics and mathematics at Balliol College, he had become a barrister, he was quite ostentatiously obsessed with the byways of philology, most notably with the finer points of Sanskrit, the languages of Norway and Finland, and the dialects of Iceland. He had a small annuity, which allowed him to indulge his philology more keenly than his law.

The first editor was Herbert Coleridge, only 27 years old, a grandson of the poet. He was a scholarly and sickly figure, and had sent the first sample pages to press when he caught a chill and died, a year into the project.

As soon as he had won entry to the Philological Society Coleridge started writing papers for its well-regarded *Transactions*—a first essay on the nature of the diminutive formed by the addition of -*let* (he wondered why, for instance, a small river was called a *rivulet*, and not a *riverlet*), and another on the Latin words *ploro* and *exploro*. His very evident erudition (and the fact that he was the grandson of the poet Samuel Taylor Coleridge) attracted Dean Trench's attention; and when Trench felt pressed by his churchly duties to bow out of the day-to-day running of the project, it was to the ever-eager young man that he first turned. Such files as the Unregistered Words Committee had collected were promptly shipped from Dean's Yard to Chester Terrace, and the dictionary work began anew, under the captaincy of a younger man.

Younger, but not fitter, Herbert Coleridge turned out to be a sickly figure, plagued by what was once called consumption but which nowadays is more generally known as pulmonary tuberculosis. The image of him that filters down through the years is of a workaholic, rarely straying from his chambers, poring unhealthily over his correspondence, his lists of words and his organizational plans, while he coughed and vomited and wheezed and in alarmingly short order grew ever weaker and weaker.

His accomplishments made under these trying circumstances, though they are widely forgotten today, are far from trivial. With the help of a committee he drew up the *Canones*—the Rules—by which the three-part dictionary he envisaged might be created. He divided the books that were to be read into three groups—those appearing between 1250 and the publication of the first English New Testament in 1526; those published between 1526 and Milton's death in 1674; and those printed between then and 1858, when the project was formally set under way. He also found in the famed Nicholas Trübner a printer and publisher[5]—a rather premature arrangement, even the most optimistic might think—who would be able to perform the intricate work that a dictionary, with its countless typefaces and foreign languages and phonetic alphabets, required.

In addition Coleridge organized the first small army of volunteer readers—he wrote around to schools and universities and members of the Society and their friends, and within a year managed to find no fewer than 147 men (and a small number of women) who happily agreed to help find quotations showing a variety of words in contexts that the editor should find illustrated their various meanings and senses. But their ardour quickly cooled. Of these first 147, the editor reported dejectedly in May 1860, only some 89 were still working—the early enthusiasm of the other 58 (he dismissed them as 'hopeless') had clearly evaporated.

Coleridge was brutally frank about the quality of the survivors, and coldly invoked a lexicographical version of the triage: Class I, into which he placed some 30 men, were 'first-rate'; fifteen belonged to Class II, being only 'of inferior merit'; and the other 44 were lumped into Class III, 'not having produced sufficient work to be able to judge'. But matters looked up again when Coleridge found an American, the Honorable George Perkins Marsh of Burlington, Vermont, who readily agreed to mastermind a transatlantic search for illustrative quotations of wanted words. He impressed Coleridge as first-rate from the very start.

Marsh was himself was a fascinating character—a Puritan aristocrat, wealthy from his dealings in wool and railways, fluent

---

5   Trübner—his firm survived until 1892, and is now subsumed into Routledge & Kegan Paul—was the son of a Heidelberg goldsmith who became the publishing friend to a score of struggling scholars. Trübner 'est une bouche d'or' it was said—and for his kindness he was awarded chestfuls of honours, including the Lion of Zähringen, the White Elephant of Siam, and Crown of St Olaf of Norway. His firm published for the Royal Society their famous report on the eruption of the volcano Krakatoa. He was never, however, to publish a single page of the Dictionary, other than by way of experiment and specimen.

in twenty languages, sent as a diplomat to Istanbul, in later life a renowned environmentalist, and for all his career sufficient of a scholar to have Coleridge select him, from all the Americans that he knew, to be the ideal leader of the dictionary effort in America. By the time Marsh died in Florence in 1882 it was said that he had assembled a large group of distinguished Americans to help him with the project—fulfilling Coleridge's early promise that the title of an *English* dictionary was 'no longer strictly applicable', since the book could now include linguistic peculiarities from well beyond Albion's shores. Little remains to record how much effort Marsh actually made, though the fact that American contributions to the later development of the Dictionary have always been prodigious, suggests that he did leave a legacy of some kind.

Coleridge also made the very first list of words that he thought should be included—he took the material, the illustrative quotations that had been sent in by his 89 volunteer readers, to Chester Terrace, and arranged them alphabetically, according to the words to which they referred. He called these organized lists his 'basis of comparison'—since he would read through the various quotations and compare the way that the target word was used in each of them, so that he could compare their various meanings and senses and find out for himself which were essentially the same and which were different, and if different, whether profoundly or subtly so. It was by way of this non-judgemental, descriptive, and manifestly non-prescriptive way that meanings were eventually discerned, and the definitions written.

It is perhaps easiest to explain by offering an example.

Because of some gaps in the early archives of the Dictionary, it is difficult to be certain which submitted quotations were actually worked upon by Herbert Coleridge himself. We do know that he worked for more than a year on words that began with the letters A to E, and that to a lesser degree he began to sift through words beginning with the letters F to L. Within that first group we know also he asked Messrs Trübner to prepare some sample pages (somewhat prematurely, critics said), the most successful apparently being those for the words between *Affect* and *Affection*. It might be worthwhile looking here.

Some few of the words in the sample pages—*affectationist* for example, 'one who indulges in affectation or artificiality'—have only a single meaning. But most of other words have many more meanings—as, for instance, the word three further down the alphabetical line, *affected*. By reading the quotations submitted by volunteer readers for this one word, any good lexicographer who was working on proper historical principles would be able to recognize and discern several different shadings of meaning.

For instance, a quotation (and these that follow were indeed all received at Chester Terrace, and were eventually included in the Dictionary) such as 'He is too picked, too spruce, too *affected*, too odde', which comes from Shakespeare's *Love's Labour's Lost*, suggests the meaning 'full of affectation; non-natural or artificial in manner; pretentious; affecting airs'. On the other hand, if the editor found, as in Milton's 1649 work *Eikonoklastes*, the phrase 'A work assigned rather than by me chosen or *affected*', he would know that affected here meant something quite different—in this case, 'sought after, aimed at, desired'. And yet again, if another volunteer reader found in the *Daily Telegraph* and submitted to Coleridge a report allowing that 'the accused was mentally *affected*, her father and three of her aunts having all been insane', he would recognize a third meaning, 'tainted, distempered, diseased'.

This is not to say that an editor, having read these three quotations, would instantly come up with three meanings for the word. He would want many more quotations—five or ten at the very least—to confirm that one meaning was indeed different from another, that each of them had some persistence in the literature, and was not just the result of carelessness, or a malapropism. Which is why the work of a lexicographer is, as Samuel Johnson had famously said, so much harmless drudgery.

A microscopically close reading of all the literature would thus throw up as many meanings as were ever intended for any particular word (there are a total of eighteen definably different meanings and senses for *affected*)—whereupon Coleridge, or his successors, would make note of them, ponder the best way of writing a definition for each, gather in the etymologies and variant spellings and pronunciations, and have everything laid down in type, before moving on to the next word (in this case, *affectedly*).

To reiterate: Coleridge saw as his principal job the discovery of as many historically recorded uses as he and his volunteers could find of each of the words destined for the Dictionary; and from the comparisons he made of how each word had been used over time, he would work out which meanings were which, and arrange his dictionary accordingly. Moreover Coleridge, just like his colleagues[6] and successors, and in deference to the ideas of Dean Trench and to the *Canones* he and his committee had written, stuck gamely to the basic principle of the project: that the more quotations that could be found, the more easily the subtle differences between the (possibly) myriad usages and meanings of any single word could be identified. This is how historical dictionaries are made: not as difficult a task today, perhaps—but Coleridge and those around him were pioneers, and every step of the process was new to him and to all who tried to help.

---

6   One colleague was his uncle Derwent Coleridge, a cleric and schoolmaster whose appetite for language was formidable: as the *Dictionary of National Biography* (*DNB*) has it, 'he could read Cervantes and Alfieri as easily as Racine and Schiller, and was well acquainted with Hungarian and Welsh poetry. Of the latter he was intensely fond. He could also read not only Arabic and Coptic, but Zulu and Hawaiian.'

To help him in arranging the words and the quotation slips[7]—the crucially important pieces of paper that would be the project's building blocks—Coleridge had a carpenter build for him, in oak, a small suite of pigeon-holes, to hold and permit the alphabetical arrangement of the various quotation slips that his volunteers sent in. The arrangement which he designed was six square holes high, nine across—giving him a total of 54 pigeon-holes, with some 260 inches of linear space that were thought sufficient to hold comfortably between 60,000 and 100,000 of the slips. No greater number could Coleridge ever imagine his having to deal with. When they were all filled with quotation slips, he was heard to tell his fellow philologists, then and only then would it be time to start proper editorial work on the big dictionary.

Herbert Coleridge was a steady and a Christian man, and he had well-developed—but, as it happened in the end, lexicographically quite unacceptable—views on the kinds of word that should *not* be in the Dictionary. He asked the Philological Society, for example, to exclude mock words like *devilship* since in this one case 'it was never intended by its author for general circulation or adoption'. The Society members politely disagreed, and voted that such words should indeed be placed in the book (*devilship* is there, with a quotation, and not a humorous one, from 1644), and that only laboured and unused puns like *hepistle* and *shepistle* should be proscribed. (Both are rightly absent, though *herstory*—the feminist equivalent of *history*—is first quoted[8] from 1970.)

In mid-April 1861 he asked Trübner to print a few pages as specimens—the page that showed the words *Affect–Affection* was

7   His rules laid down a fixed design for the slips—they should be exactly half a sheet of writing paper in size, the headword should be at the top left, the quotation from each cited author should be written below, and there should be a separate slip for each quotation.

8   It appears first as a component in the acronym WITCH—'Women Inspired To Commit Herstory'.

regarded as the best. When he was halfway through working on a second 'basis for comparison', of those words beginning with letters between E and L, he was caught in a sudden spring rainstorm as he walked to St James's Square. He sat damply through a meeting of the Philological Society, and the next day, being thin and frail, caught a chill. He was taken back to his rooms, his friends watched aghast as the chill turned to consumption, and on the quintessentially English date of 23 April—both the Feast of St George and the birthday of Shakespeare—he died. He was just 31 years old.

It is said that his final words were 'I must begin Sanskrit tomorrow'. This seems a charming but somewhat improbable suggestion, given the section of the alphabet upon which he was working and the nature of the work he was bent on completing. But the story remains, indicative of the young man's learning, but hardly a memorial to his work on the book. The only other memorial (his plan for a three-part dictionary did not survive him, nor did his plans to have Messrs Trübner be the publishers, and his idea of having quotations going back only to 1250 was abandoned too, with the present Dictionary sporting illustrations from as far back as the ninth century) was the handmade set of 54 oaken pigeon-holes. These are still in existence, dusty and neglected in a museum in Oxford. Their dimensions proved woefully inadequate, and they were soon to be replaced by a set more than 40 times as large (and yet which in due course themselves proved to be just as niggardly too).

Herbert Coleridge had found it difficult to imagine that he would ever need to find room for the 100,000 quotations that he thought were likely to be used as the basis for the Dictionary. In the event, his successors had recourse to use the better part of six million, and no set of pigeon-holes known to man could ever have accommodated all of them.

Two years after Coleridge's death, Dean Trench returned to Ireland to take up the post of Archbishop of Dublin. The inchoate dictionary project, then no more than a barely formed mess of papers and file folders on a dead man's desk, was then handed over to the third member of the founding trinity—an amazing scholar-gypsy of a man who would be intimately associated with the project for the next half century, but whose early involvement led very nearly to disaster and abandonment.

He was Frederick James Furnivall, and though perhaps the most anodyne remark ever made about him was that 'to tobacco and alcohol he was a stranger through life' he was an eccentric of the fullest flower—or, as the *DNB* puts it with exquisite tact, he 'showed a characteristic impatience of convention and an undisciplined moral earnestness'. His long life was frequently mired in scandal, he was a man given to the oddest of short-lived enthusiasms. Of all the leading players in this saga, the boisterous Frederick Furnivall remains among the most colourful, most memorable, and deservedly best loved.

His critics—and they were legion—made much of the fact that his father ran (and made a fortune from so doing) a private lunatic asylum in Egham, in Surrey. He was an indifferent mathematics student at Cambridge, and is best remembered there and later for his fondness for sculling, the solitary sport he always thought far superior to rowing (though he had made the Trinity Hall rowing club's first eight), and which he pursued as a hobby all his life. He then became a student at Lincoln's Inn, and in due course (and without much enthusiasm) he became a lawyer.

But his first passion remained sculling. He was sufficiently dedicated to the sport, and with his inherited fortune insulating him from the need to pay too much attention to legal work, that he took time to design a special outrigger for his boat, to form sculling clubs, to inveigh against clubs that forbade working men from

Coleridge was succeeded by the scandalous, irrepressible but entirely lovable Frederick Furnivall, whose caprices and poor judgement very nearly caused the collapse and abandonment of the entire enterprise.

taking part, and, most vocally of all, to protest against the then general ban on allowing women on the water. He was inordinately fond of the ladies; and in his middle years he liked to recruit pretty waitresses from the Aerated Bread Company's teashop in Hammersmith with a view to teaching them the delights of his chosen sport. There are sepia photographs of him grinning impishly, surrounded by a group of very well-proportioned (and evidently rather cold) shopgirls in their close-fitting sculling tops, and others of him speeding along the river, a pretty girl behind him, with his long white beard flowing in the wind, the two of them a picture of goatish contentment.

One of the girls, an Oxford Street waitress named Blanche Huckle, from whom (after racing up the stairs two at a time 'like a young boy') he invariably ordered 'weak coffee, rusks and butter', wrote in a memorial volume published after his death, that 'Furney' was 'one of the kindest gentlemen I have ever met'. He would regularly 'invite several of us girls to a picnic up the river', she added, and he would bring presents to the café, most often 'two pairs of stockings for each of us'.

Such images led many to suppose Furnivall a bit of a rascal—and indeed, he confirmed his membership of a flexible moral universe by committing the doubly unpardonable sin of first marrying his very young lady's maid, Lizzy Dalziel, and then, after she had borne him two children and had become, as he saw it, 'indolent and dull', cruelly abandoning her. He left her, when he was 58, for a girl 37 years his junior, his dazzlingly pretty and intellectually vibrant 21-year-old secretary named Teena Rochfort-Smith. So appalled was one correspondent on receiving word of this affair that 'he immediately stuck stamp-paper over the signature of the writer who gave him the news'. *Vivat, Victoria!* (Sadly, fate saw to it that Teena was not able to bring Furnivall happiness for very long. She was burned to death in Goole, in Yorkshire, after a flaming

Frederick Furnivall loved two things as much as the English language—the company of pretty young women and the noble watersport of sculling. He managed to combine both passions by establishing a Ladies' Sculling Club in Hammersmith, West London, and appears well contented among its membership.

match-head broke off while she was trying to destroy some letters. It was a scant two months after her lover had obtained a formal separation from his wife.)

This extraordinary, 'embarrassing but unembarrassable' man—'[this] kind, selfless, patriotic humanitarian ... [this] dedicated literary detective, collating, annotating, transcribing, deciphering and editing so that all Englishmen might read the literature of their noble forefathers ... [this] volatile, impulsive, meddling, cantankerous literary warmonger ... [this] undiplomatic, unconventional individualist in corduroy trousers and pink-ribbon tie', as a biographer put it—promptly took on the work that Coleridge's death had bequeathed to him. Technically he was a practising solicitor—though far more interested in philology, socialism, and girls—and so at first all the dictionary work was passed from Chester Terrace first to his law office on Ely Place, and later to his house in St George's Square, off Primrose Hill. In May 1862—a year after Coleridge's death—a friend[9] recorded meeting Furnivall at work:

> *Found him in a strange dingy room upstairs; the walls & floor and chairs strewn with books, papers, proofs, clothes, everything— in wondrous confusion; the table spread with a meal of chaotic and incongruous dishes, of which he was partaking, along with 'Lizzy' Dalziel, the pretty lady's maid whom he has educated into such strange relations with himself, and for whose sake he has behaved so madly to Litchfield & others of his best friends; & her brother, a student of our College. After the meal, which lasted from 7 to 9, all four of them set to work, arranging and writing*

9 The friend was the poet Arthur Munby, whose own sexual eccentricities became known only after his death in 1910. He was powerfully attracted to rough, strong, dirty women, and he married his own servant, Hannah Cullick, delighting in her covering herself with dirt and soot as, perfectly willingly, she cleaned the household chimneys entirely naked. Much of his poetry extols the virtues of manual labour and working women.

out words for the Philological Dictionary, of which Furnivall is
now Editor in place of poor Herbert Coleridge. 'Missy', as F.
calls the girl, is his amanuensis and transcribes: takes long walks
too with him and others, of ten and twenty miles a day; which
is creditable to her; and indeed she seems a quiet and unassuming
creature.

There is no doubting either Furnivall's genius, his energy, or his scholarship. He was blessed with friends who luxuriated in his many talents: Alfred, Lord Tennyson was close, as were Charles Kingsley, John Ruskin, William Morris, and Frederick Delius. And the banker-writer Kenneth Grahame, who shared Furnivall's enthusiasm for sculling, eventually succeeded in writing his friend into *The Wind in the Willows*, a book which Furnivall had encouraged him to write. He cast him as the Water Rat, a cunning and ever-keen creature imbued with a properly rattish pedantry. 'We learned 'em!' says Toad. 'We taught 'em!' corrects Rat.

But what was seriously wanting in Furnivall, in his now enforced role as dictionary editor, was any sustained sense of organization or self-discipline. He was dedicated and enthusiastic, true; and there was much early optimism about his appointment. 'I am very glad you are able to undertake the dictionary,' wrote Hensleigh Wedgwood, still stunned by Coleridge's early death, 'which must otherwise have gone to pot.' Elisabeth Murray, the granddaughter of the man who would eventually succeed Furnivall, admitted the man's 'impressive' sustained enthusiasm—but at the same time she could see that his was a much misdirected enthusiasm, and that he was sorely lacking both in patience and in an acknowledgement of a great need— extraordinary in a dictionary-maker—for accuracy.

His problem, so far as the Dictionary was concerned, is perhaps best illustrated by his indefatigable and inexplicable need to found societies. Between 1864 (when he should have been hard at work on the book) and 1886, he founded no fewer than seven of them: the Early English Text Society, the Chaucer Society, the Ballad Society, the New Shakspere Society (whose members clung to the old spelling of the Bard's name), the Wyclif Society, the Browning Society, and the Shelley Society. His involvement with the Philological Society began early on in his life, in 1847, not long after it was founded. He became its joint secretary in 1853—and later, as mentioned, one of the trinity of good men on the Society's Unregistered Words Committee.

In addition to all of the duties and responsibilities that stemmed from so much belonging, Furnivall was a deeply committed socialist and (until his later agnosticism set in), a somewhat enthusiastic Christian, and a keen believer in the right of blue-collar labourers to enjoy the benefits of a full education. His involvement with the London Working Men's College, which had been set up to take care of such needs, took up much of his time as well. He took up long-distance cycling, and would spend weekends touring southern England with his new labouring friends. He fought gamely against any injustice he perceived was visited on workers—on one occasion leading a deputation of angry ballast-heavers to Downing Street, and on another selling some of his own books to help pay the legal fees of some vexed wood-cutters.

And if all this were not enough diversion, Furnivall also managed to get himself involved in a series of the most dreadful spats and arguments, fights that would have sapped the energy of many a lesser man. The most celebrated of these fights was with the poet Algernon Charles Swinburne. It all began in 1876 with a technical dispute over the metre of lines in a play, *Henry VIII*, that had once been loosely attributed to Shakespeare. It smouldered for some years, then burst out into the open, and in a torrent of abuse: Swinburne called Furnivall 'the most bellicose bantam cock that ever defied creation'; Furnivall countered by accusing the poet of having 'the ear of a poetaster, hairy, thick and dull', and played with the origins of his name, restyling him as 'Pigsbrook'. Swinburne in turn looked up the origins of Furnivall's name, and rendered it into 'Brothel-dyke', and his gatherings 'Fartiwell and Co.' or 'The Shitspeare Society'. This undignified feud lasted for six miserable and exhausting years (great fun for all spectators, of course). It stirred up tidal waves of a lasting enmity directed at both men. And it must have had a singularly damaging impact on Furnivall's more important tasks.

The inevitable consequence was that under Frederick Furnivall's direction, work on the Dictionary in the years following Coleridge's death, staggered, stalled, and then very nearly died itself. Furnivall was 36 when he took over the job. He assumed it would take him until he was just over 40 to complete it. And so he began in earnest, assembling yet more reading lists, gutting yet more books for quotations, taking on new armies of volunteers: 'Fling our doors wide!' he wrote, exhorting readers to send in ever more, 'all—not one, but all—must enter!'

He next arranged (once Trübner had lost interest, or the firm's contract had lapsed, or both) for the much-revered house of John Murray[10] to agree to take on the task of publishing the book. He tried to persuade the firm of his seriousness of purpose by proposing they first publish a Concise version of the book, which, he promised, could be ready in three years or less. In addition he hired a new rank of employee—the sub-editor, he was called, a fairly new term borrowed from the newspaper industry—who would undertake (without pay: Furnivall was at first most persuasive) the lexicographical grunt-work that Furnivall regarded himself as too grand to perform.

---

10 Still admired today, as since 1768—though lately subsumed into the embrace of the Hodder Headline group.

But despite the burst of initial enthusiasm, little was to come of anything. The *Concise English Dictionary* never got out of the starting gates—John Murray called Furnivall a 'h'arbitrary gent', and pulled out of talks. Volunteer readers, infuriated by Furnivall's short attention span and his caprices of fascination, began deserting the programme in droves. Sometimes it was simply Furnivall's irascibility that scared them away. 'Next time,' he wrote to one, testily, 'will you be good enough to copy out each passage on a separate half-sheet of notepaper? All your former ones I shall be obliged to have cut up and pasted on larger pieces of paper.' (At least this particular volunteer did not commit what some—though not Furnivall—regarded as the heresy of cutting up the books he was reading, and pasting the quotation onto the slip. Many was the time when sub-editors would receive slips with valuable sixteenth-century black-letter cuttings stuck onto them, evidence of a book now ruined by lazy lexicographic vandalism.)

But sub-editors too, daunted by the huge number of quotation slips that had arrived by the sackful during the volunteers' more productive days, started abandoning ship as well. And though Furnivall did, as he had promised, successfully oversee the making of the third part of the Basis of Comparison, for the letters M to Z, it was not long before the Philological Society itself began to get cold feet too.

A steadily decreasing official enthusiasm for the project begins to make itself evident in the Society's journal, the *Transactions*, as the years of Furnivall's editorship continued. In the beginning the journal's pages were filled with exuberant and confident reports of the 'tremendous progress' and 'great strides' and 'significant achievements' that were being realized by the project's managers, as quotation slips were being solicited, shades of meaning determined, definitions written, entire letters ticked off the list. But slowly, towards the end of the 1860s, the purpose begins to falter.

The year-end assessments of progress became shorter, their language less robust, the show of optimism less evident. By 1872 Furnivall was forced to report to his masters that 'progress in the Dictionary has been so slight that no fresh report in detail is needed'.

Books and papers held by the volunteers—many of them had been sent volumes from the Philological Society's library, which they would use to do their research—were now being returned by readers too exasperated, weary, or disenchanted to go on. Before long the lobby of Furnivall's house at No. 3 St George's Square was 'cumbered with boxes and bundles of every size and form'; in 1879 more than two tons of papers were sent in as the wholesale abandonment of the project proceeded. Moreover, it was now clear that other disenchanted volunteers had simply left their papers and their books where they stood—had consigned them to lumber rooms, taken them away on holiday and left them behind in faraway hotels and boarding houses, dumped them in rubbish bins, lost them. By the mid-1870s, the work of thousands had been dispersed across half the world like wind-borne pollen: if the project ever were to be revived, it would take an immense amount of diligent searching to bring it all together again.

But it was worse than that. A terminal crisis was looming. 'The general belief', wrote an editor at the *Athenaeum*, 'is that the project will not be carried out.' If the great dictionary project was to continue, it would require the appointment of a far more organized, less volatile, and better-tempered leader at its helm.

The Society was already recognizing this as early as 1874, when its President, the mathematician Alexander Ellis, wailed that he thought the body 'less fitted to compile a dictionary than to get the materials [for it] collected'. Then again a year later the sub-editor who had worked on the letter F (and who had supervised a second series of specimen pages, on the words *Fa*[11] to *Face*), the Reverend George Wheelwright, suggested, in a briskly worded pamphlet, that Furnivall make up his mind about the future of the scheme.

He should, the cleric said, promptly find a new editor, assure everyone that they were not on 'a Fools chace which should end only in a general fiasco', and by so doing bring to an end 'the intolerable suspense under which we all groan'. Wheelwright had spent ten years of his life dedicated to the Dictionary: he was not about to see it fail without someone, somewhere, making an effort to save it.

As early as 1871—three years before his Society became publicly exasperated, four before Wheelwright's outburst—Furnivall himself had come to appreciate how hopeless he was at running the project, and had tried to find a replacement. He knew he had lost sub-editors who had initially agreed to supervise the words beginning with the letters A, I, J, N, O, P, and W—leaving fully one quarter of the alphabet uncovered—and he wrote that he was now bound to look 'for a fresh editor for the whole work'.

He had first approached Henry Sweet, a notoriously rude phonetician who was later used by George Bernard Shaw as a model for Henry Higgins in *Pygmalion*—later the play and film *My Fair Lady*. But Sweet had turned him down flat. Furnivall then approached Henry Nicol, another eminent and rather calmer philologist, who was amenable to the idea, and rather flattered. But when he looked at the size of the task ahead he reminded himself that he was chronically unwell, and in any case too busy with other tasks—and so Furnivall had to look elsewhere.

It was fully four years later that he at last came upon the man

---

11 *Fa* has four meanings—versions of the words *few*, *foe*, and *fall*, and the fourth note of the octave in the sol-fa system.

who would pull the project back from the brink, and propel it to its ultimate success. It began with a chance remark made to him at a Philological Society meeting. It ended with Furnivall concluding decisively that the man who had made the remark would, could, and indeed should be the ideal candidate for the post of new editor. He began immediately to work 'like a busy spider', as he later put it, spinning the web that would eventually ensnare his candidate and keep him tightly enmeshed in the Byzantine complexities of the English language for the rest of his days.

The man was James Augustus Henry Murray. What he had said to Furnivall, when he learned of the difficulties the Secretary was having in finding a new editor for the Dictionary, was simple, no more in essence than, 'I rather wish I could have a go at it.' He had not intended the remark to be taken seriously. After all, he was no more than an amateur philologist, interested in whiling away his evenings musing on the origins of dialect. He was 38 years old, a former bank clerk who was by now employed rather more happily as a teacher at the Mill Hill School in north London. He was a lowland Scot, a linen draper's son, from the Teviotdale village of Denholm, near Hawick, in Roxburghshire. He had been brought up in rural isolation, his family unmoneyed, his life unsophisticated, his future unpromising. 'I am a nobody,' he would write in later years, when fame had begun to creep up on him. 'Treat me as a solar myth, or an echo, or an irrational quantity, or ignore me altogether.'

But there was no ignoring him, for James Murray was in all ways—and in particular, in intellectual ways—unforgettably remarkable. He was remarkable even in an age that produced a disproportionate share, or so it seems today, of exceptionally clever men. He has a reputation still as a towering figure in British scholarship. He was Calvinist in his spiritual outlook, polymathic in his interests and his competences, forbidding in his appearance—a fiery red beard lent him the air of faint bellicosity—and he was all too casually aware of the combined effect that these formidable attributes of looks and brains had on those around him. He radiated a magisterial air of righteous authority—rather, as it turned out, as the dictionary that he would make would also radiate in its own time.

And he, at long last, was the man who would make all the difference.

3

The General Officer Commanding

I have to state that Philology, both Comparative and special, has been my favourite pursuit during the whole of my life, and that I possess a general acquaintance with the languages and literature of the Aryan and Syro-Arabic classes—not indeed to say that I am familiar with all or nearly all of these, but that I possess that general lexical & structural knowledge which makes the intimate knowledge only a matter of a little application. With several I have a more intimate acquaintance as with the Romance tongues, Italian, French, Catalan, Spanish, Latin & in a less degree Portuguese, Vaudois, Provençal & various dialects. In the Teutonic branch, I am tolerably familiar with Dutch (having at my place of business correspondence to read in Dutch, German, French & occasionally other languages), Flemish, German and Danish. In Anglo-Saxon and Moeso-Gothic my studies have been much closer, I having prepared some works for publication upon these languages. I know a little of the Celtic, and am at present engaged with the Sclavonic, having obtained a useful knowledge of Russian. In the Persian, Achaemenian Cuneiform, & Sanscrit branches, I know for the purposes of Comparative Philology. I have sufficient knowledge of Hebrew & Syriac to read at sight the Old Testament and Peshito; to a less degree I know Aramaic

Arabic, Coptic and Phenecian to the point where it was left by Gesenius.

(Letter of application for a post at the British
Museum Library written by James Murray,
to Thomas Watts, Keeper of Printed Books,
November 1866. Murray's application
was not successful.)

J ames Murray was very nearly appointed to direct the fortunes of quite another dictionary. In 1876 he was approached by the publishing firm of Alexander Macmillan, who had been hired to act as agents for the American house then known as Harper & Brothers. Harper were in an agitated condition over the stunning success that was currently being enjoyed in America by the firm of George Merriam, which had been making a small fortune by publishing Noah Webster's great *American Dictionary of the English Language.* They now wanted to create their own work to rival Webster's, and asked Macmillan to scout around in the salons of literary London to see if they could come up with a scholar who might be amenable to accepting the post as the new project's editor. Richard Morris, a schoolmaster and a member of Furnivall's Early English Text Society, thought immediately of Murray, the young Scot who was fast making a name for himself as philology's rising star. Macmillan approached Murray, and sounded him out.

Fortunately for the future of what would in due course become our *Oxford English Dictionary,* Murray turned down the Macmillan proposal—which came, he said, as 'a bolt from the blue'. The book that Harper had in mind, he surmised, was too short, too wanting in significance and ambition. He thought the very minimum size of a new dictionary that might rival Webster was 5,000 pages—it might not even fit into 5,500. He drew up some sample pages—they involve the early words beginning with *Car-*, such as *carabineer*, *caramel*, *carapace*, and *caravan*—to demonstrate how large a comprehensive dictionary would have to be.

But Harper had done their sums in New York, and the suits of the day would not budge from the corporate view that all could be encompassed by no more than 4,000 pages. And that is where the negotiations stalled. Murray was certain that the grand confection of a dictionary that the Philological Society had in mind—though in truth, with all of Furnivall's talk of a Concise edition, and the project's general lack of momentum, he was not exactly sure *what* the Society was now wanting—was what the English language truly deserved. So he would prefer to wait, he said, for the big dictionary to get itself under way, and he would have no truck with anything of lesser standing.

It was not quite so simple, however. Murray was notoriously a ditherer when it came to making the bigger decisions of his life—as this one was most certainly to be. And yet as so often happened, it was his wife, Ada, whose own very trenchantly expressed views eventually prevailed upon him. He should not devote his life, she said, to achieving merely a number of smaller things, if by doing so he let slip the opportunity of achieving one thing that history would regard as truly great.

James Murray[1] had been a precocious, rather solemn little boy. On the flyleaf of a copy of the *Popular Educator*, a magazine to which he subscribed in his early teenage years, he declared

---

1   It was by this name alone that he was baptized, shortly after his birth on 7 Feb. 1837. He only started to use the additional names, Augustus Henry, when he was eighteen, never giving a ready explanation for his choosing them, other than the offer of an indulgent smile when a friend remarked that the initials JAH were to be found in the 68th Psalm as a contraction of Jehovah.

quite baldly: 'Knowledge is power', and added to it (in Latin—with which, at fifteen, he was perfectly familiar, as he was also in French, Italian, German, and Greek) the motto 'Nihil est melius quam vita diligentissima' (Nothing is better than a most diligent life). And even though the two best-known works about him were both written by relations—his son Wilfrid and his granddaughter Elisabeth, who might be suspected of having rather less than disinterested views of him, produced admiring biographies—his childhood does appear to have been quite exceptional.

He was omnivorous in his appetite for knowledge, quite catholic in his range of interests—he became an adept in the details of Roxburgh's geology and botany and wildlife, he took up mapping, he became an exceptional amateur astronomer (his younger brothers complained when James shook them awake to see the rising of Sirius, the time of which he had calculated and—to the family's sleepy exultation—correctly predicted), he cherished the fact that he had managed to befriend a local ancient who had been alive when Parliament proclaimed William and Mary joint sovereign in 1689, and he urged his mother to tell him over and over again how she first heard tell of the victory at Waterloo.

He volunteered at scores of nearby archaeological diggings—since Hadrian's Wall was only a few miles to the south, the ground was littered with lightly buried artefacts from Roman times. He became fascinated with the works of an obscure French writer named Théodore Agrippa d'Aubigné (he would read his works out loud to his fascinated family, translating into English as he did so). He learned how to bind books. He taught himself how to illuminate manuscripts with elegant little drawings, fleurons, and curlicues (learning in doing so that the room in which medieval monks would do such work was called a *scriptorium*—a word that would later come to haunt him). Though being far from a mechanical man, he once tried to invent water-wings by tying bundles of pond irises to his arms (but, being a life-long non-swimmer, nearly drowned after miscalculating their buoyancy, and only escaped by being dragged from the stream by friends hauling on his five-foot-long bow tie). He gave Latin names to the individual cows in the family's small herd of dairy cattle, and he taught them to respond to his calls. And when Louis Kossuth, the Hungarian nationalist, came on an official visit to Hawick in 1856, one of the 38 welcoming banners draped across the High Street declared, with precise Magyar perfection, 'Jöjjö-el a' te orszagod!' The nineteen-year-old James Murray had thought it appropriate to welcome Kossuth appropriately, with 'Thy Kingdom Come!'.

The Murray family was far too poor (though James's maternal grandfather had once been famed across Scotland for making the finest table linen of the day) for them to be able to afford to send this 'argumentative earnest, naïve' young man to college of any kind, and so at fourteen James left school, to earn his own way. Three years later we find him teaching his local village schoolchildren, and three years later still doing the same, but for a halfway respectable wage, at a nearby subscription academy, where boys aged ten to sixteen were offered a rigorous education 'on payment of one guinea a term'. He became a member of the Hawick Mutual Improvement Institute, then helped form the Hawick Archaeological Society and in due course gave his first lecture there, on 'Reading, Its Pleasures and Advantages'. It was around this time, when he was in his early twenties, that he became fascinated by phonetics—learning more than 300 words in Romany, delighting in the mythical origins of the Scottish tongue and in the magic of Anglo-Saxon.

And then, crucially, Murray fell under the spell of the fascinations of philology, and in a fury of new enthusiasm—but one which, unlike Furnivall's, never dimmed—he pitched into a close study of the origins of Scottish dialects and the curiosities of

Scottish pronunciation. He took a course on elocution in Edinburgh, and there—yet again, crucially for this story—he met the field's residing genius professor, Alexander Melville Bell. Bell taught him something of his brand new conception known as Visible Speech, a symbolic representation of every sound the human mouth was capable of making and, supposed Bell, the likely basis for a truly global language, a kind of facial Esperanto (and which, like Esperanto, never caught on).

He introduced James to his son, Alexander Graham Bell, with a historical nicety as a consequence. Since it has long been agreed that James Murray, one summer's afternoon in 1857, taught Alexander Graham Bell the basic principles of electricity (making for the boy an electric battery and a voltaic cell out of halfpennies and discs of zinc), it is said by admirers of Murray that he is in fact the true grandfather of the electric telephone, which the younger Bell was later to invent. The first prototype telephone ever made, in fact, was said for many years to lie in James Murray's Oxford attic—though this particular anecdote, involving as it does the curious fate of the instrument, belongs rather later in this story.

Melville Bell also introduced James Murray to the existence in faraway London of the Philological Society, and showed him papers that the organization was publishing. The visitor's interest was immediately piqued—and before long he had thrown himself into the study and had taken into his head, from a paper by Prince Louis-Lucien Bonaparte, a nephew of Napoleon's, the notion of translating biblical works into Scottish dialects. After complaining that all the earlier attempts that he had read had in his view been done very poorly and inaccurately, he eventually published his own rendering of the Book of Ruth into the language of Teviotdale. The book describing how he did this[2]—*Dialect of the*

2   This was not his first book. In 1861 he had published a 50-page monograph entitled *A Week Among the Antiquities of Orkney.*

Southern Counties of Scotland—was to be published in 1873, and it fully confirmed for James Murray a reputation that had begun to grow as early as the 1860s: that he was a philologist of the first water.

In 1861 he met and the following year married a local infant-school music teacher, Maggie Scott. Their wedding pictures[3] show the 25-year-old James to have been a tall, rather unkempt figure, with a bowed, almost simian appearance, with long arms that nearly brushed his knees, a ragged beard, ill-fitting and baggy clothes, and an expression that seems to mix distracted inattention with a vague apprehension of impending gloom, as turned out to be entirely appropriate.

Two years later the young couple had a baby girl they christened Anna—but she died soon afterwards of consumption, and Maggie fell ill enough for the doctors to propose (preposterously, given the Murrays' poverty) that she travel to the south of France to convalesce. Instead they went to a small house in Peckham, in south London—a marginally better climate than the Scottish Borders, the physicians agreed—and James Murray was obliged to set aside his intellectual pursuits and to take an uninteresting job at the headquarters of the Chartered Bank of India, Australia, and China. He would perch forlornly on a high stool in the Foreign Correspondence department in the very back of the office, wearing starched cuffs and an eye-shade, and write in ledgers in copperplate script while in the company of a host of wage-slaves and Lupin Pooters, all men quite devoid of intellectual curiosity or ambition.

Except that through all these travails he did not quite abandon his high-mindedness and his sense of an impending grand

---

3   The couple were married in Belfast, to where the sickly Maggie had been advised to travel by her doctors.

purpose. As Maggie slipped closer and closer towards her early death, James kept his intellect busied: he would speak to London policemen and try to determine, from their accents, from where they came; he studied Hindustani and Achaemenid Persian on his daily commute; he lectured on such topics as 'The Body and its Architecture' before such groups as the Camberwell Congregational Church and his local Temperance League (he was a confirmed teetotaller). He learned how the Wowenoc Indians of Maine counted their sheep, and compared their peculiar brand of ovine numerology with that of the moorland farmers of Yorkshire. And, macabre though it may sound at this remove, he even took care to notice that as Maggie slipped into her deathbed delirium, she would cry out in the broad Scottish dialect of her childhood, abandoning in her misery the refined modulations of the classroom.

It cannot but have been a blessed release when Maggie Scott eventually died, though there is no doubt from his writings that James had loved and cared for her. Looking back on a time of evident desolation he would write: 'A marriage, a birth, two deaths—all in three short years! … and I was left alone in London, doing uncongenial work.' And yet it was with an almost indecent alacrity that just a year after Maggie's funeral in Hawick, James Murray married for a second time.

Ada Ruthven, who would be his companion and helpmeet (and powerful antidote to his dithering) for the rest of his days, turned out to be a woman very much more in tune with his social and intellectual needs. Her father, George, had worked for the Great Indian Peninsular Railway—he and James Murray had indeed met on a train, where Murray found that his companion was, to his delight, an admirer of and sometime scholar devoted to the great German traveller and scientist Alexander von Humboldt. Sensing James's interest in the arcane that might not so stimulate all his hearers, George Ruthven added that his wife had long claimed to have been at school with Charlotte Brontë! It then seemed no more than logical, given Murray's evident fascination with these sensational revelations in a third-class railway carriage, that he should be invited home to meet the Ruthvens' daughter Ada—with the happy result that, in short order and as all concerned fondly hoped, the couple were duly married, and became wholly inseparable.

Together James and Ada produced six sons and five daughters. To underscore the formidable intellectual atmosphere that must have prevailed in the kindly-strict Murray household (Murray had an eye that could 'both pierce and twinkle', a biographer remarked), it is worth noting how Wilfrid Murray catalogues the achievements of these children 'in whose achievements James Murray took great pride':

> *Harold, the oldest son, Exhibitioner and First Class Graduate of Balliol, was author of the* Oxford History of Chess *(1913) and, at the time of his retirement, a Divisional Inspector under the Board of Education. Sir Oswyn, GBC, the fourth son, Scholar, triple First and Honorary Fellow of Exeter and Vinerian Law Scholar, was Secretary to the Board of Admiralty from 1917 until his death in 1936; Jowett, the youngest, was a Scholar and Triple First of Magdalen and became a Professor in the Anglo-Chinese College at Tientsin; the second, Ethelbert, was at his death in 1916 Electrical Engineer for North London in Willesden; the fifth, Aelfric (Wadham College), took orders and became Vicar of Bishop Burton; the writer, also a Balliol Exhibitioner, was for 21 years Registrar of the University of Cape Town. Of the five daughters Hilda, the eldest, was a First Class Honours student at Oxford, Lecturer in English at Cambridge and Vice-Mistress of Girton College and has published several works; the second, Ethelwyn (Mrs. C. W. Cousins) was married to the Secretary for Labour of the Union of South Africa; the youngest, Gwyneth,*

(Mrs. H. Logan), a Girton First Class graduate, was married to a Canadian Rhodes Scholar who became Principal of the Prince of Wales Fairbridge Farm School in British Columbia; the remaining two, Elsie (Mrs. A. Barling) and Rosfrith, were both valued assistants for long periods on the Dictionary staff.

It was Murray's early friendship with Melville Bell in Edinburgh, and his later London encounters with the 'cross-grained' phonetician Henry Sweet and the Cambridge mathematician Alexander Ellis, that first led him to the Philological Society, and eventually to his fateful encounter with Frederick Furnivall. It was in 1868 that Bell—who had moved down to London himself, to become a lecturer at University College—first invited Murray to St James's Square, initially to hear Ellis deliver a paper on his speciality, the development of English pronunciation. At the same time, seeing Murray's huge contentment at being among the members, he formally introduced him, thus allowing the Scotsman—who still at the time was toiling in the banking house—to join a literary *corps d'élite*, about two hundred strong, whose fascination with the English language in particular was to become of historic importance. Since Furnivall was the Society's sole Secretary, the two men met, and were duly impressed with one another from the very start. So impressed, in fact, that by May of the following year Murray had been elected a member of the Council—a position that he held until his death nearly half a century later.

A year later he had left the bank, and had returned to the more leisured and rewarding world of teaching, having won a post at Mill Hill School in what were in those days the leafy suburbs of north London. The years that followed, he later wrote, were his 'Arcadian time, the happiest period of my life'. The school had given him a wonderfully comfortable house, which he named Sunnyside; his wife and family were in exceptional

81

form, comforting and supportive despite the meagre wage that had been offered; he was pleasantly occupied by his immense raft of scholarly interests; and he loved teaching polite and intelligent children who had been selected to attend what remains one of the country's finer schools.

His pupils adored him, and took great pleasure in his unconventional teaching methods. 'Dr Murray knows everything' became a watchword throughout the school. 'His classes were always intensely interesting,' wrote one boy:

> *You never knew where you might arrive before the lesson was done.*
> *A nominal geography class might easily develop into a lecture on*
> *Icelandic roots, and we often tried to bring him back to the days*
> *when the Finnish landed on the shores of the Baltic, on occasions*
> *when we had not been given adequate time to the preparation of our*
> *set lesson. Then the tricks he could play with words! Such was his*
> *skill and knowledge that many of us firmly believed that by*
> *Grimm's law he could prove that* black *really was the same*
> *word as* white; *at least that was how it seemed to our poor*
> *intelligences.*

He was troubled, however, by the simple fact that, however distinguished a philologist he might seem to be, and however celebrated a schoolteacher he appeared to have become, he felt a certain sense of ignominy mingling with his peers in the school common room because he still did not have a university degree. He in fact tried to win a degree at London University in 1871, a year after joining Mill Hill, but as his elderly father died while James was in the middle of his examinations, he was unable to complete them and only managed a humble pass degree, a kind of academic damnation with faint praise.

A campaign was promptly started to get him a proper one, though one that was honorary, requiring recognition rather than work. It was decided that a Scottish university would be the most appropriate for this Borders lad, and that of all the possible candidates, St Andrews would be the most stylish, but Edinburgh the most august. St Andrews had been criticized for having handed out too liberal a number of honorary degrees in recent years—and so Edinburgh, it was concluded, was the one. So a letter-writing blitz was begun.

It was far from difficult to write in fulsome terms of this most remarkably turned-out man. James Murray, wrote Frederick Furnivall, deserved to be granted a degree because he was 'the first living authority on our Northern Dialects', a man who 'if he lives, and I hope he will, long, will by a series of ... books ... do credit to the University that allies him to itself'. Prince Louis-Lucien Bonaparte chipped in with a supporting letter, as did Alexander Ellis and a score of other distinguished linguists and phoneticians. The university fretted for a while, and expressed its polite doubts: it was being asked to give an honorary doctorate of letters to a young man who was merely a schoolmaster, a former bank clerk and one who had left school at fourteen? To some of the elder brethren at what was Scotland's most esteemed academic establishment, this was a bit much.

In the end it was geology that came to the rescue—a drollery that would have amused William Whewell, one of the Philological Society's founders and a man who had expressed a firm belief that there were strong philosophical connections to be made between the historical development of words and of sedimentary rocks. In March 1874, when the Edinburgh University campaign was at its height, Murray had a chance meeting with Archibald Geikie, the professor of geology and a member of the University Senate. Geikie, later to become head of the British Geological Survey and a pioneer in work on evolution, remembered Murray's help as a youngster in solving various geological problems in the Teviot valley. He added his weight to the campaign, persuaded his fellow

Senators—and James Murray became an Honorary Doctor of Laws with effect from 1 April. 'It could not be *All* Fools Day when wise men do a wise deed,' exulted his brother Charles. 'What an Easter egg! Hip Hip Hip Hurrah!'[4]

And shortly thereafter, as if to confirm the wisdom of the Edinburgh award, Murray was invited by Thomas Baynes, the editor of the *Encyclopaedia Britannica*, to contribute the definitive essay on 'The English Language' for the ninth edition. He had not been the first choice—Baynes had initially asked Thomas Arnold—but he was flattered to get the invitation. 'A mere summary from you', wrote Baynes, in necessarily oleaginous tones, 'would be of more value than a longer article from a writer of less authority.' Murray wrote twelve pages, a summary that remained a classic, long in print—certainly for as long as *Britannica* remained a work of authority, a role it relinquished only recently. Murray was asked to revise his article in 1895, and it duly became part of the celebrated 11th edition, surviving intact for decades beyond, with the result that our uneducated Teviotdale draper's son was to become, in essence, the established authority on the national language for several generations.

And then came the chance remark to Furnivall, during the frustrating days of searching for a replacement editor for the Philological Society's dictionary: 'I rather wish I could have a go at it.'

By this time—it was March 1876—Murray was a rising star within the Society, was properly equipped for academe with his honorary Scottish LL D (plus his London University pass degree),

---

4   There was evidently some tomfoolery afoot during the degree ceremony, as one of the benches collapsed under the weight of seated dons, 'causing not a little merriment'.

and now, with his book on *The Dialect of the Southern Counties of Scotland* that had been published three years before and his *Britannica* article soon to be in the works, he had fully consolidated his reputation. He was, in other words, the ideal candidate. But for what? For the short Macmillan dictionary that was wanted by Harper in America? For a rather longer Macmillan dictionary that made use of the materials collected by Furnivall and Coleridge? Might Cambridge be interested? Or John Murray? Or what about the possibility that Oxford University Press might publish a dictionary for the Philological Society? More specifically, might not the project interest the Clarendon Press, the Oxford imprint which had been established a century before to produce the most learned of works, each of them so far a book 'so impenetrably erudite that it was impossible to extract from it any passage likely to entice the non-specialist reader', as Peter Sutcliffe has it in his informal history?[5]

Walter Skeat, a noted amateur philologist and Anglo-Saxon expert, approached the Syndics, as the governors were known, of the Cambridge University Press. Henry Sweet, who had excellent contacts at the Clarendon Press, was instructed by the Society to see if he could persuade the Delegates, as the Syndics' opposite numbers were called at Oxford, both to commit to the project and to cough up enough to pay an editor's salary. Five hundred pounds a year was the suggested sum. Cambridge said flatly no, and Oxford, though significantly without refusing point-blank, also balked.

So there was no option, at least at first, but to talk to Macmillan—though about a Macmillan-only project, not about

5   More than occasionally the Delegates of Oxford University Press—a firm which made a small fortune out of selling Bibles and prayer books—raised an eyebrow or two at the keen non-commercialism of the Clarendon Press. Max Muller's *Passerine Birds*, for instance, sold just 49 copies between 1860 and 1882—and 40 of these had been given away.

the cut-price scheme that had been proposed by Harper and which Murray had so swiftly rejected. And so negotiations between the father-and-son Macmillan dynasty on the one hand and the Society on the other—with Murray at its head, acting both as lead negotiator and as editor-in-waiting—began. For almost a year they staggered along with what, at this distance, looks like extreme discomfort.

The discomfort all had to do with the projected book's great size. Long beforehand Murray had warned of the scale of what he was now openly calling 'the Big Dictionary'.[6] It would, he wrote, 'be far more enormous than one would suppose could possibly *sell*—far too large to be printed at anything but a frightful expenditure of money'. Macmillan, on hearing this dismaying news, tried every imaginable way to perform the arithmetic that would make economic sense—trying to persuade Murray to pare the book to its very bones, trying to pay almost nothing to those who would be employed in making the book, trying to suggest, as Furnivall had, a shorter version to act as an *amuse-gueule* for the reading public. But Murray—'Mr. Editor', Furnivall had taken to calling him—held firm.

Or at least, he seemed to. The trouble was that while Murray was preparing specimen pages (nine of them) for Macmillan to consider, Furnivall was at the same time dealing behind his back. He was dealing still with John Murray, he was dealing anew with Oxford, trying hard to find an alternate publisher with whose offer he could shame Macmillan into paying more. And it seems that Macmillan, eager to conclude an arrangement, would in fact have paid more, would have agreed to publish more or less the number of pages, to make the book more or less the size for which Murray was arguing. Except that they found out what Furnivall was up

6   His use of the term percolated to street level. He became known, jocularly, as 'the Big Dic' and his growing army of children 'the little Dics'.

to—and they promptly exploded. 'It is a pity', Alexander Macmillan wrote to Murray, 'that [Furnivall's] pretty little ways should ever be intruded into serious business.' They pulled out of the entire deal. The only shred of politesse that emerged from the wreckage was a note from Macmillan's chief negotiator, sent personally to Murray, which said there was no doubt that the dictionary Murray had in mind would be published, would make an unassailable contribution to English scholarship, and would make Murray famous.

Even so. For a short while following the debacle with Macmillan, James Murray seems to have had some doubts, to have become more than a little discouraged. He began to toy with the idea of accepting the post as head of a boys' school in Huddersfield, somewhat closer to his family home. He complained openly to friends that the work of a lexicographer was far more tedious than he had supposed. And he grumbled further that in doing his work he felt bound by rules—principally Coleridge's now wretchedly didactic *Canones Lexicographici*—which he now felt were irrelevant to his purpose. He also felt personally cowed by Furnivall's brutal insistence and by his stubborn determination to get the Society's dictionary moving again.

Still, he refused to let the project go. Under Furnivall's urging the Society's dictionary team took a step backwards, and began to talk once again to the presses that had already turned them down. They found in very short order that the Syndics of Cambridge would have nothing at all to do with any project that had Furnivall associated with it. 'Somehow he isn't believed in at the Universities,' wrote Walter Skeat. So Cambridge were out. ('The largest wrong decision in publishing history', wrote the Press's M. H. Black some years later, wondering how differently fortunes might have turned out had we today been familiar with the *CED* instead of the *OED*.)

John Murray then turned out to be furious with Furnivall too—he had demanded they repay an advance of £600 the Society had paid at the time of the very first negotiations. So they were non-starters too. The only serious and suitable publishing house that had not given an absolutely definitive no for an answer, therefore, was Oxford.

Henry Sweet, memorably rebarbative though he may have been, was the man who first started the ball rolling. He did so in April 1877 by writing formally (the legalisms all checked by his father, who was a solicitor) to Bartholomew Price, the Delegates' Secretary at Oxford.[7] He formally suggested that first the Clarendon Press assume responsibility for publishing the Dictionary—a work that would be based, as had always been hoped, on the treasure trove of Philological Society materials, the collection of tons of quotation slips that had been assembled (and to a bewildering and distressing extent disassembled once Furnivall began to exasperate everyone) from the armies of word-searching volunteers. Sweet argued that no matter how monumental the task might seem, it *could* make money: the 4,000-page Littré French dictionary that had recently been published in Paris at the price of £4 had sold a staggering 40,000 copies. And to guarantee that the Oxford dictionary would be at the very least as successful, Sweet went on to make his second formal suggestion—that James Murray, BA, LL D, senior member of the Philological Society, be appointed editor.

It was to be a full year before the decision was made. There were some doubters—Bartholomew Price first among them. He had been bothered over the delay in a long-promised work by Murray on Scottish texts, due in 1874 but now three years late. Could a man so slow in delivering this one relatively modest work

7   He was generally known as 'Bat' Price.

be trusted to produce, on time, this much more formidable project? Then again, Max Müller, the renowned Orientalist and Sanskrit scholar, worried out loud that Murray might tend to concentrate more on the exotic words and overlook the more common, everyday terms.

Müller, seized of this idea, persuaded the Delegates to ask Murray to produce samples of commonplace words for which it was known that there were sub-edited materials (quotation slips that had been organized into their various meanings and senses) available. Murray agreed, did some experimenting, and came up with the words *arrow, carouse, castle*, and *persuade*. He wrote them up in the summer of 1877, and the Delegates looked at them and ruminated over their execution once they had begun the Michaelmas term. They pronounced themselves very much less than satisfied—with Müller in particular arguing endlessly with Murray over the etymology of one of the four words.

As if this were not bad enough, the Delegates then attacked Murray's plan for showing how each word should be pronounced, and attacked his plan for displaying the etymology—going so far as to suggest that the etymologies should be dropped entirely. This idea was germinated in part because Walter Skeat was in any case himself producing an *Etymological Dictionary of English*, making (in the Delegates' rather niggardly view) this particular feature unnecessary.

Furnivall, who had kept in the background until now, well aware of his unpopularity at Oxford and Cambridge, promptly turned himself into a Victorian Henry Kissinger. He raced up to Cambridge, persuaded Skeat to write to the Oxford Delegates insisting that they reverse their decision. (He also inquired once more whether Cambridge might like to publish, but was again rebuffed.) He then travelled to Oxford, bludgeoned Müller into relaxing his position, saw Henry Liddell, Dean of Christ Church and co-editor of the famous *Greek–English Lexicon*,[8] and told him that the dictionary team now had 393 volunteer readers at his disposal, that they should really be allowed to start work, and that James Murray was becoming weary with all the delays and with the somewhat loftily patronizing attitude that the Delegates seemed to be taking towards him. He took editors to lunch in London clubs. He wrote letters. He lobbied, persuaded, cajoled, entreated.

And all the while Murray himself was lost, deep in worried thought. Later he wrote to a friend: 'My interest ... was purely unselfish. I wanted to see an ideal Dictionary, & to show what I meant by one.'

The two weeks that spanned the last part of March and the beginning of April 1878 were, Murray would later write, 'the most anxious fortnight my wife and I passed, or ever may'. He knew full well that Max Müller had voiced the Delegates' deep concern that 'in an undertaking of this magnitude, in which one might almost say that the national honour of England is engaged, no effort should be spared to make the work as perfect as possible ...' So there was little doubt that the Delegates would permit him to *try* to create an ideal, a perfect dictionary. But was he really up to it? Could he manage the work and do it as well as it needed to be done? Would he be able to muster the energy and the time and the intellectual resources necessary to complete a task that, all of a sudden, seemed so terribly daunting? The book would not be a mere academic text—it would be of national, perhaps even international, importance. It could turn out to be the standard work, the grandfather of all word-books, the world's unrivalled *über*-dictionary for what in time might well become the world's

8   And father of Alice, to whom Charles Lutwidge Dodgson became so devoted, and about whose adventures in Wonderland we remain enthralled.

über-language. Was he, the untutored linen draper's boy from distant Teviotdale, truly the man to do it? He trembled, his confidence waning by the day, as he waited for the call.

It came, in the end, in late April—just as he was due to set out for an Easter in Somerset, where he had plans to interview a dialectician. He was minded to go; but friends advised otherwise, urged him that it would be prudent to cancel this particular West Country tour, and to report instead to Dean Liddell's rooms at Christ Church at 2.30 p.m. on Friday, 26 April 1878.

And so, nervous (having mugged up overnight on chemistry, the topic on which he felt himself the weakest), he duly travelled up from Mill Hill the night before, stayed with friends in what were then the rural surroundings of Park Town (now part of a hugely expanded city), and the next afternoon walked down the Banbury Road and Cornmarket and across Carfax and beneath Tom Tower, and climbed the staircase off the Peckwater Quadrangle to attend the Delegates in their lair, laying out for them his case for taking personal command of what was clearly to be the greatest lexicographical project ever to be attempted.

It must have been a daunting occasion. The men who assembled that week after Easter were as distinguished and intellectually rarefied a group as Oxford can ever have assembled. Liddell was there, presiding; the ever-sceptical Max Müller was at his side; the Regius Professors of both History and Ecclesiastical History were there—the former the great William Stubbs, who was credited with making history worthy of respectable academic pursuit in these muscularly philistine Victorian times; the University Vice-Chancellor, James Sewell, a high churchman of a formidably conservative bent; John Griffiths, Keeper of the University Archives;

the classical scholar Edwin Palmer; Granville Bradley, a well-known educationalist and Master of University College—and so on.

Yet in the event the encounter proved not to be in the slightest bit terrifying for any of the parties involved. They all appeared to like one another. The Delegates saw Murray as 'docile, but dogged'—and were greatly relieved that he did not seem quite so unstable as Furnivall, nor as unpleasant as Sweet. They treated Murray well, and when he emerged back out on the street it was with an evident spring in his step. He stayed an extra night or two in Oxford, but wrote immediately to Ada back in Mill Hill:

> Seen the great men—a very long and pleasant interview, increasing I think our mutual respect and confidence—but I don't think it decided anything or that we are much nearer a decision. Max Müller played first fiddle and talked as everybody's friend. It struck me that we were playing Congress [9] with myself as Russia, the Dons as England, Max Müller as Bismarck, and the result—nothing yet! Absit omen! But they are decent fellows and shook me very warmly by the hand at leaving as a man and brother.

It took one further full year before the deal was done—with the twelvemonth almost entirely devoted to wranglings about money. There were many explosions, most of them involving Furnivall. At one time he derided Bartholomew Price as a 'mean old skunk-rat'. Then he became convinced that the Delegates themselves were a byword for 'shiftiness and cupidity', or on another occasion men of 'miserable parsimony and sharp practice', and essentially told them so. In one extraordinary speech he accused the Delegates—in most un-Victorian language—of wanting to 'screw' the Society. Henry Sweet could get distempered, as well.

---

9   Murray's reference is to the Congress of Berlin, which had been called to modify earlier provisions concerning the Ottoman Empire. Bismarck was the supposed honest broker in the row between Disraeli and Russia's Alexandr Gorkashov.

At one stage in the talks he forecast that Oxford simply wanted to take charge of the Society's materials, whereupon 'Murray would be fired and some Oxford swell, who would draw a good salary for doing nothing, put in his place. I know something of Oxford,' Sweet said, ominously, 'and of its low state of morality as regards jobbery and personal interest.'

But finally, on 1 March 1879, a deal was struck. Bartholomew Price sent the package of papers to Murray at Sunnyside, Mill Hill. It was a formal, ten-page contract between the Society and Oxford University Press. The intention behind the hard-won document was to produce what would be called *A New English Dictionary on Historical Principles formed mainly on the Materials collected by the Philological Society and with the Assistance of many Scholars and Men of Science*. The book was expected to be of some 7,000 pages, and work on it, fully funded by the Press at an estimated cost of £9,000, should take no more than ten years. The editor would indeed be James Murray[10]—by now fully-fledged as President of the Philological Society—and he would be paid an annual salary (the arrangement for its payment was excruciatingly complex, involving pounds per page-published, lateness penalties, and lump sum payments for subordinate staff) that amounted to around £500. As token of the completion of the year-long marathon of talks, Dr Price enclosed a cheque for £175, and a note which ended: 'Let us all congratulate each other on having arrived at

---

10 In later years Murray liked to tell of a dream he had that illustrated Samuel Johnson's likely reaction to his appointment. Boswell seemingly asked the Great Cham, 'What would you say, Sir, if you were told that in a hundred years' time a bigger and better dictionary than yours would be compiled by a Whig?' Johnson merely grunted. 'A Dissenter?' Johnson shifted, a little uneasily, in his chair. 'A Scotsman?' Johnson started, and began to speak: 'Sir...' But Boswell persisted. 'And that the University of Oxford would publish it.' 'Sir,' roared Johnson, unable to contain himself. 'In order to be facetious *it is not necessary to be indecent.*' Safe to say the dream was apocryphal, the illustration as much of James Murray's refreshingly sportive attitude—at times—to his job.

this resting place in our enterprise. Believe me to be with the best wishes for you in the large undertaking.'

Dr Price, like almost everyone else, had absolutely no idea how magnificently wrong was the forecasting. The Dictionary took not ten years to complete, but 54. The number of pages was not 7,000, but 16,000. And the cost of the entire project turned out not to be £9,000, but £300,000.

Not that James Murray was much better informed. In all the excitement and sanguine mood of the contract-signing day, he gaily supposed that he would be able to continue as a schoolmaster at Mill Hill and simply edit the Dictionary in his spare time. He did not reckon with the terrible undertow of all those hundreds of thousands of words that lay hidden, waiting to be included in the book that would eventually contain and compass them all. He was optimistic; the Philological Society was optimistic; Oxford was optimistic; and all of them, though they were essentially right in spirit to be so, and though their rosy view of lexical ambition was to be vindicated at the very end, were nonetheless at this moment in the saga, spectacularly unrealistic. This was all going to be very much more difficult than anyone could possibly have imagined.

Let us leave it to Samuel Johnson to offer his perspective, in paragraphs taken from the deservedly famous Preface to his own dictionary of the century before. Murray could almost recite these words by heart: he would later reproduce them, as if they had been carved in stone, in his first Preface to Volume I of his great book:

> *When first I engaged in this work, I resolved to leave neither words nor things unexamined, and pleased myself with the prospect of the hours which I should revel away in feasts of literature, with the obscure recesses of northern learning which I should enter and ransack; the treasures with which I expected every search into these neglected mines to reward my labour, and the triumph*

with which I should display my acquisitions to mankind. When I had thus inquired into the original of words, I resolved to show likewise my attention to things; to pierce deep into every science, to enquire the nature of every substance of which I inserted the name, to limit every idea by a definition strictly logical, and exhibit every production of art or nature in an accurate description, that my book might be in place of all other dictionaries whether appellative or technical.

But these were the dreams of a poet doomed at last to wake a lexicographer. I soon found that it is too late to look for instruments, when the work calls for execution, and that whatever abilities I had brought to my task, with those I must finally perform it. To deliberate whenever I doubted, to enquire whenever I was ignorant, would have protracted the undertaking without end, and, perhaps, without much improvement; for I did not find by my first experiments, that what I had not of my own was easily to be obtained: I saw that one enquiry only gave occasion to another, that book referred to book, that to search was not always to find, and to find was not always to be informed; and that thus to pursue perfection, was, like the first inhabitants of Arcadia, to chase the sun, which, when they had reached the hill where he seemed to rest, was still beheld at the same distance from them. I then contracted my design, determining to confide in myself, and no longer to solicit auxiliaries, which produced more incumbrance than assistance; by this I obtained at least one advantage, that I set limits to my work, which would in time be ended, though not completed.

Perhaps no more eloquent a testament to the trials of a lexicographer—a man performing 'the work of a poet at last doomed to wake'—has ever been written. James Murray chose these paragraphs as his set of guiding principles, words which seemed somehow designed by the Fates to inspire him, but also to remind and to warn him.

For he in his work now vowed absolute perfection, no matter that it involved the asking of uncountable questions, nor boundless quantities of time. He said to himself that in making this new work he would brook no expedience, he would take no short cut, he would turn away from no unsolved enigma, no unexplained mystery. James Murray vowed, in short, to complete the work that Samuel Johnson could only claim to have brought to an end that was convenient for himself and his small band of scriveners; that he would, eventually and once and for all, fix and enumerate and catalogue all of the English language, no matter if it seemed that he was thereby bound, endlessly, to be chasing the very same sun that Samuel Johnson had so signally failed to reach.

4

Battling with the Undertow

The writer of a dictionary rises every morning like the sun to move past some little star in his zodiac; a new letter is to him a new year's festival, the conclusion of the old one a harvest home.

(Translated from Jean Paul Richter's *Levana*, 1807)

'There are two beginnings to every year,' says an old Irish proverb. The *Oxford English Dictionary* had the first of its beginnings in 1861. And now, with James Murray's formal appointment in 1879 as editor, it was having its second almost twenty years later. But it was not quite so simple, getting matters under way again after so long a period of quietude.

First, there was the small matter of what everyone called quite simply 'the slips'. These were the quotation slips, the morsels of paper on which the brief—but to a dictionary editor absolutely essential—pieces of information that had been gleaned from all those years of volunteer reading of the core books of English literature, of the newspapers[1] and learned journals and railway

---

1 Furnivall made liberal use of the *Daily News* in citing words for the Dictionary. Close students of the *OED* may notice that some later periods make greater use of the *Daily Chronicle*. This, it turns out, is simply because Furnivall changed his daily paper.

timetables and technical manuals and navigational almanacs and collections of *belles lettres* besides. Within the sentences that were written onto these slips, and which were waiting to be sifted and sorted and discovered by dictionary editors, lay all the subtle and not-so-subtle shades of meaning and sense of the various words that the quotations illustrated.

There were said to be something like two million of these slips already collected, tied together in rough order, no doubt covered in dust and lint, curled and yellow, and perhaps even crumbling themselves with age and decrepitude. It was already twenty years since Herbert Coleridge had begun to amass them at his house on Chester Terrace, and fifteen or so since Frederick Furnivall had entreated his scores of readers to 'copy and burrow' in the literature, to write out the slips, and to send them in to him to St George's Square. Some were therefore very old indeed, and by now a good number of those gentle readers who had collected them had perhaps not survived to see them put to use.

Many of those worthies whom Furnivall had appointed as subeditors for individual letters had taken away their bundles of slips for sorting; and when Furnivall's attention settled on one of his other enthusiasms—Amazonian scullers from Hammersmith teashops, for example, or practising with early English balladeers, or setting up Working Men's Clubs—many had stopped working on them, had squirrelled them away somewhere, and everyone involved had forgotten about them.

Most of the slips were simply half-sheets of white writing paper, each of them (if properly filled in by the volunteers who submitted them, though not all complied) with the headword—or the catchword, or the lemma, as it is now generally known—at the top left, the date and author and precise source of the quotation that contained it written below, and then the quotation itself, either in full or in what the rules were pleased to call an 'adequate form'. Two million of such slips, weighing the better part of two tons, were in existence.

But where in God's name were they? To begin work properly on his dictionary, Murray needed to find them, and given that the contract clock was running, he needed to find them fast. Frederick Furnivall, it will be remembered, had entirely lost the will and concentration that was necessary to run the project, and had quite frankly lost track of all the scores of volunteers, the hundreds of thousands of slips, the pages of schedules and proofs and specimen pages and type designs and other details of dictionary assembly, such that the entire enterprise under his care had been reduced to a sorry shambles of decay and desuetude.

The slips were the most important asset of Furnivall's legacy, such as it was. His headquarters had been in Primrose Hill. James Murray's were now in Mill Hill. The tons of slips had perforce to be moved across the outer villages of London town—if only, that is, they could be found.

In anticipation of Murray's editorship, a somewhat embarrassed Furnivall had already been scratching his head and wondering where the missing sub-editors and thus his missing slips might be. Come the spring of 1879, when the final contracts were exchanged with Oxford, and with James Murray champing at the bit, he made a big push—and slowly but surely, from the recesses of the scholarly universe, many of the packages of slips began to come to light.

First, he sent a van with everything that had accumulated in his own house. The van was late—'things must be got away from here on Friday, as my wife is coming home from the seaside'—but eventually, after he had found a willing local man (but he demanded that Murray pay him) who piled into his cart everything that Furnivall had stacked in his hallway, the load was dispatched. Along with it came a note, suitably cryptic, which hinted at the state of affairs Murray was in short order to discover (and also, in the chiding italicized passage that is included, reminded the new editor why so many people found Frederick Furnivall a meddling and cantankerous old fool):

> *You'll want a Secretary and Sorter at first besides H,[2] in preparing the A work for you. You shd have all the A slips pickt out first, they're in packets, except such as are in the 2 or 3 G. Eliot packets whose slips want written catchword ... I hope you have, or very soon will have your whole room shelved. It is the only plan of keeping the slips easily accessible and moveable.*
>
> You've never acknowledged receipt of any of the little Dicty packets I've posted to you. Pray don't treat stranger contributors so, or they'll put it down to indifference or rudeness. Have some receipt Post Cards or forms printed, & let H. acknowledge the receipt of everything ...
>
> *Some of the outer slips have got torn, &'ll need mending. You've probably laid in a supply of gum.*

Once the carrier had dumped the enormous pile, Murray ferreted around in it for a few hours and then stood back—professing himself shocked and appalled by the condition of it all. There were boxes of slips, neatly arranged, to be sure. But some of the subeditors had put their hundredweight collections of papers into hessian[3] sacks, and then left them to rot. Murray found a dead

2　This was S. J. Herrtage, arguably the first true assistant employed in the service of the Dictionary. Three years later he was discovered to be a kleptomaniac, and was thus also the first employee to be summarily dismissed. He went to Cassell's, and worked on the lexicography of another multi-volume dictionary. The firm of Cassell therefore had unhappy associations for Murray: it was perhaps appropriate that Philip Lyttelton Gell, who as we shall see was later to become such a thorn in Murray's side, came to Oxford University Press—from Cassell.

3　Technically untrue, since the word *hessian*—meaning 'a coarse cloth composed of a mixture of hemp and jute'—did not enter the language until 1881, two years after the first sacks (then made of what was called sacking) were piled up on Murray's office floor.

rat in one of these, and then in another a live mouse with her family, all of the creatures contentedly nibbling away at the paper, making bedding for themselves out of years worth of lexical scholarship. Many of the sacks had been left in damp basements and stables for ages, and their contents were damp and mouldy. The writing had in many cases faded, or else was so illegible that Murray said it would have been far better for them to have been written in Chinese, since he could always obtain the services of a translator.

One sub-editor had delivered his slips in a baby's bassinet; another—responsible for headwords beginning with I—had left his in a broken-bottomed hamper in a long-empty vicarage in Harrow. Furnivall had tried to keep a list of the addresses of all those to whom he had entrusted slips, but his minuscule address book (bound in wrinkled brown leather with a white paper label stuck to its side—infuriatingly he remembered it all too well) had gone missing, and the two men had the devil's own time tracking the various men who, if still alive, had a fair chance of still retaining the papers. But even that wouldn't have been entirely useful, since many sub-editors had died or moved (a large number of vicars, for example, were already venerable when Coleridge made contact back in the 1850s), leaving behind them piles of slips 'to tender mercies of indignant tenants or grasping landlords', as Murray was to write.

By the early summer of 1879 the severity of the situation seemed all too clear. The letter H was missing in its entirety, as was the slightly less important Q and Pa. The slips for G were very nearly burned with the household rubbish when one Mrs Wilkes turned out the house in the wake of her husband's death.

And yet in fact things turned out to be—at least in these three instances—not so bad after all. H was found in Florence—it had been given to the American businessman and diplomat George

Perkins Marsh, who took the slips to Italy and then found that his eyesight was too poor to work on them any more, and left them in his villa in the Tuscan hills. Q turned up in the English Midlands town of Loughborough, in the care of one J. G. Middleton, who thought the project had been abandoned. And Pa (Furnivall could never explain how it came to be separated from the entirety of P–Py) was found in a stable in County Cavan, where some of the slips had already been used for lighting fires. The Mr Smith to whom the relatively small selection of slips[4] had been entrusted was an Irish clergyman who had been obliged to quit his living on the disestablishment of the Irish church, and had then died; his brother had taken charge of them and in due course handed them over to a complete stranger for what was laughably supposed to be safe keeping. It was from this stranger's stable that the housemaids mistook the slips for spills. Not all of the Pa slips were burned, but it took fresh volunteers many months of hard reading to re-place the quotations that had been lost in a succession of Cavan hearths.

The sub-editor for the letter O also proved to be something of a nuisance. He was called W. J. E. Crane, and he lived in Brixton, and it was there that he resolutely kept hold of his slips, being obtusely and mysteriously unwilling to relinquish them. Entreaties seemed not to work; a visit by one of Murray's assistants proved fruitless because Crane was away and no one in his household would release the papers; and then lawyers had to be hired, and everyone became insanely worried lest Crane, in a fit of rage, make his whole collection into a bonfire. In the end, 'by great importunity', Murray got the papers out of Crane's hands and into

---

4 Essentially Pa runs from (if we exclude the diminutive for *father*) the Tonga monetary unit, the *pa'anga*, to a bovine stomach concretion—like a bezoar, used in medicine— known as a *pazar*. The *OED* uses 350 pages to cover all the words that start with Pa—so although the find in an Irish stable was of a relatively small number of slips, in terms of this mammoth dictionary even small turns out to be rather huge.

Mill Hill—but it was, at one time, touch-and-go for a letter that was to occupy 356 pages, from *O* itself, via *Oaf* to *Ozonous*.

(In later years there were further trials, as might be expected with so vast a project. Words beginning with the preposition *in-* vanished when they were in proof and on their way to the printers, but eventually turned up. A policeman happened to find a packet of copy dropped in the street, and restored it to its editors unscathed. And at the very end of the enterprise one entire word— *bondmaid*—was found to have been left out of the first edition altogether: its slips had fallen down behind some books, and the editors had never noticed that it was gone.)

But now where, once the great pile had been found and gathered and assembled, to put it all? 'Sunnyside' was a pleasing and comfortable Victorian house, true; but by 1879 James and Ada already had six of their eventual eleven children, and some of them were at nursery age, others ready for the schoolroom. The idea of having the family house filled to the brim with two tons or more of dusty paper piles was pure anathema to the houseproud Ada, no matter how supportive she might have been of her husband. He had, quite simply, to find somewhere else to do his work.

His first thought was to rent a neighbouring cottage. Mill Hill in those days was a village on the edge of London, and there was indeed a small house with a thatched roof on Hammer's Lane that seemed suitable for the purpose. But the thatch was the problem: it created, Murray thought, too much of a fire risk. If he took it, it would only be to house one of his assistants.

And then Ada saw in one of the illustrated gardening magazines an advertisement for a new type of small shed-like structure, ugly and made of corrugated iron, and which the wealthier type of people used for potting, or storage, or housing their lawn-rollers or their diligences. The Sunnyside back garden, it turned out, was large enough to accommodate one of the larger models; the school governors, perhaps unaware of just quite how ugly it was, gave their sanction to its construction; and so at about the time that the first piles of slips began to come in from Primrose Hill, from Florence, from Brixton, and from all other points of the compass, the shed was bought (for £150) and swiftly put up. It took three weeks to build. It had skylights and was lined with deal, and was painted grey with a brown roof. Some said it looked like a Methodist chapel.

Murray had his brother-in-law Herbert Ruthven build and install on the walls a set of no fewer than 1,029 pigeon-holes—it will be remembered that Coleridge, twenty years before, had optimistically imagined that his nest of 54 would be sufficient. Visitors remarked on how in this new incarnation pigeon-holes seemed to dominate everything in the little building—every available wall was either covered with them or with plain deal shelving, some of which was horizontal and some sloping, and with a beaded edge to prevent books falling to the floor. There was a look of studied purpose in all that Murray did.

He bought desks and tables—and, in a nod to the way Samuel Johnson is supposed to have worked, he had the chippy build a foot-high dais at one end of the room, on which he could place his own chair and desk, and from which eyrie he could survey the work of his helpers. He decided that while everyone else seemed to call this nasty and damp and unhealthy little building 'the Shed', he would dignify it by the name monks gave to the room in which they prepared illuminated manuscripts: 'the Scriptorium'. The name stuck—to this building in Mill Hill, and later when the project moved to Oxford.

All that remained was for James Murray to put on top of his greying head the black silk velvet biretta that had been part of his vestments when he received his Edinburgh LL D. He had remarked then that the cap was modelled on that worn by his hero

John Knox (although the founder of the Church of Scotland was also the author of the phrase 'the monstrous regiment of women', which did not reflect the thinking of Murray, for whom women were a boon in myriad ways). No matter its origin: James Murray was to wear his old Knox cap for every one of his 35 years of editing that followed. Pictures of him clad thus, surrounded by row upon row of slip-filled pigeon-holes and against a background of shelves of learned books, and with a group of suited and scholarly looking helpers in the background, remain classic illustrations of the lexicographic art, as well as being an image of Murray from which he, a proud man now not entirely unaware of his growing worth, derived great pleasure.

So now, come the late spring of 1879, the Scriptorium—*the Scrippy*—was declared by Murray to be 'in full orderly work'. He was ready, he announced, to receive interested visitors, and to show them himself and his general staff beginning their formidable battle.

Once he had settled down to draw breath and plan his campaign, Murray realized that, voluminous though the mass of material now arranged along his Scriptorium walls was, it just was not enough. One problem was that readers had never bothered to consider with much enthusiasm what might be called the *ordinary* words of the language—they had succumbed to an understandable temptation to send in slips for interesting words, but not for the prosaic ones. So the supply slips for these banal words was meagre, almost useless. 'Thus of *abusion*,' writes Murray, referring to an unusual word that means deception or outrage, 'we found in the slips about 50 instances: of *abuse*, not five.' It was clear that to solve this problem, fresh instructions to readers needed to be

Murray (centre) in his first Scriptorium in his garden at Mill Hill School. Already one of his children can be seen working for extra pocket money.

issued, and, what is more, that very many more volunteers needed to be pressed into service.

Within weeks of taking on the job, Murray acted. He first persuaded the Clarendon Press to issue his now-famous Appeal, and had it published quickly, at the end of April 1879. This was a four-page printed document entitled '*An Appeal to the English-Speaking and English-Reading Public* in Great Britain, America and the British Colonies to read books and make extracts for the Philological Society's *New English Dictionary*'. Readers were wanted, Murray wrote, 'to finish the volunteer work so enthusiastically commenced twenty years ago, by reading and extracting the books which still remain unexamined'. So there were four further pages that listed the 'unexamined' books that Murray thought it might be useful for volunteers to read. Two thousand copies of the Appeal were printed, with Murray pleading in each that 'a thousand readers are wanted, and confidently asked for, to complete the work as far as possible within the next three years'.

He summarized the kind of reading that needed to be done:

> In the Early English period up to the invention of Printing, so much has been done and is doing that little outside help is needed. But few of the earliest printed books—those of Caxton and his successors—have yet been read, and any one who has the opportunity and time to read one or more of these, either in the originals, or accurate reprints, will confer valuable assistance by so doing. The later sixteenth-century literature is very fairly done; yet here several books remain to be read. The seventeenth century, with so many more writers, naturally shows still more unexplored territory. The nineteenth-century books, being within the reach of everyone, have been read widely; but a large number remain unrepresented, not only of those published during the last ten years while the Dictionary has been in abeyance, but also of earlier date. But it is in the eighteenth century above all that help is urgently needed. The American scholars promised to get the eighteenth-

AN APPEAL

TO THE

ENGLISH-SPEAKING AND ENGLISH-READING PUBLIC

TO READ BOOKS AND MAKE EXTRACTS FOR

THE PHILOLOGICAL SOCIETY'S

NEW ENGLISH DICTIONARY.

In November 1857, a paper was read before the Philological Society by Archbishop Trench, then Dean of Westminster, on 'Some Deficiencies in our English Dictionaries,' which led to a resolution on the part of the Society to prepare a Supplement to the existing Dictionaries supplying these deficiencies. A very little work on this basis sufficed to show that to do anything effectual, not a mere Dictionary-Supplement, but a new Dictionary worthy of the English Language and of the present state of Philological Science, was the object to be aimed at. Accordingly, in January 1859, the Society issued their 'Proposal for the publication of a New English Dictionary,' in which the characteristics of the proposed work were explained, and an appeal made to the English and American public to assist in collecting the raw materials for the work, these materials consisting of quotations illustrating the use of English words by all writers of all ages and in all senses, each quotation being made on a uniform plan on a half-sheet of notepaper, that they might in due course be arranged and classified alphabetically and significantly. This Appeal met with a generous response: some hundreds of volunteers began to read books, make quotations, and send in their slips to 'sub-editors,' who volunteered each to take charge of a letter or part of one, and by whom the slips were in turn further arranged, classified, and to some extent used as the basis of definitions and skeleton schemes of the meanings of words in preparation for the Dictionary. The editorship of the work as a whole was undertaken by the late Mr. Herbert Coleridge, whose lamented death on the very threshold of his work

The first page of the Appeal for Readers, written by Murray and sent to bookshops and libraries across the English-speaking world, with which he assembled the immense army of unpaid helpers for the making of the *OED*.

century literature taken up in the United States, a promise which they appear not to have ... fulfilled, and we must now appeal to English readers to share the task, for nearly the whole of that century's books, with the exception of Burke's works, have still to be gone through.

This formula cast the net: but what exactly was to be swept up into it? To widen the selection—to make sure that *abuse* got treatment as fair as *abusion*, for instance—Murray offered some gently phrased guidance:

Make a quotation for every word that strikes you as rare, obsolete, old-fashioned, new, peculiar or used in a peculiar way.

Take special note of passages which show or imply that a word is either new and tentative, or needing explanation as obsolete and archaic, and which thus help to fix the date of its introduction or disuse.

Make as many quotations as you can for ordinary words, especially when they are used significantly, and tend by the context to explain or suggest their own meaning.

The leaflet was distributed first to newspapers, who treated it as a press release and printed extracts as they saw fit. Then it was sent off in bulk to bookshops and libraries, in the United Kingdom and America, in Australia, Canada. Anyone borrowing or buying a book would likely find, tucked between the pages, this small and elegantly designed little document. The first 2,000 were swiftly augmented by a further print run of 500. And the leaflet found itself, evidently, in many other places besides those to which it was first sent. More than 800 men and women responded in total, saying that they were happy to help—and by squinting at their names written in the small type of the various Prefaces to the very first finished parts of the Dictionary we may learn something of who they were, as well as the success of the brochure's scatter-shot landings.

Aside from the hundreds of towns and villages in the British Isles that provided enthusiastic new readers, there are submissions written from would-be volunteers living in Austria, Ohio, Pennsylvania, Holland, New South Wales, Indiana, Calcutta, New York, San Francisco, Ceylon, Arkansas, New Zealand, and Wisconsin, and a dozen other places besides.

Murray decided that the American efforts, which were very large and involved many hundreds of readers, should be locally superintended (as they still are today—for, as we shall see, the process of reading for the Dictionary still goes on, as it always must). He first appointed the great Pennsylvania-based literature teacher Francis March[5] to run the American reading programme—an inspired choice, and one that redeemed a pledge made by Herbert Coleridge twenty years before, which was to have American readers exclusively responsible for reading eighteenth-century English literature (the era being one in which Americans would be naturally peculiarly interested) as well as all American-born literature thereafter. Murray had voiced some dissatisfaction in his Appeal; once March was in place and working hard, all his earlier misgivings evaporated.

(Few readers, at least in those early days, seemed to admit to coming from France and Italy, however. One has to assume, if unkindly, that those living under the heel of firmly prescriptive linguistic authorities like the Forty Immortals of the *Académie* in Paris and the members of the *Accademia* of Florence, were a little unsure how prudent it might be to read for a book that would

---

5   March was as polymathic a figure as Murray, teaching to his students at Lafayette College, Pennsylvania, a range of topics that included Latin and Greek, French and German, botany, law, political economy, 'mental philosophy', and the Constitution of the United States. He also edited, in 1902, the most useful of all thesauruses, which outclasses Roget in being a dictionary as well, but which, regrettably, has long been out of print. March is a forgotten figure, omitted both by *Britannica* and by the *American National Biography*.

be so wildly different in its constitution from those they were used to.)

In any event, the speed of the response was staggering. Within a month of sending out the pamphlet Murray was able to report that 165 people had signed up to do work; 128 of them had chosen the books they were going to read (a total of 234 books had been sent off); all had been sent their slips[6] and so were now presumed to be beavering away. Some who had volunteered to read very large or important books—such as the fourteenth-century northern poem the *Cursor Mundi*, which in time became the most-quoted work in the entire *OED*—were sent pre-printed slips, designed by Murray to free these particular volunteers from the labours of writing each time the title and the edition for each of the quotations they found.

A year later the number of readers had more than quadrupled, to 754; 1,568 books had been sent for reading, and 934 of these had been thoroughly combed through and finished. This was work on a scale and at a pace of which Coleridge and Furnivall had never dreamed: within just a year of signature of the contract the number of quotations returned on slips had increased by 361,670, and a year later still, by 656,900. Within a matter of months a further ton of material had been received in the Scriptorium, and Murray and

6   Murray, in a moment of organizational brilliance, decided that he would change, very slightly, the requirements for the size of the slips his readers might use. Where Furnivall and Coleridge had asked them to set their quotations out on half-sheets of writing paper, Murray demanded instead that his contributors write lengthways across quarter-sheets of foolscap, oblong pieces of paper that would measure about 6⅝ inches by 4¼. He would send out bundles of blank slips of this size—*fiches* to French workers, *zettelen* to Germans—to newly signed-up volunteers. This new size, still in use today, would offer his editorship two advantages. First, it would allow him and his colleagues to recognize which slips came from the previous era (the larger ones) and which from his. And second, it would perhaps minimize the infuriating habit of those few readers—Furnivall most notorious among them—who would send in their quotations on anything that came to hand, be they the backs of envelopes, old laundry lists, or scraps of newspaper. Murray wanted to impose rules and order—if not on the language itself, then at least on the way that examples of its use were collected.

his tiny band of workers were kept furiously busy sifting, sorting, and deciding, day after day after day.

Indeed, the first three or four years of the enterprise in Mill Hill were completely dominated by the seemingly incessant processes of sorting and classifying slips and then reading the quotations written on them. The idea of actually producing even the first volume of the mighty work seemed still very distant, no more than a chimera, a mirage, a phantasm.

About 1,000 slips arrived at the Scriptorium every single day. Each time a packet of slips was received—maybe one particular reader had sent but a single slip in his envelope, more probably he had saved up his efforts and sent in a brown-paper parcel that held fifty or more—it was opened up, and the slips examined to see if there was any egregious error—an obviously misspelled word, say, or if a reference was clearly less full than would be useful. If that were the case, the slip would be set aside and Murray would write a letter asking the reader to rectify matters.

Then the sorters—two young Mill Hill village women employed, a Miss Skipper and Miss Scott, at fifteen shillings a week—arranged the slips into the alphabetical order of their headwords. The two were the uneducated daughters of local tradesmen, and they cheerfully admitted little knowledge of what it was that they were sorting; but they learned an extraordinary dexterity in shuffling the slips into order, and proved themselves invaluable.[7]

After these, in the ascendant pecking order, came the rather more learned (and, as it happens, male) helpers, like the thus-far-unmasked kleptomaniac Mr Herrtage, or James Murray's

---

7 The efforts of these two young women, however, pass unacknowledged in any of the earlier volumes of the completed Dictionary—a mordant commentary on the realities of Victorian life. However, when the complete *OED* was published in the more liberal and enlightened year of 1928, their names did appear on the list of Assistants.

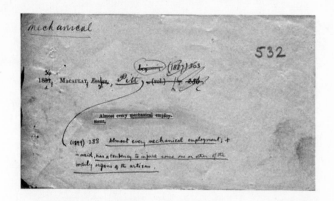

A selection of slips—some handwritten, some cut from books, some printed—for the word *mechnical*, which would have been housed in the Scriptorium pigeon-holes, waiting to be examined, considered and finally perhaps used in the pages of the Dictionary.

Mechanical
Lawrie T. V. ii. (1830) II. 115¼

1830 Galt Lawrie T. V. ii. 545

settlers of the mechanical orders.

The sagacity with which Mr Hoskins had chosen the site of
Judiville became every day more manifest, by the
preference given to it by settlers of the mechanical orders.

mechanical (calculated by aid of the science of Mechanics).

1777 T. Percival ; Essays (1777) I. 21 589

Equally false and absurd is the mechanical
hypothesis concerning the operation of medicines,
which is supposed to depend upon the size,
figure, and gravity of their constituent particles.

Mechanical

1848 Leigh Hunt, Jar of Honey iii. (1848) 31 602

Archimedes — His wonderful mechanical
inventions are among the daily instruments
of utility all over the world.

mechanical 555

(1874)

1874 Whyte Melville Riding Recoll. VI. 98

... most of us can remember / the
mechanical horse exhibited in Piccadilly
some ten or twelve years ago, a German invent[?]
Ib. p. 100
[99] No gentleman who fancied he could " ride a
bit" was satisfied till.... [100] the mechanical horse
had put him on his back.

brother-in-law Herbert Ruthven, Alfred Erlebach, and John Mitchell (who was to be killed mountain climbing in Snowdonia). This team looked closely at each headword and sorted those that were spelled the same way into their different parts of speech—for example, *lie* the verb, as in to lie down, or *lie* the noun as in falsehood. Once this was done, the slips were further arranged within the new categories such that the quotations written on them were in chronological order.

The most crucial stage came next. An editor-sorter of even more experience—James Murray being *primus inter pares*, of course—would then look carefully at the quotations and from them attempt to discern the differences in the meanings and senses that the quotations showed had been used over the centuries. For an important word there might be several hundred quotations—and it would only be by the very slow and painstaking reading of these quotations that a skilled editor could discern, could see in his mind's eye, the various ways the words had been employed over the centuries.

Sometimes the differences were obvious; sometimes they were more subtle; occasionally the differences were the merest shadings of meaning, the discernment and determining and defining of which were to make this one dictionary so infinitely superior to all others. And to make sure the quotations did each reflect the meaning that a sagacious editor thought they did, each and every quotation would have to be checked. Was what the volunteer reader had written accurate? Was the date he had assigned to it correct? If there were errors here, then the whole basis of the definition and the history of the word would be thrown into disarray, and any dictionary based on such inaccuracy would be made useless. Checking and rechecking the original sources, however tedious it might seem, and however seemingly disrespectful to the volunteers, was essential.

The assistants—or the sub-editors or that special sub-class called re-sub-editors—who did all these determinings would pin together the slips that fed into each category of meaning and attach with the same pin[8] a piece of paper that showed a first attempt at a definition of what the slips' quotations appeared to show the word to mean. And then the sub-editor would take all the small pinned bundles for any one word and arrange these bundles chronologically, so that the lexical history of the word could be ascertained as well.

Finally in this multi-layered process, the gently fierce-looking, pepper-and-salt-bearded (the red had faded to brown and was now beginning to grey itself), and black-velvet-capped James Murray, working steadily away up on his foot-high dais and from behind a semicircular and seemingly machicolated fortress wall of reference books, would receive the pinned bundles. He would make such further subdivisions as might seem to him appropriate, work into the mix the etymology of each word, add its alternate spellings and then the way that the Philological Society and common sense suggested that it might best be pronounced. He would number the bundles from 1 to 1,000 (in case they were ever to be dropped by a clumsy sub-editor or a compositor), and eventually he would perform the most important of all the tasks that a dictionary editor must accomplish—he would write and polish and fuss with and burnish, for each one of the words and senses and meanings, what he divined as their definitions.

Defining words is a rare and special art. Some rules for the process have evolved, the earliest of them Aristotelian in origin. A word—let us take the noun[9] *cow* as an example—must first be

---

8   The paperclip was a newfangled invention, the word first appearing in the language
    around 1875. The *OED*'s editors, however, had little use for them and, for all business
    concerned with the sorting of slips, made do with pins.

9   Or what Oxford, perversely, chooses to call a *substantive*, and gives the abbreviation *sb.*

defined according to the class of things, by the genus, to which the chosen meaning belongs (mammal, quadruped, hooved), and then differentiated—defined by *differentiae*, in Aristotelian terms—from other members of its class (bovine, female). The definition must be written to show what the thing signified by the word *is*, and not what it is *not*. And all the words used in the definition must appear elsewhere in the dictionary, so that any reader's puzzlement can be rectified by his simply looking those up as well—to repeat, the rule of thumb has it that no word in the definition should be more complicated than the word that is being defined. (Samuel Johnson broke this rule on numerous occasions. In his definition of the word *elephant*, for example, he writes of the animal's *pudicity*— few know at first blush that this word means shyness, making the definition, and thus by extension Johnson's entire dictionary—less than ideal. Which is, of course, what Dean Trench pointed out in his famous paper of 1857.)

James Murray's definition of *cow* (or one of its many meanings—*cow* has about nine, though *cower* has only two) is a model of elegant simplicity, as were most of the hundreds of thousands he wrote: 'The female of any bovine animal (as the ox, bison or buffalo); most commonly applied to the female of the domestic species (*Bos taurus*).'

Once having completed his definition, and having assembled in bundles enough work to make the next part of the venture worthwhile, he would tie them together, place them in a large brown package marked, triumphally, with the simple word 'Press'—and send them post-haste to the printers.

Murray's son Wilfrid, who spent much of his adult life in Cape Town, employed a delightful South African English word *inspan*— it means to yoke up a team of oxen or horses, and it has *outspan* as its opposite—to describe how the editor would employ his children in the service of the Dictionary. 'They were inspanned', he writes, 'as soon as they were of an age to be trusted.' What he meant was that as soon as they seemed able to read they were asked to report to the door of the 'iron room' (the inside of what their father called the Scriptorium was out of bounds to them), collect from an assistant some newly arrived packets of slips, and take them back to the Sunnyside breakfast room for sorting.

'We received no pocket money as a matter of course,' wrote Jowett, the youngest Murray boy, 'but had to earn it by sorting slips.'

> Hours & hours of our childhood were spent in this useful occupation. The motive actuating us was purely mercenary: we wanted money for our Christmas or our birthday presents, or to spend on our summer holidays, & the only way to get it was to sort slips. We were paid according to age, not according to skill or speed. The standard rate was one penny an hour, but this rose to two-pence, threepence or even sixpence, as you mounted up in your teens.

Wilfrid, who sounds to have been something of a playroom lawyer, brought in a spoof bill to regulate the practice, reading it as a motion before what was called the Sunnyside Debating Society. He called it the Appropriation Act, and it read: 'That the members of this House to steadily henceforth keep to the work of half an hour's slips per day for the gain of sixpence a week.' The children passed it *nem con*. James Murray appears not to have taken the slightest notice of it. Jowett was obliged to continue writing his description of the trials of the task:

> The sorting into first letters was easiest: that into second letters was a little harder, because you often had to read the whole catchword. The final sorting and combining two or perhaps three bundles were hardest of all; but we became very skillful with practice &, I believe, quite as quick as the junior assistants in the Scriptorium. ... Financially considered, I am sure the Oxford University Press did very well by our labour.

The work was not uninteresting if done for only an hour or two at a time. But when we wanted to earn half a crown or even five shillings in the space of a week, we had to work long hours. We enlivened the task by reading out tit-bits from Dr. Furnivall's newspaper cuttings, & bundles of slips from Dr. Furnivall were in demand, in spite of the bad handwriting.

However, just as at first with the poor Misses Skipper and Scott, none of the labour of the young Murrays was to be publicly acknowledged. It seems a rather ungracious Victorian attitude, but evidently one that had precious little to do with gender. More than likely this conferring of invisibility was just the result of James Murray's whims and caprices, and not based in any kind of settled policy.

There was, though, one unforeseen bonus to be derived from all their labours. In their old age, and when such puzzles became a regular feature in the newspapers, the Murray children turned out to be brilliantly adept at solving crosswords. They also—though this could perhaps hardly be termed a bonus—derived from their work one splendid phrase of insult. They had found the word *toe-rag* in one of Furnivall's newspaper cuttings, and decided to make adolescent use of it themselves. The halls of Sunnyside would re-sound with cries of 'You dirty toe-rag!'

And all the while, Murray was inching towards the moment when he would be able to offer up his first publication—the first real indication of progress, and one which he could share with all the interested world.

He began working on his words at what suddenly seems to have been a rare old clip. As early as May 1879—not three months following his appointment—he had advanced from the letter A^{10} as far as *Aby*, covering 557 words, which made up enough copy (depending on the design, the number of columns, the size of the typeface) for perhaps 36 pages of the completed Dictionary. By May 1880 he had struggled through a further 124 pages, reaching as far as *Al-*. In 1881 (by which time he had sent out fifteen hundredweight of paper, in the shape of 817,625 of the pre-printed slips, to his readers) he had begun thinking seriously about typography, and in June 1881 there was talk of making specimen pages.

The design of the Dictionary occupied his mind for many months—and the fact that the design he eventually came up with has lasted for so very long since those Mill Hill ponderings points up the extraordinary prescience of Murray as a bookmaker, as well as a lexicographer. For in all his decisions he seems to have achieved a rare perfection—the form of the book is one that no designer since has had reasons either to tinker with or to complain about.

The Periodical, the in-house journal of Oxford University Press, understandably gave much of the credit to their own printers, who were regarded as men possessed of an unusual degree of skill and taste. Their compositors and readers, said the journal, puffing out its chest, had bestowed the greatest care upon the Dictionary:

> *The variety of type used, the many languages involved, and the multiplication of 'arbitraries'[11] have demanded technical knowledge and minute accuracy to an extent probably unequalled in any*

10 Murray defined *A* as 'the first letter of the Roman Alphabet, and of its various subsequent modifications (as were its prototypes Alpha of the Greek and Aleph of the Phoenicians and old Hebrew); representing originally in English, as in Latin, the "lowback-wide" vowel, formed with the widest opening of jaws, pharynx and lips. The plural has been written aes, A's, As.' The first illustrative quotation comes from a fourteenth-century Northumbrian poem called *A Pricke of Conscience* by Richard Hampole.

11 Printers use the word 'arbitrary' to signify a character not customarily in their job trays: an example is the mixed question-mark-cum-exclamation mark known as an 'interrobang'.

other work. The typographical superiority of the Oxford Diction-
ary over works of comparable scope is everywhere acknowledged.
One has but to turn to great books like Littré and Grimm to be
impressed once again with the choice of type and the disposition of
the page which have made the Oxford book easy and pleasant to
read.

Whether it was Murray who made the final design decision or the then Printer to the University, Edward Pickard Hall, is a little difficult to discern.[12] And certainly the celebrated Vice-Chancellor of the University and Master of Balliol, Benjamin Jowett—for whom there was a rhyme using his name and which ended 'there is no knowledge but I know it'—was deeply (and, to Murray, annoyingly) involved as well. But whoever of these was properly responsible for the look of the finished product, the result was then, and remains today, unutterably pleasing.

The book is laid out in three columns, each essentially ten inches tall and two-and-a-half inches wide. The body type is a classic British Imperial-era face called Clarendon, which had been designed and the punches cut in 1845 by Benjamin Fox for Robert Besley at London's renowned Fann Street Foundry: it used boldface for the headwords, and then a variety of styles (light and italic among them) and a variety of fount sizes for the various elements that Murray decided required illustration.[13] The

---

12 Hall was in any case soon to be dismissed and replaced in 1883 by the man who is probably still revered as Oxford's finest printer, Horace Hart. Hart, who was Controller of the Press until 1915, made many decisions relating to Murray's dictionary, and printed many of the early volumes. He is best known for his *Rules for Compositors and Readers*, a once privately printed manual which remains—as *Hart's Rules*—the single greatest authority on style for writers, editors, and publishers. He died tragically in 1916, found floating in a pond called Youlbury Lake near Oxford. His gloves were folded neatly on the bank; it was said that he had suffered a series of nervous breakdowns.

13 Robert Bringhurst, an authority on typography, says that the suite of Clarendon faces 'reflect the hearty, stolid, bland, unstoppable aspects of the British Empire. They lack cultivation, but they also lack menace and guile. They squint and stand their ground, but they do not glare.'

Benjamin Jowett, the towering intellect of Balliol College, who initially became an infuriatingly meddlesome nuisance to Murray, but who ended up one of his most stalwart supporters and a champion of the *OED*.

definitions are set in Old Style; the quotations in a smaller fount size of the same. All kinds of typographical device—daggers, parallels, inferior and superior stress marks, numbers—are there to mark various elements of each word. A bewildering variety of other typefaces are used as well—not the least of them Arabic, Hindi, Icelandic, Greek, and the various symbols of Old English (such as thorns, yoghs, wyns, ashes, and eths), and, in the dictionary section that is devoted to what lexicographers call 'orthoepy', and which all else call 'correct pronunciation', the equally arcane and irritatingly non-intuitive symbols of the phonetic alphabet.

It was on 19 April 1882 that Murray sent off a first batch of all-but-finished copy to the Clarendon Press printing house at Oxford. Things were now moving, and in terms of the glacier-like mobility of the dictionary world, they were moving fast. Some days later, in early May 1882, he signalled the epochal moment of possible publication to his fellow members of the Philological Society. It had been three years since his appointment as editor: now at last he was able to employ the words that have been already used as the epigraph to Chapter 2: 'The great fact ... is, that the Dictionary is now at last really launched, and that some forty pages are in type, of which forty-eight columns have reached me in proof.'

Since he was now in the business of editing the book, rather than collecting material for it, he decided that he could now call a halt—or at least a temporary halt—to the main volunteer reading programme. 'The general amassing of quotations *must cease* with the present year,' he declared. By now he had enough slips (about three and a half million) to be going on with, and he decided he would in future ask for more books to be read only when he needed to fill a gap, or when he was uncertain whether the quotations he already had truly did represent the full history of a particular word. He would also make up lists of those words for which he felt he needed citations earlier than those his volunteers had already found. He called these lists his *desiderata*—and such lists also still exist today, as the modern editors of the *OED* entreat today's volunteers to see if they can spy any uses of words at earlier dates than so far found.

Meanwhile, the proof pages began to come back from the compositors' stones. Each page was set by hand. So complex was the typesetting that every sheet was reckoned to cost about £5 to make up.[14] Dozens of compositors were involved: one of them, James C. Gilbert—a slender man, balding with a regal-looking and very tidy white beard—appears, remarkably, to have worked on the entire run of the Dictionary. He joined the Press as an apprentice in 1880, then, according to a brief appreciation of his almost unimaginably long tenure, he recalled how he 'lifted his first take … in 1882, at an early stage of the letter A', and was still working 36 years later when the final words (which all began with W, not Z, as will be explained) were set in January 1928. 'James Gilbert had worked for a greater length of time and had set more type for the Dictionary than any other compositor,' the brochure records.

The return of the proofs sparked off one of the many internal schisms that seemed to plague the early days of this great enterprise. They were, said one of those who glimpsed them, perhaps 'the most heavily corrected proofs ever known', and had been covered with pencil corrections on almost every one of 2,600 lines of type that, on average, make up an eight-page sheet of

---

14 It is not quite as costly as it sounds. One sheet pressed for the Dictionary would encompass eight double-sided pages of the finished book—so the cost per page would be only 12s. 6d.

1593 NASHE 4 *Lett. Confut.* Wks. (Grosart) II. 224 ~~The next weeke..hee will haue at you with a~~ cap case full of French occurrences .. When that fly-boat of Frenchery is once launcht, your trenchor attendant..intends ~~to tickle vp a Treatise of the barly kurnell.~~ **1826** H. N. COLERIDGE *West Indies* 149 ~~Still kindly good-bye,~~ bright island; I have a nook in my heart for thee with all thy Frenchery.

French hood. A head-dress worn by women ~~during~~ the sixteenth century and ~~the beginning of the~~ seventeenth.

1541 *St. Papers Hen. VIII*, I. 695 To the Quenes Grace ye must appoynte six frenche hoods, with thappurtenaunces. *a* **1553** UDALL *Royster D.* II. iii. (Arb.) 35 We shall go in our frenche hoodes euery day. **1636** JACKSON in *Hygiasticon* To Translator, For these loose times, when a strict sparing food More's out of fashion then an old French hood.

b. ?A head-dress worn by women when punished for unchastity.

1568 *Durham Depos.* (Surtees) 89 A whipe and a cart and a franc hoode, waies me for the, my lasse. ~~1615 OVERBURY Char., Common Lawyer, But now being enabled to speake in proper person, he talkes of a French-hood, in steede of a Ioynture, wages his law, and ioines issue.~~

Frenchification (fre·nʃifikḗ·ʃən), ~~vbl. sb.~~ [f. ~~FRENCHIFY,~~ see -FICATION.] The action of the vb. FRENCHIFY.

1834 *New Monthly Mag.* XL. 226 They had assumed all the Frenchifications possible. **1863** ~~Blackw. Mag. Sept. 269~~ Where he [Pope] was deemed by his contemporaries to have improved upon Dryden, it was in the more complete Frenchification of Dryden's Style.

Frenchified (fre·nʃifəid), *ppl. a.* [f. ~~FRENCHIFY~~ + -ED [1].]

1. *contemptuous.* Having French manners or qualities; French-like.

1597 B. JONSON *Ev. Man out of Hum.* I. i, This is one Monsieur Fastidious Brisk, otherwise called the fresh Frenchified courtier. **1606** *Sir G. Goosecappe* I. i. in Bullen *O. Pl.* III. 8 Can yee not knowe a man from a Marmasett, in theis Frenchified dayes of ours? **1717** D. JONES *Secr. Hist. Whitehall* II. 328 Which Procedure thunderstruck the King and his Frenchify'd Council. **1770** J. LOVE *Cricket* 4 The Frenchifi'd Diversion of Billiards. **1819** *Hermit in Lond.* III. 116 Frenchified John Bull is a would-be butterfly, and a positive blockhead. **1861** THACKERAY *Four Georges* ii. (1876) 51 The home satirists jeered at the Frenchified .. ways which they brought back.

+2. (See quot. 1659).

Scores of factors caused the project to take as long as it did: not the least was the prodigious complexity of proof-reading and correcting, as this one page, shown halfway through its progress from first assembly to final printing, will suggest.

James Gilbert, a compositor at Oxford University Press appears, uniquely, to have worked on the entire Dictionary—lifting the first type for the letter A in 1882, and working until the completion of the final volume in 1928.

the Dictionary. Many lines had themselves twenty changes to them—meaning that every single sheet could have as many as 10,000 proof marks, necessitating alterations, the expenditure of much time—and great cost.

It was this particular prospect that apparently raised the hackles of Benjamin Jowett, in his capacity as ex officio chairman of the Delegates. Both he in particular, and the Delegates in general, began behaving in a way that Murray found most disturbing. Jowett—whose publicly stated aim was 'to arrange my life in the best possible way, that I may be able to arrange other people's'—embarked on a sudden campaign of highly aggressive interference. Towards the end of July 1883 Jowett invited Murray to come up from London and stay in a guest room at Balliol; the next day he took Murray with him when he went to visit both the full body of the Delegates and then, more ominously, to see members of a hitherto moribund subcommittee that had been set up three years before specifically to look into any problems which might arise with the Dictionary. Jowett showed them all the massively corrected proofs for part of the first section, he explained how much it would cost the Press to deal with all of them, and, in an autocratic style for which he was notorious, he argued fiercely that changes needed to be made. He handed Murray a document: 'Suggestions for Guidance in Preparing Copy for the Press'.

Murray, who was already upset, and by turns furious and dismayed by his treatment, went through the roof. He spluttered, he fulminated, he raged in public and in private. How dare Jowett and his minions—men who had not the faintest notion of the way that Murray worked or of the methods of the men and women in the Scriptorium—tell him how to run a dictionary? How dare some anonymous Delegate suggest, for example, that the words *aardvark* and *aardwolf*, words that are meat and drink to any beginning lexicographer, be omitted because they were deemed too scientific or too foreign? How dare Jowett suggest that newspapers not be used as source material? that only the works of 'great authors' should be cited? that there should be no illustrations of words quoted from later than 1875 (nothing *modern*, in other words)? And that scientific and 'slang' words be omitted unless they had appeared in the better sorts of literature?

'I am sure', Murray said when he had cooled down a little, 'the time will come when this criticism will be pointed out as a most remarkable instance of the inability of men to acknowledge contemporary facts and read the signs of the times.' What the Delegates were demanding was a series of economies that would surely rob the book of its likely authority. 'The Dictionary can be made better in quality', Murray wrote, 'only by *more* care, *more* work, *more* time.' This was not the moment to try to speed things up, to cut corners and trim fat, and to risk making a shoddy book in place of the great one Murray had in mind.

But the 'Suggestions' were not all, were not the worst of Jowett's supposed crimes. In October, even closer to the publication date of the first part of the Dictionary, Jowett perpetrated the ultimate impertinence by trying both to rewrite Murray's Preface and to change the Dictionary's title. The new Preface, which was sent to Murray without comment or explanation, was unrecognizable, and moreover—as an added insult by the meddlesome Jowett—his own effort was not returned to him. And the great book was no longer to be *A New English Dictionary on a Historical Basis*, but was, in Jowett-speak, *A New Dictionary Showing the History of the Language from the Earliest Times*.

If Murray had gone through the roof at the time of the 'Suggestions'—and he was no martinet; had Jowett's criticisms been fair he surely would have accepted them—now he turned positively apoplectic. 'I object emphatically to anybody altering it without consulting me … I shall write my own preface, *or it shall remain unwritten*.' He threatened to resign. He planned to tell his American friends that he was available to take up the many offers of professorships with which universities in the United States were already showering him. 'The future of English scholarship lies in the United States,' he said with an uncanny prescience. 'The language is studied with an enthusiasm unknown here.'

His friends rallied round him, and many agreed that he ought to go, and not let Jowett have his way and become, de facto, the editor of Murray's great work. 'I boil over,' wrote Alexander Ellis from Cambridge, 'to think of the misery of it … the utter shipwreck which one self-sufficient man can accomplish. It may be—I think it is—the best thing for your health and wellbeing to give it up, & insist on the removal of your name from the title page.'

But the crisis did eventually blow over—and it did so largely because of the energy, kindness, and immense tact of one of the *OED*'s great unsung heroes, the merchant and merchant banker Henry Hucks Gibbs, later to be ennobled as the first Lord Aldenham. He was the man who, 'if the inner history … ever comes to be told in full', in the words of Wilfrid Murray, 'saved the Dictionary'. Or, as another writer has it, 'whoever takes the credit for inspiring the Dictionary as a piece of scholarship, it is he who should receive it for maintaining the book as a business proposition'.

Hucks Gibbs was 40, wealthy, and splendidly aristocratic when he joined the Philological Society in 1859. His family had made much of their money from working the vast deposits of guano in Peru. (Doggerel of the day referred, not unkindly, to 'The House of Gibbs that made their Dibs by selling Turds of Foreign Birds'.) He was fascinated by the economics of bimetallism, that (now discredited) monetary system based on the equal footings that could in theory be enjoyed by both gold and silver.

'The man who saved the Dictionary'—the kindly and solicitous merchant banker Henry Hucks Gibbs—later ennobled as Lord Aldenham—who loaned money, intervened in disputes, and generally helped James Murray each time the mercurial editor threatened to resign.

He was a keen huntsman and a good shot.[15] He collected books with a fury. He regarded himself as a Liberal Conservative. He paid for the restoration of a number of English churches and cathedrals, and essentially funded the building of Keble College, Oxford. He was, in other words, the perfect saviour for a project as English and as worthy as Murray's Dictionary.

Murray was a neighbour on Mill Hill, as well as a leading light in the Philological Society, and so it was not too surprising that the two men became friends, and Murray came to regard Hucks Gibbs as a confidant. The problems faced by Murray in pioneering the work on the Dictionary became particularly acute once the proof sheets were returned for his inspection: three hours would be needed, he estimated, for him to examine every single sheet—and yet there were new sheets to prepare, new words to define. Sometimes the 'terrible undertow of words', as he wrote, seemed to present an impossibly powerful and ever-running tide; to try to halt it was a never-ending battle that an ordinary mortal could never hope to reverse or to win.

It was not just that. Mill Hill was a good distance from central London with its libraries and museums, both essential to his work; and Oxford was nearly a day's travel away too. The Delegates had started to become difficult, Jowett was impossible, the post was so often late and packages were lost; and then there was the money. Always the money. Oxford was grudging in parting with it, niggardly in budgeting for it, parsimonious in demanding detailed accounting for it. The undertow of words seemed sometimes as nothing when compared to the debilitating miseries of having to pay for so much effort with such deeply diminished funds.

Hucks Gibbs stepped smartly into the breach, lending Murray £400 so that the editor could pay his assistants and settle other

---

15 Fairly good: he blew off his right hand in 1864, but remained keen on the sport.

expenses, and he made no immediate demands for repayment. He worked eagerly as a sub-editor, on the letters C, K, and Q—with critics later saying that his work on C resulted in one of the best-furnished sections of all. He also mediated the dispute between Murray and Jowett—having already established some credentials for doing so, since much earlier on he had brought Jowett down to see the Scriptorium. Murray's diary records the meeting: 'Prof. Jowett. A week past on Wed. Mr. Gibbs showed him everything as well as his patience would allow, not very great—jumping at con-clusions.' Hucks Gibbs remembered both men as having been 'rather heated'.

By now the heat between the pair had become unbearable, and Hucks Gibbs had to employ all his reserves of diplomacy and tenacity to prevent Murray resigning, sailing off to America in a huff, and leaving the Dictionary to be completed by no doubt lesser men. By dint of a cascade of letters, by dining Jowett in the finest London clubs, by smothering him with aristocratic ad-miration, he eventually won the day.

The Vice-Chancellor wrote to Murray explaining that the Delegates now wanted the editor to write his own Preface, and implying that the 'Suggestions'—'good authors', no newspaper quotations, no words to be included post-1875—were essentially now moot. Murray, returning the favour, rewrote his Preface to include as many of the Vice-Chancellor's suggestions as seemed prudent—and the matter was closed. Jowett was widely seen as an irritating nuisance, and Murray as a man to be reckoned with—stubborn, principled, and right. But for the wise and steady inter-vention of Henry Hucks Gibbs, the rightness that led Murray to make so fine a dictionary might have been of no value at all.

The upshot of all the argumentation was that the first part of the great work was slightly delayed. But on 29 January 1884—five years after James Murray had signed his contract and started battling with the undertow—the messengers from the Press delivered to the Scriptorium at Sunnyside a bundle of bound copies of what all the lexicographic world had been waiting for. Part I of the *New English Dictionary* was, at last, officially, and as the phrase of the day had it, uttered for publication.

5

Pushing through the Untrodden Forest

I think it was God's will. In times of faith, I am sure of it. I look back & see that every step of my life has been as it were imposed upon me—not a thing of choice; and that the whole training of my life with its multifarious & irregular incursions into nearly every science & many arts, seems to have had the express purpose of fitting me to do this Dictionary … So I work on with a firm belief (at most times) that I am doing what God has fitted me for, & so made my duty; & a hope that He will strengthen me to see the end of it … But I am only an instrument, only the means that He has provided, & there is no credit due to me, except that of trying to do my duty; Deo soli gloria.

(Letter from James Murray to the politician Lord Bryce,
15 December 1903)

Murray was sustained for the rest of his life by an illusion that time, however quickly it ran out, was on his side. For a moment in history the language had paused and come to rest. It could be seized and captured for ever.

(Peter Sutcliffe,
The Oxford University Press: An Informal History, 1978)

Inside the bundle delivered to the Scriptorium were a dozen copies of a flimsy but curiously heavy volume, which measured some twelve inches along its spine, was eight inches deep, and, with 352 half-uncut pages between its flimsy covers, was a little less than an inch thick. It was bound in an undistinguished, muddy-looking off-white paper cover. Had it come from a later era, it might well have been mistaken for a telephone directory for a smallish city—Cincinnati, perhaps, or Nottingham, or Marseilles. But it was nothing so slight. This was a work that had been designed and made with immense care, its contents the consequence of years of scholarship and furrowed brows, and intended to have value for scores of generations to come.

Its title page, grandiloquent in tone but discreet in presentation, announced itself to the waiting world: *A New English Dictionary on Historical Principles, Founded Mainly on the Materials Collected by the Philological Society. Edited by James A. H. Murray, LL.D., President of the Philological Society, with the Assistance of Many Scholars and Men of Science. Part I. A–Ant. Oxford: At the Clarendon Press. 1884. [All rights Reserved.]*

It was in summary a slender, somewhat undistinguished-looking paperback book. It looked as beggarly as it did—more a publisher's starveling, not at all like the more traditional Clarendon Press books, bound as they all were in dark blue cloth or in red morocco, with handsome fleurons stamped onto the spine in gold and with marbled endpapers and silk headbands and page-markers—because Oxford, perpetually strapped for cash, had insisted that it should.

The department of the University called the Oxford University Press—together with its more academically inclined offspring, the Clarendon Press—had long made the bulk of its money from the publishing of Bibles, hymnals, and prayer books. Its buildings in Walton Street in west Oxford, designed in 1827 to look as collegiate as possible, were divided (they merged in 1906) into the Bible Side and the Learned Side, the profitability of the former subsidizing the indulgent obscurities of the latter. The irony of the Bible Side's unconscious reliance on the marketplace of Mammon was noted by one historian of the Press, who wrote of the early nineteenth century: 'Within the huge building the industrial revolution steamed and roared:[1] an outward front of dignified piety advertised its evangelizing mission: a Bible in every home in Christendom.'

But by the nineteenth century, as the pace of learning and scientific discovery quickened and the pace and volume of production from the Learned Side expanded to keep up with it all, so the Delegates began to insist on a much higher rate of return from the books that were commissioned and made. The *New English Dictionary*, so immense a Learned Side publishing project, and one that seemed unlikely to offer up even a penny piece as return on the thousands of pounds of investment that the Press would be enduring for years, for decades (and how optimistic even those forecasts turned out to be!), ran the risk of proving an enormous financial trial for the Press, perhaps even a financial

---

1   The Steam Press, once housed in a small building that jutted out into the OUP main quadrangle, used to obtain its water from a circular reservoir in the quad's centre, a body of water now converted (with a fountain) into a pastoral ornament. The only reminder of this pond's former purpose is a notice, warning the employees who take their summertime ease beside it, that it is 'unusually deep'.

embarrassment for the University. Some kind of device was needed, some kind of publishing gimmick, that would make it possible for this one project to bring as much money back into the Press's coffers as could be managed, and as quickly as possible.

And so Oxford, in an unusual (though not unheard-of) step, took a leaf from the peculiar way that magazines and newspapers were just then publishing new works by authors like Dickens and Trollope. These publishers were doing so in serial form, putting out a chapter a week, or a section a month, and permitting the reading public to spin out their buying over many months or years, keeping the costs down and in theory making everyone—the accountants most of all—content.

Oxford, a house of great dignity and gravitas, would never of course publicly countenance anything so vulgar. And yet the idea of publishing the Dictionary bit by bit had for the Delegates considerable commercial appeal. So as a means of priming the pump and allowing money to start flowing in to the great project as early as possible, the Press had demanded that the Dictionary be turned out in fascicles, sheaves of pages that were collected together to form distinct parts, but which could themselves be bound together later between hard covers and thus made into whole volumes.

This somewhat ordinary-looking and—at twelve shillings and sixpence, somewhat inexpensive[2]—book was thus the first morsel of substance to have emanated from the works of Coleridge and Furnivall, the Philological Society, and James Murray. This was *it*—publication number one, a volume that included, to the best of the editor's knowledge, every single one of the English words that

---

2 The American equivalent, distributed by Macmillan from New York, was priced at $3.25 a copy.

lay between and included *A* and *Ant*. It was woefully late—Oxford
had expected (and indeed, the contract had specified) that publication would begin in 1882, and that once matters were in
high gear, the Dictionary team would be able to churn out some
704 pages of completed work each year, almost two pages a day.
Murray had done his gallant best—Jowett's interference
notwithstanding—but at one stage, he wailed piteously to a friend
that though he tried to meet a personal target of completing 33
words a day, 'often a single word, like *approve* ... takes ¾ of a day
itself'.

However, the eventual appearance of the first fascicle did a
great deal to buck up Murray, who was at the time—on the eve of
his 47th birthday—feeling more than a little intimidated by the
scale of the task ahead of him. A few weeks later he would refer to
'the difficulty of pushing our way experimentally through an untrodden forest where no white man's ax has been before us'. But
now, and here, there was the first appearance of a pathway
through the confusing and unfamiliar thickets. It was, he told
the scores of admirers who wrote in with congratulations, 'my
offering to the world, which must be taken on its merits and de-
merits and with the tolerance which is the mature fruit of culture.
It will improve with age.'

The way that this first part of this great—and, as it happens,
essentially ageless—book was organized, the way that the 8,365
words included in it were arranged and defined and otherwise
dealt with, was to set the pattern for the future of the big Dictionary itself, the path that would eventually have an end. Maybe,
Murray supposed, he would get there in ten or eleven years' time.
The fact that it would take the 31 years left to him, and still not
be completed, might not have dismayed him had he known the
fate of the other great multi-volume European dictionaries that
were under way at around the same time. Although Emile Littré's

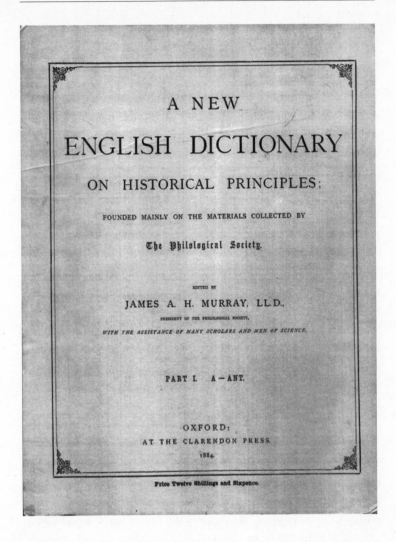

A NEW

ENGLISH DICTIONARY

ON HISTORICAL PRINCIPLES;

FOUNDED MAINLY ON THE MATERIALS COLLECTED BY

The Philological Society.

EDITED BY

JAMES A. H. MURRAY, LL.D.,

PRESIDENT OF THE PHILOLOGICAL SOCIETY,

WITH THE ASSISTANCE OF MANY SCHOLARS AND MEN OF SCIENCE,

PART I. A — ANT.

OXFORD:
AT THE CLARENDON PRESS.
1884.

Price Twelve Shillings and Sixpence.

The first fascicle, containing the 8,365 words which James Murray and his colleagues declared was the entire sum of the English words between *A* and *Ant*, was published in January 1884—27 years after Dean Trench's speech.

rather short *Dictionnaire de la langue française* took only a decade from publication of its first volume to the last—though 32 years from the conception of the plan—the Grimm brothers' *Deutsches Wörterbuch*, which was six times bulkier than its French equivalent, was begun in 1838 and fully finished only in 1961. If that was not long enough, the Dutch dictionary known as *Woordenboek der Nederlandsche Taal* was started in 1851 and completed in 1998, 147 years later. And a nineteenth-century attempt to fix the entire Swedish tongue between hard cover continues today into the twenty-first century, with scholars still stuck on the complexities of Swedish words beginning with the letter S.

Murray's seemingly dilatory state was as nothing when compared to the molasses-in-January progress in the scriptoria over on the European mainland. And he eventually realized it when, some years later, he was able to write approvingly of the speed with which his own dictionary-making machine was functioning. 'We have already overtaken Grimm, and have left it behind.' But that was in the future: just now, matters seemed to grind exceeding slow. These first 8,365 words had been won with the expenditure of Stakhanovite degrees of labour.

Before describing just what was in—and what was not in—Murray's first fascicle, a small but significant fact needs to be pointed out: something that will make rather more sense when we come to the very end, or least to the most modern part, of this story. A detailed textual analysis throws up in these very early parts of the Dictionary certain slight idiosyncrasies of style, a certain lack of consistency, a vague impression of (dare one say it?) *raggedness* that, while invisible to all but the most critical readers, suggests a degree of editorial hesitancy, an unease, a lack of complete confidence, a quite understandable sense of the editor perhaps not yet being fully into his stride. With the publication of each successive part, and, when in later years, whole volumes of the Dictionary appeared, so Murray's confidence and that of his colleague editors became, as one might anticipate, ever greater; the curious details and faint clues that occasionally give slight pause to those lexicographers who study the work's early parts vanished clear away. The early letters of the alphabet might fairly be said to be the dictionary equivalent of a 'Friday car'—fashioned not quite as perfectly as were some of the later letters, in much the same way that a car made moments before everyone leaves for the weekend might not be quite as fine as that produced when the assembly line was working at its best.

All of which serves to explain why the editors of the third edition of the *Oxford English Dictionary*, working to Murray's template, decided at the end of the twentieth century to begin their work with the letter M, not A. That way two things would happen: their own unadmitted inconsistencies at the start of their labours would be balanced by the perfection of Murray's middle-alphabet work; and by the time they reached a point of what they considered 'stability'—most probably the end of the letter R—and then turned to Murray's perhaps ever so slightly ragged A, their own system would be so firmly in place as to negate any shortcomings from the nineteenth century.

What we are talking about here is slight and subtle, idiosyncrasies that would pass unnoticed by almost all readers. But the reputation of the Dictionary centres about its majestic degree of accuracy and perfection: it was to obviate any possibility of a shortfall in standards that the new editors decided to begin their effort in the middle, and not at the beginning.

There were more than a thousand columns of type set out in Part I, and a total of 8,365 words. Murray separated these into three types. There were 6,797 instances of what he liked to call 'Main Words', each of which in his considered judgement deserved a separate article—words like *advance*, to pluck one at random from the fascicle, which has an 'article' that illustrates sixteen meanings for the verb form and ten for the noun, and which takes up very nearly a full page of the Dictionary. Then there were a further 570 'Combinations'—doubled-up words (to follow the chosen article to its end) like *advance-guard*, *advance-party*, and, peculiarly close to home in the case of James Murray, *advance-proofs*. And then another 998 entries, in those early days identified by being printed in smaller and fainter type, were deemed to be 'Subordinate' words, which were cross-referenced to the Main Words—subordinates like *advant*, which is an obsolete version of the verb *to advance*, subordinate to and therefore cross-referenced to *advance*, and which was first used by the poet and translator George Chapman[3] in 1605.

Almost a third of the 6,797 Main Words—1,998 of them, to be exact—were now obsolete themselves. They were all well worthy of inclusion in the Dictionary, however, for heaven forfend that anyone might ever stumble across a printed word in a book no matter how old or obscure and *not* find it in the Dictionary—it must be remembered that it was the intended function of a work like this to capture the language in its entirety, remembering all the while that one man's dead word may yet be another's still alive.

A further 321 of the words found lying between *A* and *Ant* Murray deemed 'foreign or imperfectly naturalized'. By that he meant they were not entirely English, in other words—rather more tied still to their origins in French, Italian or 'East Indian', but more or less current in contemporary usage.

---

3   The same Chapman of 'On First Looking into Chapman's *Homer*', by Keats.

The first part's first word—once the four pages devoted to the simple letter A had been accounted for, and after the entry for an occasionally used means of spelling the long *a*, *aa*—was the obsolete word for a stream or a watercourse, the noun spelled in the same way, *aa*. There was just one quotation supporting its use, taken from 'The Muniments (the deeds or official documents) of Magdalen College, Oxford', referring in 1430, and in a Norman-French–Latin hybrid tongue, to a widely used communal waste channel in the Lincolnshire marsh-town of Saltfleetby, as '*le Seventowne aa*'.

The first properly current word in the fascicle was *aal*, the Bengali or Hindi word for a plant similar to madder, from which a dye could be extracted for colouring clothes. One of Murray's readers had found the word in Andrew Ure's *Dictionary of Arts, Manufactures and Mines*, published in 1839, in a sentence that provided a nice example of a classic illustrative quotation: 'He has obtained from the aal root a pale yellow substance which he has called morindin.'[4]

Then, notwithstanding the objections of Benjamin Jowett's anonymous Delegate friend, the words *aardvark* and *aardwolf* are both included, with three quotations for the former and two for the latter: Murray had evidently seen off with quiet dispatch the lunacy of the idea of omitting such words. *Aardvark* is particularly lovingly chronicled, as the first familiar and properly English word in the book should perhaps be: it comes from the Dutch word *aarde*, meaning earth, combined with a series of Old English

---

4 And even though the word *morindin* must be rare indeed, the *OED* lists it—though (as occasionally occurs) without a definition—Murray simply noting 'See quotations'. There are two: the first is from an 1848 issue of the *Transactions of the Royal Society of Edinburgh*, in which a man named Anderson refers to 'The colouring matter of sooranjee, to which I give the name of Morindine', and the second in a chemicals manual a decade later, with a reference to 'Morindin ... yellow crystalline colouring matter'. The trail doesn't run cold at *sooranjee*, either: this, a further cross-reference has it, is the root of *Morinda citrifolia*, and is used in the dyeing of calico.

and Old High German forms of the Latin word *porcus*, a pig:
Murray's definition, suitably scholarly and concise, reads:

> *A South-African quadruped (Orycteropus capensis Cuv.) about
> the size of a badger, belonging to the insectivorous division of the
> Edentata, where it occupies an intermediate position between the
> Armadillos and Ant-eaters.*

By chance, the fact of Murray writing this summary of the
famous Cape Colonial earth-pig points up one of the short-lived
eccentricities of the early days of the Dictionary, a personal foible
of Murray's own which was to land him in no small amount of hot
water. Although by coincidence and chance he writes in the definition the hyphenated phrase *South-African*, he does not in fact
permit the word *African* to appear, as a headword, as a listed ad-
jective, in his Dictionary. He tries to explain why in his Preface,
and one can feel him squirming uncomfortably as he does so:

> *…the word African was one of the earliest instances in which the
> question of admission or exclusion arose with regard to an import-
> ant adjective derived from a geographical proper name. After much
> careful consideration, and consultation with advisers, it was de-
> cided (perhaps by a too rigid application of first principles) to omit
> the word, as having really no more claims to inclusion than Al-
> gerian, Austrian or Bulgarian. But, when American was
> reached, some months afterwards, it was seen that Americanize
> and Americanism must of necessity be included, and that these
> ('with the Americanising of our institutions') could not be ex-
> plained without treating American, and explaining its restricted
> application to the United States. American was accordingly ad-
> mitted. Then the question arose, whether the exclusion of African
> was consistent with the inclusion of American; but the question
> came too late; African had been actually omitted, on its own
> merits.*

Murray realized his misjudgement swiftly. He eventually overruled himself, and decided that *African* was after all to be included in the first Supplement, which would be published some five years after all the work on the Dictionary had been done in 1933. But its absence from Part I, and then again from the First Edition's Volume I which was published in 1888 and which includes all of the 31,254 words that begin with A and B, is very noticeable. (It should by rights have been located between an obsolete word for 'devour', *afrete*, and the word for 'face-to-face', *afront*. There is otherwise no word listed that begins with the letters *Afri-*, and most decidedly not that which describes what once was known, from H. M. Stanley's popular book, as 'the Dark Continent'.[5]) It can be seen today as an error—or a wrong-headed judgement-call—which stands as mute testimony to the complexities of the decision-making which so stimulated, and yet so wearied, James Murray, as he steadily and manfully wound his way through the untrodden forests of the language.[6]

Murray himself—a man never averse to revealing to all the trials of his task—offers in the Preface a snapshot of the difficulties involved in being so much of a pioneer:

> *Our attempts lay no claim to perfection; but they represent the most that could be done in the time and with the data at our command. The … direction in which much time has been consumed is the elucidation of the meaning of obscure terms, sometimes obsolete, sometimes current, belonging to matter of history, customs, fashions, trade or manufactures. In many cases, the only thing known about these was contained in the quotations, often merely allusive, which had been collected by the diligence of our readers. They were*

5 Nowadays there are two such words: *afrit*, an Islamic mythological demon; and *Afridi*, the name of a tribe that lives near the Central Asian homelands of the Pathans.

6 Murray very nearly included by mistake the noun *alliterates*, which a reader came across in an essay by the American poet James Lowell. Lowell wrote in answer to a puzzled Murray—who could find no other citation—saying it was clearly a misprint for *illiterates*. The verb *alliterate*—meaning to constitute alliteration—does of course exist.

to be found in no dictionary, or, if mentioned in some, were ex-
plained in a way which our quotations evidently showed to be
erroneous. The difficulty of obtaining first-hand and authoritative
information about these has often been immense, and sometimes
insurmountable. Ten, twenty or thirty letters have sometimes been
written to persons who, it was thought, might possibly know, or
succeed in finding out, something definite on the subject; and often
weeks have passed, and 'copy' advances into the state of 'proof',
and 'proof' into 'revise', and 'revise' even into 'final', before any
results could be obtained. It is incredible what labour has had to be
expended, sometimes, to find out facts for an article which occupies
not five or six lines; or even to be able to write the words 'Derivation
unknown', as the net outcome of hours of research and of testing the
statements put forth without hesitation in other works.

Elisabeth Murray, in her classic biography of her grandfather,
recalls a lecture in which he listed a typical daily bout of letter-
writing:

I write to the Director of the Royal Botanic Gardens at Kew about
the first record of the name of an exotic plant; to a quay-side
merchant at Newcastle about the Keels on the Tyne; *to a Jesuit*
father on a point of Roman Catholic Divinity; to the Secretary of
the Astronomical Society about the primum-mobile *or the solar*
constant; to the Editor of The Times *about a letter of the year*
1620 containing the first mention of Punch *[the beverage]; to a*
Wesleyan minister about the itineracy; *to Lord Tennyson to ask*
where he got the word balm-cricket *and what he meant by it,[7] to*
the Sporting News *about a term in horse-racing, or pugilism; or*
the invention of the word hooligan *in June 1898; to the Librar-*

---

7   The word—it means the common cicada—is a mistaken translation from the German
    Baumgrille, meaning tree-cricket, though it was not Tennyson who made the original
    error in his poem *Dirge*, but the eighteenth-century author from whom he had bor-
    rowed the word. The exchange of letters between Murray and the ennobled poet
    figures prominently in the Dictionary's public archives; and the *OED*'s notes of the
    etymology take on a rare personal tone by writing that it is all explained 'as Tennyson
    tells us'.

ian of the Cambridge University Library for the reading of the first edition of a rare book; to the Deputy Keeper of the Rolls for the exact reading of a historical MS which we have reason to suspect has been inaccurately quoted by Mr. Froude; to a cotton manufacturer for a definition of Jaconet, *or a technical term of cotton printing; to George Meredith to ask what is the meaning of a line of one of his poems; to Thomas Hardy to ask what is the meaning of a word* terminatory *in one of his novels; to the Editor of the* New York Nation *for the history of an American political term; to the administrator of the Andaman Islands for an exact reference to an early quotation which he has sent for the word* Jute, *or the history of* Talapoin; *to the Mayor of Yarmouth about the word* bloater *in the herring fishery; to the Chief Rabbi for the latest views upon the Hebrew* Jubilee; *to a celebrated collector of popular songs for the authorship of 'We don't want to fight, But by* Jingo *if we do,' which gave his name to the political* Jingo.

It is worth remembering that all of this correspondence had to be written by hand; and that the letters had, what is more, to be written twice. Although carbon paper had been invented by an Italian in 1806, its use for the making of copies of handwritten letters had not been perfected, and most courteous correspondents—like Murray, who was notably so, and who wrote in some kind of elegant copperplate—preferred the tribulations of simply writing everything out once again, of making a fair copy.

Many of the letters he wrote were to celebrated figures—Lord Tennyson preeminent among them. Once he had to write to Robert Browning, asking the meaning of the word *apparitional*. Browning's reply confused him, and in later years Murray was mildly scathing about the poet's constant use of words 'without regard to their proper meaning'—a habit, Murray complained, that 'added greatly to the difficulties of the Dictionary'.

Yet for all these vexing aspects of his work, the triumph of the first part of the Dictionary was plain to see. It was abundantly clear, even from this one small part, that what would eventually be published was the catalogue of a truly vast emporium of words. Here were the wonderful and the ordinary, cheek by jowl—*acatalectic* and *adhesion*, *agnate* and *allumine*, *animal*, *answer*, and *ant*. And by *ant* Murray did not only define the 'social insect of the *Hymenopterous* order'—he included the prefix *ant-* as a contraction of *anti-*, and used in words like *antacid*, and the suffix *-ant*, attached to form words like *tenant*, *valiant*, *claimant*, and *pleasant*.

True, there were critics aplenty, and as soon as the work was published letters started trickling in to the Scriptorium, triumphantly listing earlier quotations than those used, or alleging (usually erroneously) that words had been missed out. Murray, a prickly man at the best of times, was extremely sensitive to any criticism. But his confidence in his work was clearly burgeoning—and it allowed him (or so a few fans of Murray like to think) the luxury of inserting within the scores of pages and definitions and quotations in that first fascicle one of the very few witticisms that is known to exist in the complete work.

When pressed, lexicographers involved in the making of the book remark that such humour as is to be found in the *OED* was placed there 'only inadvertently', and so there almost probably was never any humorous intention on Murray's part—none, for instance, as there plainly was in the writing of the single-volume *Chambers's Twentieth Century Dictionary* of 1901, which had droll entries such as that for *éclair*: 'a cake, long in shape but short in duration'.

Nonetheless, in this first fascicle of the Philological Society's work we find what some might regard as a classically Oxford sense of amusement when we encounter the following, buried in the second sense of the very rare noun *abbreviator*:

> *An officer of the court of Rome, appointed … to draw up the*
> *Pope's briefs …*

Would James Murray have inserted that definition, heavily freighted with its double entendre, deliberately, and out of a sense of fun? Probably not: *briefs* meaning underwear did not come into use until 1933—in all likelihood its inclusion truly was inadvertent, reflecting only the splendid innocence of the utterly aloof. And yet I like to wonder. There are more than a few photographs of Murray wearing a decidedly impish grin behind his beard, and I like to imagine that, from time to time, this increasingly confident man allowed himself the pleasure of teasing his otherwise rather stern and exacting readership, just a little.

Many eminent figures read that first part of the great Dictionary. Some were admiring. A few of them carped. The Delegates—to Murray's chagrin, hurt, and disappointment—said nothing, offered no note of congratulation or encouragement. But there was one outsider who did read it, and who, moreover, did so with the greatest dispatch and eagerness. He was someone quite unknown to Murray: an outsider, an apparently unqualified critic with no track record in any of the lexical skills. He was, in fact, no more than a former corresponding clerk in a Sheffield cutlery firm, recently made redundant, a 39-year-old Nottinghamshire farmer's son named Henry Bradley. His reading of it changed everything.

On close scrutiny it would seem that Bradley's life and career to this point was in many respects rather like Murray's (except that Bradley had had far better than a rural Scottish village education—he had been at a grammar school in Chesterfield, a very traditional and well-regarded academy sited in the shadow of the curiously twisted spire of the town's Church of St Mary and All Saints[8]). At the time of the publication of the Dictionary's first fascicle he was living in London and working as a freelance writer. He had been forced by impoverishment to take his previous job, and it was one that he didn't like (Bradley had counted shipments of spoons and knives that had been sent off to foreign clients, Murray had, prior to his schoolmastering days, written ledger entries for the foreign department of a bank). He had a sickly wife who needed to be moved to the warmer airs of the south (hence London, once the cutlers had sacked him). And, most importantly, he had an extraordinary and Murray-like aptitude for language.

And an aptitude, as it happened, for much, much more. Just as with James Murray—and, so it seems, with so many of the men and women involved in the dictionary project—Henry Bradley had a range of interests and a level of scholarship in each (except music—he could only recognize one tune, 'God Save the Queen', and that he knew only because everyone stood up when it was played) that was almost unimaginable. He had taken only fourteen days to learn Russian, it was said—'with no help but the alphabet and a knowledge of the principles of Indo-Germanic philology'. He also had an uncanny ability to read a book when it was upside down. He had learned to do this, he said, by looking at the Bible perched on his father's knees while he sat before the family reading prayers; it was a facility which, once learned, he was never to lose.

A friend once stumbled upon some of Bradley's childhood notebooks, which, he noted, included

8   The use by its fourteenth-century builders of too much green wood is said to be the explanation for the spire's extraordinary crookedness. Locals like to suggest that it bent itself to take a peek at the highly unusual sight of a virgin being married in the church below. Should it happen again, they say, it will straighten itself back up in astonishment. Until then it remains the symbol of this Derbyshire county town.

Henry Bradley, a remarkable linguist and amateur lexicographer, first came to Murray's attention after writing a two-part critique of the first fascicle. He soon joined the staff as an assistant, and was appointed joint senior editor—though still doffing his cap to Murray—in 1896.

> *facts of Roman history, scraps of science, lists of words peculiar to
> the Pentateuch or Isaiah, Hebrew singletons, the form of the verb
> to be in Algerine, Arabic, bardic and cuneiform lettering, Arab-
> isms and Chaldaisms in the New Testament, with vocabularies
> that imply he was reading Homer, Virgil, Sallust and the Hebrew
> Old Testament at the same time. In another group the notes pass
> from the life of Antar ben Toofail by 'Admar' (apparently of the
> age of Haroun Arrashid) to the rules of Latin verse, Hakluyt and
> Hebrew accents, whereupon follow notes on Sir William Ham-
> ilton and Dugald Stewart and a translation of parts of Aeschylus'*
> Prometheus ...

This dauntingly learned early middle-aged man, understandably weary of clerking in Sheffield, arrived in London, along with
his fragile wife Eleanor and their four children, at the end of 1883.
They took rooms in Fulham, on the Wandsworth Bridge Road,
and Bradley started pounding the pavements in search of freelance writing assignments. Before long he befriended a man
named J. S. Cotton, who then ran an elegant weekly magazine
(thirteen shillings a year, published every Saturday) called the
Academy.

In every sense the journal was a perfect outlet for the talents of
a figure like Bradley. It was styled *A Weekly Review of Literature,
Science and Art*—it was kept mercifully free of the canting irrele-
vancies of politics—and it usually ran to sixteen or twenty pages. A
typical issue might have a dozen book reviews, a number of the-
atrical notices, and columns filled with delicious arcana—essays
on the latest developments in France ('160,000 francs subscribed
for a statue of Gambetta at Cahors') and America ('Matthew Arnold reportedly taking elocution lessons in Andover, Maine, to
prepare himself for an American tour'), jottings on scientific advances ('new fossils discovered in the Bagshot Beds to the south of
London'), philological studies ('fresh information on the number

of Greek words in the Karlsruhe Priscian No. 132'), and count-less other oddities besides.

In early February 1884 Cotton called Bradley to his offices on Chancery Lane and handed him a single copy of Part I of James Murray's *New English Dictionary*, suggesting that the cutlery clerk might like to try to write a five-column review of it, both to test his abilities of comprehending so complex a book and then to see if he might be capable of organizing some sensible thoughts about it.

Bradley took the thick slab of printed pages back to Fulham, exultant at the chance. He had not fully moved in: he had only a tea-chest in his living room to use as a desk; but he nonetheless wrote his review and handed it in within days. Cotton found it far too long—but quite fascinating, and extraordinarily well written. Rather than return it to Bradley to cut it down—Victorian editors were more lenient about allotting space than their counterparts today—he decided he would divide it into two parts. These duly appeared, edited in double-quick time, in the issues of Saturday 16 February and Saturday 1 March.

The appearance of the notice—written as it was by a hith-erto quite unknown figure, by someone well outside the philo-logical priesthood—provoked an instant small sensation. It was an essay that in due course changed Bradley's life—plucking him from the tiresome trajectories of freelancing into the highest realms of academe and establishment. It was an essay that in due course changed James Murray's life too. And it changed—most happily—the fortunes of the Dictionary, like almost no other event before or since.

The most notable characteristic of Bradley's review was that it managed to be admiring and yet neither slavish nor sycophantic in its admiration. To be sure, there was no doubt that Bradley liked the book: 'the present specimen affords every reason to hope that the skill of Dr Murray and his assistants will prove equal to the arduous task which lies before them,' he said in his first paragraphs. It could be confidently asserted, Bradley continued, 'that if the level of excellence achieved in this opening part be sustained throughout, the completed work will be an achievement without parallel in the lexicography of any living language'.

He used the essay to work his way in detail through the design and structure of the book. Nothing much was quoted before what Murray chose as the linguistically epoch-changing year of AD 1150—when standard English had finally wrested itself free from the strictures of Anglo-Saxon—this, Bradley noted with singular approval. The pages were far more elegantly designed, he said, than the typographic 'chaos' of M. Littré's French dictionary. Murray had been much more sensible in his relatively economical use of quotations—he had been wise not to pile on simply repetitious examples, as Littré had done (we can feel the anti-Gallic gorge rising in Bradley's throat), and he cited, in a sideswipe at the Frenchman, his 'twenty-three numbered senses of *eau*'—which just had to be an 'over-refinement, which is rather confusing than helpful'.

He was not entirely enamoured, however, of some of the lesser details of Murray's work. He chided the editor gently for somehow failing to include all the phrases with which he, Bradley, was familiar—why was the phrase *acting edition* not included? What about *free agent*, for example? Where was *alive and kicking*? The idiomatic nature of the phrase *old age* was not explained, and Bradley could not fathom why. And as for Murray's habit of including a very large number of quotations from the two or three years before publication—what, pray, was the point? 'It seems to savour too much of "bringing the work *down to the latest date*" '—a phrase which critics of Bradley's essay might think was a piece of verbal clumsiness for 'bringing it *up to date*', until we learn (from the modern *OED*) that the phrase *up to date* did not itself become current until around 1888, four years after Bradley wrote his review.

There were other cavils. Bradley wondered if it was right to remark that the word *anemone* signified 'daughter of the wind', since the Greek suffix was not, he said with the casual confidence of one who knew, 'exclusively patronymic'. The first syllable of *alpaca* was probably not Arabic, as Murray had written—and Bradley went on to argue why it was much more likely, in fact, to be Spanish. Nor was the *Academy*'s essay entirely sure that it was wise of Murray to quote himself (from the Mill Hill school magazine) using the word *anamorphose*; warming to this theme, and slightly facetiously, Bradley then wondered whether Murray might do likewise in Part II, when it came to the word *aphetize*, a favourite word of Murray's, and one he was often heard to use when making speeches devoted to etymology and philology.[9]

All told, the 4,500-word review, with its broad and measured praise and its cleverly detailed and quietly stated criticism, was very evidently the work of a figure of rare intelligence and judgement. The tone of the piece seems to have been unaffected by Bradley's obvious delight at seeing the book in print at last, and by his expectation that it would, when completed, be a masterpiece. It was, in short, just the kind of review that any intelligent editor might dream of—and it had a singular impact on James Murray.

It made him want, all of a sudden, to accomplish two related things. He wanted to find out who on earth this unknown and mysterious writer for the *Academy* was. And once he had found that out, he wanted to hire him. A man of his evident perspicacity, and

9 Bradley's prescience was amply confirmed: not only does Murray quote himself for *aphetize*—he quotes an entry he had written, a definition for *acute*, in the Dictionary's very Part I that was under Bradley's review: 'In the sense of sharp in business, shrewd, it [*acute*] …is often aphetized as *'cute.'* The word *anamorphose*, which still sports a Murray quote today, means 'to distort into a monstrous projection'.

fondness for the book, should be taken on to help. So Murray wrote from Mill Hill to Fulham, commended and thanked Bradley for his review—and then without further ceremony began to ask him a number of complex problems of etymology of words that began with B. Bradley wrote back, unfazed and helpful; and in June he wrote to Murray asking whether, in the event of some vacancy in the Scriptorium, there might be a place for him on the staff. The job had to be full-time, and salaried, he said: he had a wife and four children, and the life he could live on the proceeds of freelancing was a modest one indeed. He needed a sense of security.

And in due course, Henry Bradley did indeed join the staff of the Dictionary. He eventually presided over vast numbers of pages, becoming the most critically important of Murray's colleagues. In time, with Murray's death, he succeeded him as senior editor. Yet history has perhaps been less kind to him than he deserves: fate has consigned him to remain permanently memorialized in Murray's shadow, and his reputation, by comparison with that of Murray, has never been able truly to flourish. More of the details of his work belong to the next chapter: suffice to say here that his nearly 40-year connection with the Dictionary began modestly enough, with Mr Cotton's invitation in February 1884 to write an experimental book review for his small London literary magazine. The story of what then befell Henry Bradley should serve as encouragement for today's writers, one might think, and prompt them to consider the possibilities and opportunities that might yet come from the vagaries of the freelance life.

There was one unanticipated reward for Murray, one that was specifically timed to coincide with the appearance of Part I. Henry

Hucks Gibbs had been working behind the scenes for the past year, trying to persuade the government, no less, to help alleviate Murray's troubling personal financial position. (Furnivall, Trench, and Prince Louis-Lucien Bonaparte had added their support to the campaign as well.) And in the end, it worked. At the beginning of 1884 Gladstone, the Prime Minister, even though he was then deeply embroiled in the nation-gripping saga involving General Gordon of Khartoum,[10] agreed to award the editor a pension from the Civil List—even though the List was a body set up in the late seventeenth century to pay the costs of the Royal Family and high officials of the government, like judges and ambassadors. The idea of paying the editor of a book was eccentric, to say the least—but Gladstone was clearly sufficiently impressed with the worth of what Murray was doing to persuade Queen Victoria to make an exception.

> *I am directed* [the Downing Street private secretary wrote] *to acquaint you that having given further consideration to the question of affording you additional aid in the work upon which you engaged of editing the* New English Dictionary, *he has received the Queen's approval to his recommendation that you should be granted a pension from the Civil List of £250 a year. He hopes that this proposal may be agreeable to you, and he wishes you all success in your important task.*

Murray was thrilled, and wrote back to Gladstone saying that he accepted happily, though not for himself, but for his staff—the number of which he would now be able to increase. Hucks Gibbs added to his improving state by setting up an Indemnity Fund in Murray's name, to which others of his admirers contributed. And

---

10 A half-mad, alcoholic, but inescapably heroic Christian imperialist whom Gladstone and his ministers tried—and failed—to control. He died in Khartoum after a 320-day siege by Sudanese rebels, and is remembered still by all British schoolboys, along with other tragic heroes like Scott, Oates, and Lord Cardigan of Crimea.

Oxford, too, chipped in, by revising its budget to make a total sum of £1,750 available each year. Of that sum, £1,175 would cover the wages of up to eight assistants. Seventy-five pounds would go for postage and stationery. And fully £500 would be earmarked for the editor—which meant that, together with the subvention from the Civil List, Murray would earn the not-so-trifling sum of £750 a year. Back in 1879 it had been suggested that he might be earning one pound for every page of the book: if he could keep to the Oxford target of 700 pages each year, then he would indeed be earning just what had been forecast, back when he had first signed the contract to start his work.

There were, however, two conditions applied to the seeming generosity of the Press. First of all, Murray had to agree that, were he to find himself falling short of producing 704 pages a year—two fully finished fascicles of 352 pages each—he would be obliged to hire a second senior editor, someone who would, in the pecking order, enjoy essentially the same standing and authority as himself. Murray agreed—hoping, if matters did demand it, that his new-found friend Henry Bradley would become available. And secondly, said Oxford—if the new funds were to be forthcoming, then James Murray would have to give up his schoolteaching in Mill Hill, and he would have to move himself and the entire dictionary operation to the city of Oxford, where logic and expediency had long suggested it should be shifted. The *New English Dictionary*, and all of its staff, together with its shelves of reference books, its hierarchy of desks and tables, its suites of pigeon-holes, and, most important, its ever-growing tonnage of quotation slips, should be removed in short order to a new location 56 miles to the west, to Oxford.

James Murray had been expecting this requirement for some time, and he was barely troubled by it. His response—or, at least, a response that coincided with the request—came with his inclusion of a quotation in the next part of the Dictionary that was as celebratory as it was entirely invented.

He was working on the word *arrival*, in the sense of 'one that arrives or has arrived'. His new (and ninth) daughter, Rosfrith Ada Nina Ruthven Murray, happened to be born on 5 February 1884, just a week after the birth of Part I, and as he was dealing with *arrival*, he inserted into the proofs of the Dictionary the sentence *the new arrival is a little daughter.* He had done this once before, when Elsie Mayflower was born in May 1882, when he was working on A: he inserted into the list of illustrative quotations *as fine a child as you will see.*

In time Elsie Mayflower began to work on the Dictionary (and when she was eighteen, so did Rosfrith Ada Nina—despite her left-handedness, which made for some early difficulties). Elsie worked for her father for most of the rest of his life. The quotation announcing her birth survives in the *OED* to this day.

6

So Heavily Goes the Chariot

Only those who have made the experiment know the bewilderment with which the editor or sub-editor, after he has apportioned the quotations for such a word as above ... *among 20, 30 or 40 groups, and furnished each of these with a provisional definition, spreads them out on a table or on the floor where he can obtain a general survey of the whole, and spends hour after hour in shifting them about like pieces on a chess-board, striving to find in the fragmentary evidence of an incomplete historical record, such a sequence of meanings as may form a logical chain of development. Sometimes the quest seems hopeless; recently, for example, the word* art *utterly baffled me for several days; something* had *to be done with it; something was done and put in type; but the renewed consideration of it in print, with the greater facility of reading and comparison which this afforded, led to the entire pulling to pieces and reconstruction of the edifice, extending to several columns of type ... those who think that such work can be hurried, or that anything can accelerate it, except more brain power to bear on it, had better try.*

(James Murray,
Presidential Address to the Philological Society, 1884)

I t was Benjamin Jowett of Balliol who first formally suggested that James Murray should move full-time up to Oxford. Yes,

Jowett, the infuriating, arrogant, self-regarding, and yet quite un-speakably brilliant martinet whose interference in the early stages of the Dictionary's planning very nearly caused Murray to resign. By now, however, the two men had more or less settled their differences—Henry Hucks Gibbs had seen to that—and were, des-pite all early appearances to the contrary, fast becoming the very best of friends. And Murray, despite his self-evident fondness for Mill Hill School and the increasingly well-oiled machinery of his little Scriptorium, accepted that it was mightily inconvenient for him to live so far away from where his Dictionary was being type-set, printed, and published.

However fast the ice might be melting between Murray and Jowett, the fact is that the mills of Oxford themselves grind ex-ceeding slow, and it took some months of negotiation and argu-mentation about money—and reams of correspondence with the always annoying Frederick Furnivall, who was not at all keen to see Murray taken away from him and his own headquarters in Primrose Hill—before everything was agreed. Jowett had made his first suggestion of the move in the autumn of 1883; Murray was not to shift until the summer of 1885.

Mill Hill School bade him a heartfelt farewell at a ceremony in that year's Foundation Day. The little iron hut that had served as the first Scriptorium was presented by Murray as his valedictory gift, and after the Old Boys raised the necessary cash, it was moved from the Murrays' garden to the grounds of the main school itself. It was to be a reading room for the boys, Murray said, a memento of his mastership among them,[1] and a place where, especially on the Sabbath he still held dear, they could enjoy peace and time for reflection. And as a pleasing coda for the departing family, Harold

[1] The deal panelling caught fire in 1902, the corrugated iron melted, and the building was consequently ruined. But a replacement was opened the following year and still stands as the Murray Scriptorium; and a block built later to house the school's day-boys was christened the Murray Building.

Murray, the oldest son, who was a senior pupil at the school, distinguished himself in appropriate fashion by carrying off most of that year's academic prizes.

In short order Murray managed to find a house, an ideal house in fact, for Ada and himself and his (thus far nine) children in Oxford. It was a substantial and newly built structure in brick and Cotswold stone, set on the east side of the Banbury Road at the very edge of town (Oxford City's old boundary stone can still be seen in the front garden wall). There were open fields to the north, the University Press half a mile away by foot (a little longer on Murray's infamous Humber tricycle, which he pedalled furiously all around town) to the west, the Bodleian Library and the colleges (the house was built on St John's College land) a short step to the south. It was in most ways ideal—with plenty of room for the family's children, books, and lumber, and with a garden of a size that was perfect for recreation, relaxation, and privacy.

He named it 'Sunnyside'—both after his first home back down in Mill Hill and also because, at least once noon had passed, it had been built on the sunny side of the north-bound street. It still stands, at No. 78—home now to an eminent anthropologist who has taken the greatest of care to memorialize the three astonishingly productive decades that James Murray spent there,[2] not least

2 Murray's already-mentioned childhood friendship with Alexander Graham Bell—Bell had been best man at Murray's wedding to Ada—continued to flourish when Murray lived in Oxford, with the consequence that after Bell had invented the first working telephone he presented it to Murray in gratitude for teaching him about acoustics and electricity back in their younger Edinburgh days. Murray found the wood-and-bakelite arrangement somewhat uninspiring, and consigned it to an attic. In the 1980s the present occupant of 78 Banbury Road found himself at the AT&T Museum in New Jersey, where the curator was bemoaning the fact that Telephone Number One had never been found. A search of the Oxford attic turned up nothing; but the elderly gentleman who had bought the house from Murray's widow was found, and reported that during the Second World War soldiers had been billeted at the house and, during one exceptionally frigid winter, had used all available bits of rubbish they could find in the attic as firewood. If this story is to be believed, the world's first telephone appears to have gone up in smoke, to keep a party of ice-cold infantrymen from freezing.

'Sunnyside'. The house on Banbury Road, Oxford, where Murray worked on the *OED*, an endeavour now memorialized by a blue plaque beside the famous pillar-box that was erected—to the gratitude both of Murray and of Sunnyside's current owner—by the city's Post Office.

163

by placing an extremely rare first edition of the Dictionary in what was once Murray's dining room, purely as 'a sentimental gesture'.

James went first, along with the older children, the bulk of the furniture, and the family's collection of pet doves. Ada remained for a while with the younger children and the family cat, and supervised the assistants in their dismantling of the Scriptorium, collecting all the papers and books into 40 tea-chests. She grumbled in a letter to James about the hardness, the coldness, and the loneliness of the marital bed, though, and by mid-June she had joined her husband in Oxford, to begin what was to turn out a long and generally contented life in the comfortable penumbra of academe.

However pleasant a home for Murray and his family, Sunnyside turned out not to be an ideal headquarters for the making of the Dictionary. There was only enough room for the eleven Murrays, let alone for the assistants—eight of them, eventually—who were required for the project. So it was decided that a new Scriptorium had to be built—and this proved initially something of a trial. St John's College—acting wisely, since the Banbury Road was then and remains an exceptionally pleasant-looking thoroughfare—would not permit Murray to put up his monstrous-looking corrugated iron structure in the front garden. It had to go behind the house—so long as the next-door neighbour, the Vinerian Professor of English Law, Albert Dicey, did not object.

But Professor Dicey did object, and strenuously. In his short history of the University Press, Peter Sutcliffe writes that, to an astonished Murray, Albert Dicey was 'a raving lunatic ... the absent-minded professor incarnate [who] gibbered and stared at him across the garden wall'. The *DNB* is somewhat kinder, explaining that Dicey had 'a lack of control over his muscles which hampered him in childhood and, indeed, throughout life'. He was far from mad, insists the author of the article, but rather

The second Scriptorium, established the back garden of Murray's Oxford home soon after he moved in 1885, had a far more elaborate arrangement for filing slips.

had 'a lovable simplicity of character and a lively wit', and once told his students that it was 'better to be flippant than dull'. One can imagine that a flippant, witty man with poor muscle control might well seem something of a tall order for the punctilious and rather shy Scotsman to accept as his next-door neighbour.

A tidal wave of complaining letters promptly swamped the unsuspecting Murray, with Dicey insisting that the planned iron hut would ruin his view. And so modifications were made: the hut was sunk three feet below garden level, and the large pile of clayey debris from the excavation was turned into a hillock on which Ada Murray planted flowering shrubs (it still stands in the anthropologist's garden, though the Scriptorium has been replaced by a sunken garden and a limestone plaque on the garden wall). Murray had his own views as to why Dicey had insisted on his half-burying his building: it was so that 'no trace of a place of real work shall be seen by fastidious and otiose Oxford'.

But though the Murrays and the Diceys later became firm friends, the legacy of the arguments remained: the Oxford Scriptorium, 50 feet long and fifteen wide, not only was deemed ugly ('like a toolhouse, a washhouse or a stable', said a passer-by, sniffily); because it had been built in a three-feet-deep trench, it was cold, damp, and positively unsanitary. On many a winter's day Murray and his colleagues were forced to sit with their feet in boxes filled with newspapers, to protect them from the chill and the draughts, and more than a few times Murray caught cold, and several times contracted pneumonia. He no longer sat, elevated, on a dais, as he had in Mill Hill: his only sign of authority in Oxford was that his stool was a little taller than those supplied to his assistants. So he was afflicted by the piercing cold just like everybody else—a melancholy note which gave Furnivall more ammunition with which to attack the Oxford move: the 'horrid corrugated den' that had been dug into the Sunnyside back garden was quite unsuitable, he said, for the nationally important work on which Murray and his assistants were engaged.

Despite Furnivall's carping, and despite Murray's own dejection at having to leave the teaching he loved and to reconcile himself to becoming, and probably for the rest of his days, a lexicographer—Samuel Johnson's 'harmless drudge', he had cause to remember bitterly—there was one development that somewhat sweetened the pill. Benjamin Jowett directed the full force of his charm on the Murray family, and made sure that the Balliol College of which he was Master was always available as a comfortable sanctuary.

'Welcome to your own College,' Jowett proclaimed, grandiloquently, when James and Ada arrived to dine at his High Table on the first June Sunday of their residence. He later arranged for Murray to be granted an Honorary MA—rather less for any dignity it bestowed than for the right it conferred to make use of the Bodleian Library. The friendship that developed between the two men because of gestures like these turned out to be an enduring one—so much so that when a boy, the tenth Murray child, was born in 1886, he was given Jowett as his third Christian name, and with the names Arthur Hugh before it, in memory of two of Jowett's closest friends.[3]

---

3   Benjamin Jowett and Balliol College might have been close to Murray—the University, however, was not and never really would be. Oxford in Victorian times was a highly exclusive body, upper-class, rigorously classical in its intellectual bent, and un-ashamedly Church of England. James Murray was, on the other hand, the son of a provincial draper, had interests in European philology, and was an unabashed Congregationalist. He also had the terrier-like Frederick Furnivall constantly interfering on his behalf—anonymous letters to the local press his speciality—and annoying the grandees of the University by doing so. For all of these reasons, and despite his august position as editor of the greatest of all English-language dictionaries, he was never offered a University position, not even in an honorary capacity. He kept a dignified silence about having to endure the cold shoulder, other than to remark in passing, two years before his death, that he was 'to a great extent only a sojourner' in Oxford, never truly a part of the fabric of the place.

And as with Balliol, so with the Oxford Post Office, which, in a gesture it would be hard to imagine today, tried to make Murray's life a little easier. As soon as he was settled at Sunnyside, engineers came and erected a bright red pillar box on Banbury Road, right outside his front gate. It was recognized that the editor sent immense volumes of post each day, and the local postmaster wanted to make sure that it was as convenient as possible for him to do so.[4]

Congeniality and collegiality and pillar boxes and the Christiannaming of children were one thing, all part of the consummate pleasantness of the move to so civilized a city as Oxford. The number 704 was quite something else, however, and was the principal reason that, despite his outwardly agreeable situation, James Murray was wretchedly miserable during the first few years of his time in the city.

The number 704 was engraved on his heart in those first years, it seems. For this, as mentioned, was the number of pages of completed dictionary that Murray was expected—contractually expected, the Press liked to remind him—to produce for them each and every year. If he managed that—if he managed to give Oxford enough material for them to publish two finished fascicles of 352 pages each year—it was calculated that there was an outside chance that the complete work might be finished before all who were presently working on it were safely in their graves.

But Murray was finding it ever more difficult to complete 704 pages a year, or anything like it. The job was simply far too

---

4   It still stands, and when I last saw it the current owner of Sunnyside was busy stuffing his just-written quota of Christmas cards into it. He was wearing his carpet slippers as he did so, having stepped out of his living room a moment before. He said he regarded the siting of the box as 'one of the greatest conveniences imaginable'.

complex—and his own quest for absolute perfection so time-consuming and demanding—to undertake at the rate that he, and Oxford, in the heady early days of the project, had thought might be reasonable. True, now that he was free from the demands of schoolteaching, he could give an extra twenty or so hours each week to dictionary work. But even this was not enough—and the money made available by the Press would not allow him to employ more than a handful of assistants. So as the work became ever more complex, as the press of words became ever more intolerable, Murray began to fall short of his contracted targets by ever wider margins.

As if this were not enough, it was becoming abundantly clear that the sales of the Dictionary parts were not going nearly as well as had been expected. Part I had sold only about 4,000 copies—the sales estimate had suggested ten times as many—and when Part II, *Anta–Battening*, was published in November 1885, it sold only 3,600. However friendly Henry Bradley's review in the *Academy* might have been, his words were not exactly persuading legions of readers to rush out and slap down twelve shillings and sixpence for a fascicle. This sombre fact was now exercising those in the Press who took the increasingly fashionable view—first adumbrated by Jowett—that its first business was not so much to publish fine books, but to make money, and to survive commercially.

One might have supposed Murray would have been exultant to see the second part complete. He wrote his Preface at the Oxford Scriptorium[5] in September. 'This part completes the letter A, and extends nearly to the end of Ba-,' he reported, sounding, if not smug, then at least moderately well satisfied.

Of the 9,135 words that the soft-bound book contained—

---

5 He signed his Preface from 'The Scriptorium, Banbury Road, Oxford'. On all subsequent occasions he dropped the street address.

words that brought the total in the Dictionary's first two parts to well over 15,000, more than a third of the number of words in the whole of Johnson's dictionary of a century before—some were exceptionally difficult. The prefix *anti-*, for example, occupied 42 columns of the completed book, *back* spread over 24 columns, and words such as *as, at, art, ask, bail, band, bank,* and *bar* proved complicated because of their 'multitudinous ramifications of meaning': the task of determining their mutual relationships had 'hardly been more intricate than that of exhibiting the results'. In addition, words that begin with *Ba-* turned out to have fearfully difficult etymologies—'among the most obscure in the language'—and that slowed them down as well.

But he was sanguine in his forecast. 'I hope that the result of my removal to Oxford, and of the labours of the much larger staff of assistants with which the liberality of the Delegates of the Clarendon Press has furnished me, will be to make it possible to produce the following parts of the Dictionary at much shorter intervals, and that we may reach the end of Part III, finishing B, early in 1886.'

It was either very tactful or very cunning of Murray to mention in his Preface what he liked to call the generous liberality of the Press. The Press saw it rather differently: it was only a most reluctant liberality, and a liberality of which, in the lofty judgement of the official *History of the University of Oxford* written a century later, the Dictionary was during the 1880s the most chronically needy recipient. 'What makes our chariot go so heavily is the fact that it is always carrying the dead weights of scores and scores of matters which no-one will nerve themselves to finish,' wrote the Delegates' Secretary. It must have been crystal clear to Murray as he wrote those words—gratefully, or with tongue in cheek—that his project must have seemed a dead weight, and that there was not the slightest chance he would ever make his deadline.

Nor did he. Part III, which inched the alphabet forward only as far as *bozzom*—and so did not 'finish B', not by a long chalk—was due to appear in April 1886. In March, however, it was found that only a paltry 56 pages of its contracted-for 352 had been sent from final proof stages and into the hands of the printers. In the end the part was not to be published in the spring of 1886, nor anywhere near: it was a full year later, in March 1887, when it did appear; and the Part IV that did indeed complete B—and thus the first 1,240-page actual volume of the book, *A–Byzen*—was finished as late as June 1888.

Murray blamed much on the enormous difficulties involved in dealing with specific words—such as the 'terrible' word *black*, and its scores of derivatives, which took his best assistant, the Revd C. B. Mount, fully three months of non-stop work.[6] As if the lexicographic trials were not enough, there was always the 'intolerable trouble about assistants'. Murray said that he kept trying to recruit suitable people, but found in almost every case, after each had worked no more than a week, that he or she (usually he) was completely useless. One of them, despite having an Oxford MA, was found to be, in Murray's uncharacteristically dyspeptic report, 'an utter numb-skull … a most lack-a-daisical, graspless fellow, born to stare at existence'.

But few were persuaded to listen to this litany of gripes. Many critics were coming to regard Murray's complaints as a querulous whining; and a considerable number of subscribers, those who had paid ready money to get their hands regularly on the Dictionary parts as they tumbled hot off the presses, were getting restless,

6 Murray's definition of this most ancient word (it appears in *Beowulf*) runs: 'The proper word for a certain quality practically classed among colours, but consisting optically in the total absence of colour, due to the absence or total absorption of light, as its opposite white arises from the reflection of all the rays of light.'

their disappointment palpable, their annoyance recorded in ever-more angry correspondence. Bookshops who had placed regular orders stopped placing more, and cancelled those already in place. The *Athenaeum*, a journal which had always been supportive, wondered if the endless wait for the first parts of the work suggested that it might not be finished in the lifetime of most readers, if ever. Certainly it supported the desire for perfection—but if the risk was then 'the unattainability of *zyc*,'[7] might it not be sensible to cut corners, just a little? Delegates recorded their 'great anxiety' at the situation. It was indeed a truly dreadful time for Murray, and for the Dictionary.

Each one of the early ages of the Dictionary has its mascot of a villain—there was Frederick Furnivall making mayhem and scandal during the first decade, and then Benjamin Jowett, interfering and pettifogging, when the first part was about to appear. Now, once Murray had moved up to Oxford, there came a new problem in the shape of the Secretary to the Delegates who had been appointed in 1884 as successor to Bartholomew Price: he was a Balliol man whose appointment had been engineered by the meddlesome Jowett, and he was named Philip Lyttelton Gell. Not one history of this man, who in essence ran the Press for the thirteen years up until 1897, is kindly: he was widely seen as an unpleasant, idle, incompetent, and quarrelsome, and was near-universally loathed.

He was also an outsider, something the English of the time generally did not care for. He had not read Greats—which was then, and remains, the University's heavily loaded by-name for the study of classics—but history, and though he had achieved a First, in the view of the Press scholars even this was clearly not

---

7   An odd error. There is no such word *zyc*; the last in the completed *OED* is *zyxt*, an obsolete Kentish dialect word for the past participle of the verb *to see*.

credential enough. He had come from a London-based publishing firm, Cassell, and had no experience of the curious ways of publishing in Oxford. Moreover, his election had been rushed through, sneakily, during the summer holidays by a Jowett who was determined to get his way, to put his own man to run the Delegates, and thus allow Jowett to have a discreet hold on the Press, for what he arrogantly considered would be the good of all.

Gell chivvied Murray endlessly and at times most cruelly. He disagreed totally with Murray's approach, and could not fathom why, despite the increased money being paid to the project, despite the additional assistants who had been hired, and despite the move to Oxford, progress was so glacially slow. In his view Murray was to blame, and Murray alone. He began to harass him, yapping and snapping at his heels like a sheepdog, badgering him to produce more, finish more, send more completed pages down for printing.

In 1886 Gell insisted that Henry Bradley be brought in to help with the letter B—a move that initially flummoxed Murray, who had no experience in delegating work, and would brook no rival to his own authority. Yet Bradley's inclusion in the project made no discernible difference at first—perhaps because he was still based in London, and was initially given work by Murray which an ordinary assistant could do just as well. In the first six months after his appointment progress actually slowed—only fifteen pages were completed, less than five per cent of what had been targeted and outlined in the contract of 1879.

The intractability of B was a nightmare in more ways that one. Gell had wrongly assumed that B would be no more difficult than A—that it would, like all consonants, produce a slew of words that would be lexically and etymologically far simpler than any words headed by a vowel. Everyone expected that Q, for example, would be a simple letter, and that S would be formidably difficult. But B—surely it should be easier than A, at the very least. Yet this turned out not to be the case: B had many more words of far greater complexity and age than anyone had ever dared to imagine: it was just desperately unfortunate that at the very time the Press was beginning to complain at the slowing of the project, the very letter on which the editor was working turned out, unanticipatedly, to be among the most difficult of all to fathom.

Murray was now in the direst of straits, at his wit's end, and in a letter to Gell he begged for mercy:

> *I wish from the bottom of my heart that I could do without your money, and honestly give you what you would consider a commercial equivalent for it. It is an embittering consideration for me that while trying to do scholarly work in a way that scholars may be expected to appreciate, circumstances place me commercially in the position of the* bête noire *of the Clarendon Press, who involves them in ruinous expenditure.*

When B was finally done with, there was no congratulation: Gell and the Press maintained a stony silence. Murray—who was now in his 50s, and who had taken only two weeks off in the past three years, was on the verge of breaking down. Gell insisted—the only moment of humanity anyone remembers him displaying—that he take a short break; but he then swiftly reverted to type by overruling Murray's plea that the Scriptorium be closed down for a fortnight in August, when even the English sun made working inside the corrugated iron box like roasting in an oven. His staff went away on their own holidays, leaving him alone to contemplate an 'accumulation of proofs, revises, 2nd revises, finals … to say nothing of the pile of letters etc. a yard deep … so appalling that I feel inclined to sit down and weep'.

But then the overlooked, derided, and unmemorialized Philip Lyttelton Gell introduced what posterity would show was his master stroke. In November 1887, with progress down to the merest trickle—a single sheet of the Dictionary produced between May and June, a fresh forecast showing that Part IV might well take four years to finish, instead of the six months previously agreed—he demanded that Henry Bradley be promoted from being a London-based assistant editor to being a full-time (and in due course Oxford-based) senior editor. He insisted further that Bradley should have his own staff and offices, and that the two men, Murray and Bradley, should take independent responsibility for producing one part of the Dictionary every year from now on.

Murray was initially thrown off balance by the news. Gell tried his best to get Murray on side, by arranging first that Bradley produce a specimen sheet for him, and for Murray to approve it—so that Murray could be certain that Bradley was capable of working well independently. But Gell's was only a momentary lapse into geniality: within days of the appointment he was publicly threatening that the pair must produce a pair of parts per year, or else. Murray countered by insisting there be no lowering of standards: if Gell insisted on his cutting corners, then he might have to resign.

But he did not resign; and with the benefit of long perspective, it appears now that it was Gell's cruelly and tactlessly implemented reforms that did, in the end, permit the Dictionary to turn the corner that it had perforce to turn in order to survive. Even today Gell is seen by admirers of Murray as having been his lifelong enemy and his potential nemesis. But perhaps he was more sinned against than sinning, for the fact remains that when Gell assumed the leadership of the Press, the Dictionary—'the dead weight that made the chariot go so heavy'—was headed for certain disaster and for probable death; when he left the Press during Victoria's Jubilee year thirteen years later, there was no doubt that the Dictionary was in rude good health, that Murray was firmly in charge, that the project was one that would continue to completion, and that it now enjoyed the blessings of Oxford, the monarchy, and the nation, all rolled into one.

It took longer than expected for Bradley to set up an Oxford office—he lived for almost the first decade of his appointment in Clapham, and worked in a room provided for him by the British Museum. He came to Oxford only when he was needed, and by train. Furnivall was highly critical of this arrangement, regarding it as unseemly that a man of Bradley's delicacy was 'rattling his nerves to pieces in incessant railway journeys'.

When he finally did consent to come, in 1896, it was not at the Scriptorium that he worked, but in the Old Ashmolean Building in central Oxford, a classically designed and roomy structure next door to Christopher Wren's magnificent Sheldonian Theatre, in the very beating heart of the University. A later admiring biographer noted that this unassuming and always available man had no need of elaborate paraphernalia, but set himself up before a plain deal table, 'without a drawer'. Many years would pass before this changed; his assistants, thinking it more proper for an editor to have a kneehole desk, arranged a whip-round and presented one to him.

Despite the origins of his appointment, it swiftly transpired that Bradley himself as well—to whom the completion of the entirety of the letter E was entrusted as his first editorial mission—became the frequent target of Gell's scourgings, which continued mercilessly so long as this irrepressible martinet remained the

By the time Henry Bradley became a full-time senior editor in 1896, he set up shop in the Old Ashmolean Building: his first task, the editing of E, was accomplished there.

Delegates' Secretary. Bradley was in no temper to deal with it, and in consequence fell ill—he was in many senses less durable than Murray, which Murray's admirers put down to the tenacity and durability of the Scots temperament—and he had to go off to Norway for three months' sanctioned leave.

Yet inch by column inch, the work went on—with everyone looking on in wary amazement, everyone waiting for someone to resign, for someone to pull the plug, for someone to go mad. Slowly, very slowly the parts emerged. *C* to *Cass*, then *Cast* to *Clivy*, *Clo* to *Consigner*, *Consignificant* to *Crouching*, and then with the addition of the relatively small number of words between *Crouchmass* and *Czech*, C was all done, by 1893. While he was working on *Cu-* the ever-cheerful Walter Skeat tried to encourage Murray by inviting him up to Cambridge. 'I could find enough talk to *cumber* you. You could come by a *curvilinear* railway. Bring a *cudgel* to walk with. We have *cutlets* in the *cupboard*, & *currants* and *curry* & *custard* & (naturally) *cups* … say you'll *cum!*'

When C was all done, it was realized that it had been, said Murray, 'a typical letter'. (It had also the virtue that the beginning and end words of the parts were generally recognizable to most intelligent readers. The fact that so many of the B words had been wholly unfamiliar—*battentlie*, for example, *byzen*, *bozzom*—tempted some critics to say that Murray was so slow simply because he was searching out obscurities, and was moreover doing so deliberately, to annoy and obfuscate. The relative simplicity of the top-and-tail words of his C fascicles suggested otherwise, suggesting that he was dealing with the varied ordinariness of an extraordinary language—and so that particular objection, at least, could be withdrawn.)

Walter Skeat was exultant at its completion. He wrote a ditty, both to cheer up Murray and to give a fillip to Bradley, who was at the time labouring in solitude down in Clapham on the immense complexities of E. The poem, like so many written to celebrate parts of the Dictionary, is fairly execrable:

Wherever the English speech is spread,
And the Union Jack flies free,
The news will be gratefully, proudly read
That you've conquered your A, B, C.
But I fear it will come
As a shock to some
That the sad result will be
That you're taking to dabble and dawdle and doze,
To dolour and dumps, and—worse than those—
To danger and drink,
And—shocking to think—
To words that begin with D-.

D duly came and went, successfully—and the letter E, on which Bradley had been cutting his teeth, was incorporated into the same volume, so that both men shared the honours of the title page. When they counted, there were found to be 13,478 main words beginning with D, but only 9,249 that started with E. (S is by far the largest letter of the alphabet, by which it is meant that words beginning with S are the most numerous in the lexicon, occupying two full volumes of the Dictionary. C is the second largest letter, with almost as many words as are begun by A and B combined. The smallest letter sections are—in order—X, Z, Y, Q, K, J, N, U, and V. E is a moderate letter, sitting at around the middle of the league table.)

Murray was never happy with the way the Dictionary initially covered E. It is perhaps not that he regarded himself as in any-thing but good-humoured competition with Henry Bradley—he was almost equally unhappy with the way that he himself had managed A.[8] He wrote to Walter Skeat, his trusted confidant, that E was so poor because

> *the Delegates were in such a hurry to get Mr. Bradley on, to show that he could (as they thought) work twice as fast as I, that he had neither the practice, the knowledge of the weakness of the Philological Society slips, nor the resources of the Scriptorium to help him … I have always said that the letter ought to be done again. A is not quite so unsatisfactory because I had been working provisionally for a year when I began to print it, and had learned how much had to be done to supplement the slips … It was a pity to start Bradley so.*

If there was a certain waspishness about the last remark, it rarely showed itself more outwardly than this. Murray and Bradley invariably got on well. It was Murray and Gell who were so frequently at daggers drawn.

And the daggers continued to be flashed from time to time, as slowly, imperceptibly slowly, the Dictionary got onto its feet. New schemes were implemented—bonuses to encourage the staff, smaller-sized fascicles published more often to keep the subscribers and booksellers on side, and a firm agreement on how much more comprehensive the new Dictionary was going to be than was Webster, which up to this point was regarded, if somewhat disdainfully by the Oxford men, as the high-water mark of the lexicographers' art.

The row over the 'Webster ratio' consumed much time and energy during the 1890s. Everyone agreed that the new Dictionary

8 Which is why, as mentioned in an earlier chapter, the present-day editors decided against beginning their work by starting with the letter A. They feared that any hesitancy that they might display in their early work should not be allowed to compound any of Murray's perceived hesitancy that he admitted was a small problem with A. They began instead with M in 1993, so that by the time they were due to have reached R in perhaps 2005, they would have spent a good dozen years perfecting their lexicographic techniques.

(with the words *Oxford English Dictionary* now appearing, as they did first on the loose paper cover of a fascicle in 1894, and then on the title page of all volumes after Volume III) was superior in all ways to Webster—not least in the number of quotations offered and the number of senses and meanings that were discerned from them. But more comprehensive meant much bigger—and the question that bothered Gell and his commercially minded colleagues was essentially: how much bigger?

There was little anyone could do about the additional number of headwords that Murray and Bradley were determined to include: between *A* and *Age*, for example, Murray identified almost twice as many headwords as were to be found in Webster. There was simply no possibility that a dictionary like the *OED* could possibly economize by dropping words altogether—and to be fair, not even the most philistine critic of the *OED* ever thought this should happen.

But economy could be won by limiting the number of quotations, by simplifying the explanations of etymology, and by curbing prolixity in definitions. Murray tried this, and while he was working on A, managed to keep a ratio of six of his pages to one of Webster's, which most thought manageable. But gradually, as his enthusiasm for the project increased, so did his page ratio. By the letter B he was running at seven to one; by C, eight to one; and a number of delegates began to accuse him and Bradley—particularly Bradley, who seemed to be especially undisciplined in this regard—of 'systematically neglecting' the limits which had been informally imposed on him, of keeping to about six to one, and certainly no more than seven. The Delegates who warned the editors of their profligacy did, however, agree to an increase in the overall size of the *OED*: it could, they said, be published at 12,900 pages total, which was more than half as many pages again as had been agreed back in 1884.

Throughout all these rows and dramas, James Murray kept threatening his resignation; Oxford kept implying that it would suspend publication; Bradley was told he would be fired unless he contained himself; whole years went by without volumes appearing; and the project—though it had begun to sputter into life in the early 1890s—seemed mired once again, or to be running out of fuel, or on fumes, or into brick walls. The metaphors for the imagined fate of the *OED* in those years are many and various.

But, as before, it never did die. It kept itself alive, just—and then two things happened in quick succession. First, the news of the rows and the threats spilled out into the daily papers; second, in a perhaps not unconnected development, Philip Lyttelton Gell was summarily dismissed, and everything, suddenly, became a very great deal better.

The press—the *Saturday Review*, specifically, was most detailed in its commentary—got hold of the story in April 1896. Oxford, the papers said, was planning to suspend publication of the Dictionary, because of money troubles, because of the indisciplined fractiousness of its senior editors, because of the unexpectedly vast complexity of the language that the immense book was seeking to catalogue and to fix.

The *Review* immediately professed its stunned astonishment: to close down the *OED* would be nothing less than 'a national calamity ... an indelible disgrace to the University'. The Press was vilified, accused of philistinism and greed. Murray, by contrast, was transformed overnight into a noble and lonely hero, a man battered by the parsimony of a ragged army of crabbed, short-sighted, and money-obsessed zealots. And in consequence letters poured in to the Scriptorium—a building from which, on Gell's specific orders, members of the public had lately been excluded—all of them supporting Murray and Bradley in what was perceived to be their indomitably honourable quest.

Such was the outburst of public feeling that Gell had to reverse his decisions. All of them were suddenly remade, whether they were the most trivial of his instructions—passers-by were from henceforward most welcome once again to drop in to see how Murray was working, though 'Hush, please!' if the old man had a furrowed brow—to the most serious—the Webster ratio could from henceforward be more or less what the editors decided it should be. Seven to one, eight and three-quarters to one—whatever it took was, all of a sudden, just fine. It was up to the editors to run their Dictionary; Oxford just had to accept that in the short term, it probably never would make money. Thus far it had cost £50,000; and thus far it had sold enough to bring in £15,000. It would take more than a change in the Webster ratio and a ramping-up of the production schedule to close a gap such as this.

No—it was the long term that counted, and the reputation of the University. Once that philosophical hurdle was cleared, once this extraordinary sea change was effected, a new sense of purpose, direction, and energy could and did begin to infuse the project.

And as symbol of the new ideals, Gell was indeed dismissed. The Dictionary parts that appeared in his final year of employment—*Distrustfully–Doom, Doom–Dziggetai*[9]—sounded peculiarly ominous. The fascicles were made in smaller parts now, appearing more frequently, not necessarily in alphabetical order, but in the order of their completion. There was an ordered disorder to the making of the Dictionary in these newly exuberant days, and slowly, everyone began to allow a sense of sunny optimism to prevail, a sense much missed for far too long.

---

9   'A species of equine quadruped native to Central Asia, *Equus hemionus*,' says the *OED*. 'It approaches the mule in appearance.'

And even the life of poor Philip Lyttelton Gell was made marginally more easy. He was dismissed after he had fallen ill and while he was convalescing in the south of France—he was simply told not to come back to work. A friend (one of a precious few, by all accounts) tried to cheer him up by suggesting that there was no fate so enviable 'as to be unjustly "sacked" in a civilized country'; and Gell himself expressed some relief that he was no longer bound up with all the rows that had attended his time at the Press. When he had joined, he recalled, the Press was

> in a medieval muddle, with no telephones, no speaking tubes, no typewriters … Do you recall the monotony of the old Press type, and the traditional Clarendon Press page, and all the efforts you made to equip the Press with the variety of Type which has lifted up its Typography up to its present level? … that 'dead-lift' required to modernize the Press would not have to be faced twice … It took a good deal out of all concerned.

Gell left behind him a legacy of distemper and dismay such that all connected with the Press sought actively to erase him from Oxford's collective memory. When he died in 1926 he was not even given the dignity of an entry in the *Dictionary of National Biography*—he was not even short-listed, so venomous was the feeling towards him by almost all of those he touched. All that Gell could do from the Derbyshire stately home to which he retired was to point to the 'enormous stride' which separated the condition of the Press when he left it from its state when he had joined it back in 1883—the year when Benjamin Jowett, as he said of his sponsor, 'first stirred the fire and set us all running'.

He could point to that, and if he chose, he could point to the Dictionary, a work that was now on the very brink of being accepted as a lustrous achievement and as a permanent monument to scholarship—or, in words that were written just as Gell was shamefacedly making his exit, was likely to be revered for being 'not the least of the glories of the University of Oxford'. At this remove, the hapless Philip Lyttelton Gell seems deserving of at least some small credit, a muted acknowledgement that his time at Oxford was not entirely misspent.

7

The Hermit and the Murderer—and Hereward Thimbleby Price

Thos. Austin, 165,000 quotations; Wm. Douglas, London, 136,000; Dr. H. R. Helwich, Vienna, 50,000; Dr. T. N. Brushfield, Salterton, 50,000; T. Henderson, MA, Bedford, 40,000; the Rev. J. Pierson, Ionia, Michigan, USA, 46,000; R. J. Whitwell, Kendal, 36,000; Dr. F. J. Furnivall, London, about 30,000; C. Gray, Wimbledon, 29,000; H. J. R. Murray, Oxford, 27,000; Miss J. Humphreys, Cricklewood, 18,700; the Rev. W. Lees, MA, Sidlow, Reigate, 18,500; the Rev. B. Talbot, Columbus, Ohio, USA, 16,600; the late S. D. Major, Bath, 16,000; Miss E. Thompson and Miss E. P. Thompson, Wavertree, Liverpool, 15,000; G. H. White, Torquay, 13,000; Dr. R. C. A. Prior, London, 11,700; Miss E. F. Burton, Carlisle, 11,400; G. Apperson, Wimbledon, 11,000; Miss A. Foxall, Edgbaston, Birmingham, 11,000.

H. H. Gibbs, MA, London; Miss J. E. A. and Miss E. Brown,
Cirencester; Dr. W. C. Minor, Crowthorne, Berkshire; the Rev.
Kirby Trimmer, Norwich; the Rev. W. B. R. Wilson, Dollar.

(Appendix to the Preface to Volume I, listing a small
fraction of the volunteer readers, James Murray,
The Scriptorium, Oxford, 1888)

J ust who *were* these people? This question invariably forms
whenever a curious and distracted reader takes a good, close
look at the details of the great completed Dictionary. It is more
or less impossible *not* to wonder—impossible not to be curious
whenever one takes from the shelves any one of the 47 paper-
bound parts; or whenever one finds, buried in the basement of
one of the world's better libraries, some of the 128 slender paperbacked sections, with their inadvertently wonderful titles—*Sweep*
to *Szmikite, Onomastical* to *Outing, Invalid* to *Jew*, or *Gaincope* to *Ger-
manizing*—by which the Dictionary was originally offered to the
world.

Readers have to wonder because, on the opening pages of
Volume I of the completed work, and at the front of every part
and of almost every single section of the work in progress, there is
an elegant and utterly absorbing introductory essay, explaining
how this volume or this part or this section was actually put together. The essays are essential reading: they tell of fascinations—
like how the word *set* was so much more difficult than *is*, how
unexpectedly tricky *marzipan* was, or how *fraternity* turned out so
much longer and *monkey* so much more ancient than anticipated,
or that C was so much more complex than D, and how the compilation of J turned into a lexicographic bloodbath and Q was
(though the editors would never say such a thing) really an absolute dog.

But the puzzled wonderment begins for a quite different reason: for in each of these essays, at a point usually towards their end and following the description of the cat-herding trials that were involved in gathering in all the words, there is a collection, usually in small print or in a different fount, of scores and scores of names.

These are the collected names of everyone who was involved in the project and, more importantly, whose involvement was worthy of the editors' gratitude. Without regard to class or standing, qualification or creed, and certainly disregarding gender (which in Victorian times was unusual, to say the least) here are listed the names of, on the one hand, the paid helpers, the sorters of slips, and the expert advisers, and on the other the unpaid readers, the checkers of proofs, the suppliers of quotations, the bringers of sustenance, and the boosters of morale—the men and women without whom, quite literally, the immense project could not have been begun, let alone ever finished.

Above all, the unpaid, volunteer readers. It has to be remembered that this was a dictionary that relied, quite centrally and pivotally, on its amassment of readers, on the hundreds upon hundreds of readers who were cajoled into action by the public exhortations of the editors, and who then supplied the slips and presented the quotations that revealed the meanings that were ultimately to be defined in the thousand of pages of the Dictionary. Their names are all recorded in the prefaces and introductions and acknowledgements; there are lines upon lines, paragraphs upon paragraphs of names, lists of old-fashioned names that look likely to be sonorous if read out loud, like those of Beachcomber's 'Huntingdonshire Cabmen', the famous *Daily Express* column, and fascinating to behold in print—and yet at the same moment in some strange way mysterious, tempting of speculation, and utterly intriguing.

Who could not first be mesmerised and then intrigued by any list that included the names, for example, of Professors Johann Strom and S. Bugge of Christiania; Gudbrandr Vigfusson of Oxford; the Norroy King of Arms; Professor Julius Zupitza of Berlin; the Very Reverend the Dean of Canterbury; Eduard Sievers of Halle (formerly of Tübingen); the Hon. Whitley Stokes; and W. Sykes, Esq., MRCS, of Mexborough? What, for instance, of such as W. Beck, author of *The Draper's Dictionary*; of Professor Axel Kock, of Lund; of Prince Louis-Lucien Bonaparte; of R. H. Davies, Esq., of the Apothecaries Hall; of J. A. Kingdon, Esq., Late Master of the Grocers' Company: P. L. Sclater, Esq., FRS, Secretary of the Zoological Society; and of the frequently mentioned but little-known spinster, Miss Lucy Toulmin Smith?

These were the grandees (a tiny fraction of them: the lists went on for columns), the fully established figures from whom Murray and Bradley and the other senior editors sought intellectual succour and enlightenment—and for most of them there are entries in directories and obituaries in newspapers which speak at length of their achievements and renown. But it is the less well-known, the more anonymous helpers who present an even more fascinating face—a raft of personalities whose collective portrait tells us something of the times when this book was assembled, and of the kind of men and women who were content to devote their lives and waking hours to helping with its assembly.

So, to repeat the question—who exactly *were* these people? Where did they all come from? What did they do? How and why did they become involved, and how did they know so much that they felt able to make so memorable a contribution to so extraordinary a work?

It is perhaps easiest to explain about the people in just the same way that the Dictionary explained about its words—by way of illustration. Two men in particular offer a portrait of the extremes with which Murray and his colleagues found they had to deal.

One—perhaps the man who is today best known to those who are captivated both by the mechanics of lexicography and by the curious personalities of those who find its disciplines and details so attractive, and so who eagerly signed on as volunteer contributors for Murray's great work—is a man whose name sounds more like that of an institution than of a sentient being: Fitzedward Hall.

He was an American, he was colourful, and he was by all accounts exceptionally difficult. He was also perhaps the most steadfast of all Murray's volunteer helpers, devoting at least four hours of every day for twenty years, mainly to examining and critically reading the Dictionary proof sheets. Murray praised him unceasingly for his 'voluntary and gratuitous service to the English language'—and yet never once met him.

It is the strangest story. Fitzedward Hall was born in Troy, New York, in 1825. Twenty-one years later, as he was about to begin studies at Harvard, his father demanded he instead board an eastbound clipper ship and sail from Boston to Calcutta, to try to find his elder brother, who had absconded. The ship promptly foundered in a typhoon in the Bay of Bengal, and Hall was washed ashore. He made his way up the Hooghly River to the British Indian capital and, having no vessel on which to sail home (nor any brother—he never found him) decided to stay awhile, and learn languages. He became fluent in Hindustani, Bengali, Sanskrit, and Persian, and made a respectable income translating into these languages books written in English, as well as in French, Italian, and modern Greek, all of which he spoke fluently.

After three years in Calcutta he moved to the holy city of Benares, on the Ganges—now Varanasi—and taught Sanskrit at

The American Fitzedward Hall, a self-taught philologist, was by far the most assiduous volunteer, writing daily to Murray from the East Anglian cottage to which he had exiled himself after a furious row with a rival academic in London. He was a lifelong recluse, and he and Murray never met.

the local government college, and then became an Inspector of Schools, a senior position in the Imperial government of the day. He got himself into all manner of scrapes—he narrowly avoided death when a dynamite ship blew up beside his house, and he was caught up in the Indian Mutiny of 1857,[1] and spent seven months besieged in a fort. But he survived, married well (the daughter of a colonel in the British Indian army), and came to live in England— taking up a post as Professor of Sanskrit and Indian Jurisprudence at King's College, London, taking a position at the India Office, and being awarded the degree of Doctor of Civil Law at Oxford. All seemed set fair for Dr Hall to pursue from now on a life of dignified and estimable scholarship.

Except that then, in 1869, when in quite another circle the Dictionary was just bestirring itself, he became embroiled in an almighty row. We do not know the specifics, other than that it involved another philologist well known to Murray and his colleagues, Theodor Goldstücker, who taught Sanskrit at University College. The upshot was disastrous for Hall: he was dismissed or suspended from his various posts, thrown out of the Philological Society, and accused (unfairly, as it happens) of being a drunkard and a foreign spy, morally unsound, and an academic charlatan. The viciousness of disputes in the rarefied world of academia can on occasion be legendary, and irreversible, and this dispute evidently was one of those. Hall fled with his family to a remote cottage in the village of Wickham Market, in East Anglia; a year later his own family left him, and he remained for the rest of his life a hermit, rarely emerging from his cottage for the better part of the next 32 years.

He discovered the potential for work with the Dictionary,

---

1 These days the rising against the British *Raj* is termed the First Indian War of Independence.

and the unquestioningly sympathetic attitude of Murray—who minded little of the personal trials or failings of a helper, so long as he *helped*—in 1881, just two years after Murray's appointment. From that moment onward he wrote every single day, with quotations, clippings, suggestions—and then with sheet after sheet of proofs, corrected, changed, closely read and carefully parsed, just as Murray wanted.

On those few occasions Hall fell ill, Murray was frantic:

> *The everyday wish which I have from visitors to the Scriptorium, or correspondents on the subject of the Dictionary, is 'May you live to see Zymotic'; that wish, I most heartily transfer to you, for I really dread to think of the falling-off in our work, which the failure of your help would mean. It is true that you have spoken of leaving materials at my disposal, but alas! how little worth are the best materials without the master-mind that knows how to use them, and make them useful.*

And so Hall recovered, and went on helping—'I have to record with deepest gratitude', Murray wrote at the end of D, 'our obligations to you for your superb help, which has so enriched the 3 volumes now finished, and to express with trembling the earnest desire that you will be able to give us your help for a long time to come.'

He did just as everyone hoped. Letters record the specific assistance he gave—over words like *develop* (which caused the editors no end of difficulty), over *Devanagari* (the script in which Hindi, among others, is written), over *diagram, diaskeuast,*[2] *handsome,* and the pronoun *He* (he provided quotations for *he* being used as a word for mountains and rivers, for the redundant or pleonastic *he* being used in phrases such as *the noble Murray he,* of the combin-

---

2   The word, a Greek combination, means a reviser—which, since Fitzedward Hall was one, happened to be peculiarly suited for his attention.

ations *he that* and *he who* or the slightly different *he who*, in the sense of *anyone who*, and of *he* combined in a prepositional phrase like *he of Oxford* or *Henry VIII, he of the six wives*). Reading the Hall letters, and the Hall books that were recovered from his little cottage after his death, reminds one forcefully of the richness and complexity of the work that all were engaged upon.

When he died, on 1 February 1901, the Scriptorium staff were stunned. 'It is with the profoundest regret that we have to record his death,' Murray wrote in his Preface to Volume VI. Fitzedward Hall, for all his troubles, had 'rendered invaluable help in all the portions hitherto published of the Dictionary'. The section in which Murray wrote these words concludes with definitions of the noun *lap*—'a liquid food for dogs, that part of a railway track used in common by more than one train, the front portion of the body from the waist to the knees of a person seated' ... to all of which lexical complications this remarkable, unforgettable, and deeply troubled volunteer had devoted his time.

The other most celebrated of the volunteers—though as a reader of books and provider of quotations, and not as a critical student of the proofs—was an American also. He was a troubled man too— William Chester Minor, a former surgeon-soldier in the United States Army, a survivor of the Civil War who in the autumn of 1871 had been sent by his family in Connecticut across to London, to convalesce after falling desperately ill at home. Some weeks before he had been dismissed from the army because of his strange and erratic behaviour. Since he was well born and well connected, he was, however, allowed to keep his pension; and since he was a talented painter and flautist, and a collector of rare books, it was expected that he would improve.

One of the thousands of volunteers was the American army surgeon and murderer William Chester Minor, who worked tirelessly for the Dictionary from his cells at the Broadmoor Asylum for the Criminally Insane at Crowthorne, in Berkshire.

The calming airs and cultured society of London did not improve his condition, though. He became even more ill, and in February 1872, during an attack of what now looks to have been paranoid schizophrenia, he shot and murdered an innocent working man on a night-time street in Lambeth. He gave himself up to the police, and was tried—found innocent of wilful murder by virtue of what by now was his very evident insanity. He was still sentenced to be put away, for the public good: he was ordered to spend the remainder of his life—or at Her Majesty's pleasure, as the court's archaic language had it—in one of Britain's then most up-to-date asylums for criminal lunatics, Broadmoor, in the Berkshire village of Crowthorne.

The story of Fitzedward Hall might seem one of anger, bitterness and yet an obsessive devotion to duty; that of W. C. Minor, by contrast, is one of dangerous madness, ineluctable sadness, and ultimate redemption—redemption in which his work for the Dictionary became in time his therapy, a labour that he needed to perform in order to remain halfway sane. If the outward parallels between the two men—both Americans, both learned, both with Eastern connections,[3] both troubled in the mind—are intriguing, the different ways in which the two made their separate contributions to the Dictionary—and the ways in which the Dictionary in turn made improvements to their lives—seem even more so.

Minor discovered the Dictionary in 1881, or thereabouts—we cannot be entirely certain, but at almost the same time as Hall wrote his first letter to the editor. The way in which Minor made the connection is uncertain, too—he may well have seen a mention of the project in the *Athenaeum*, to which it is known he subscribed from his cell, and which urged Americans to help. The

3   Minor was born in Ceylon, the son of Connecticut missionaries.

story I prefer to believe is that the widow of the man he murdered, Mrs Eliza Merrett, who (somewhat improbably) came regularly to visit him at Broadmoor, carried without knowing it a copy of Murray's famous Appeal for Readers in a pile of books she had brought for the prisoners' library. It is said that Minor found the small slip of paper between two volumes, read it, and exclaimed that this, this dictionary work, was how he could to some extent now redeem himself.

However the connection was made, Minor worked assiduously for the next 21 years until he fell ill, in 1902, after cutting off his own penis during a fit of insane self-loathing. Murray paid endless tributes to him: one read, 'Second only to the contributions of Dr Fitzedward Hall in enhancing our illustration of the literary history of individual words, phrases and constructions have been those of Dr W. C. Minor, received week by week.'

Minor's technique of word-gathering was very different from those of most other readers—and though he rarely equalled the totals of the super-contributors (such as those noted in the epigraph, like the also apparently often insane Thomas Austin, who had already contributed 165,000 slips by 1888, with more to come), he performed his work in such a way as to make himself uniquely useful to the dictionary makers.

He read, prodigiously. He had two cells at Broadmoor, one in which he ate and slept and painted and played his flute, the other which he had shelved as his library, and in which he kept his very considerable collection of antiquarian books. Knowing that all of the books he had collected were likely to be of use to the Dictionary, he created a potentially very useful way of reading them.

He would first prepare, by folding a number of sheets of paper together, a small eight-page quire of blank writing paper. He would then open the chosen book from his library, one that he suspected might hold a number of interesting words,[4] and begin reading. When he came upon a word that interested him and which he thought, in time, might interest the Dictionary staff, and which, moreover, was used in what he considered to be 'an illustrative way' in the book, he would write it down in tiny letters—he was capable of the most minute legible handwriting—in his folder-like booklet.

Let us say, for sake of argument, that the word was *bungalow*, and that it appeared in the self-evidently illustrative sentence: 'Every day I stopped once or twice at a travellers' bungalow, or rest-house' (which is a quotation that Minor did indeed find in an 1875 copy of *Lippincott's Magazine*, and which the Dictionary later used). He would place the word in his booklet so that it was likely, eventually, to occupy its logical place in what he was in essence creating, an alphabetical index of the main book. Hence he would place *bungalow* on a very early page (since its first letter was *b*) somewhere towards the bottom (since its second letter was *u*) of the page.

If the next word-and-quotation he found interesting was *bread*, he would position this word somewhere above *bungalow*, leaving enough space for words whose second letters lay within the range *-re* to *-un*, words like *broken*, *bubble*, and *bully* and which, if he happened upon them later, would slide in between those he had already found. If the next word that intrigued him was *chortle*, he would place this on a page or so a little further on; and if it was *youngster*, say, then it would go on the middle part of a page towards the end of the book. Against each word he would write the page

4 Minor had a literary taste that tended to the obscure, the foreign and the old—all very much to his credit as a word-hunter. For instance, he liked *The Complete Woman* by one Jacques du Bosq, published in 1639, Thomas Wilson's *The Rule of Reason* of 1551, and Francis Junius, *The Painting of the Ancients*, 1638, as well as any number of eighteenth-century travellers' tales of the East, especially India and his birthplace, Ceylon.

number and line on which he had found it, so that he could find the sentence that included it in just a matter of moments.

After some weeks of work—being a prisoner who was, essentially, serving out a life sentence, he had a limitless number of weeks ahead of him, so time was not a problem as it might have been for others—he would find he had completed a full word index for the book. He would head it with the title of the book; and then begin work on another, making another booklet for that, and then another and another, and so on.

He would then wait for a communication—a letter or a postcard—from the editors. Rather than contribute quotations as he came across them—which is what almost all the other volunteers did, and often in vast numbers—he would bide his time until the editors asked him to solve a problem which immediately confronted them. A card would come in: the staff were just then working on the word *bungalow*—had Dr Minor by any chance any illustrative quotations for it? Had he by happenstance something in his index books that would satisfy what the editors were calling their *desiderata*—had he something (in this case a word, a quotation, or the solution to some lexicographical puzzle), which the labourers in the Scriptorium wanted, required, or desired?

And the doctor—no one in Oxford in those early days knew he was in an asylum cell; it was supposed by those who knew what Broadmoor was that he worked on the asylum staff—he would go to the index folders, look up those entries for *bungalow*, find the relevant quotations noted in his index—often there would be scores of entries, perhaps dozens in one book alone—write each on a separate quotation slip, and put the bundle in the post for the Scriptorium. The editors would duly receive the bundle the next morning, and would ease them into the very page of the Dictionary on which they were then working. Working with Minor was just, one of them said, like turning on a tap. Whenever the

Dictionary wanted specific material for words, an editor had merely to send a postcard to Broadmoor, and out the details flowed, in abundance and always with unerring accuracy.

Murray and Minor did meet, and under unusual circumstances—no one at the Dictionary, least of all James Murray, had hitherto suspected that their most assiduous contributor was a madman, a murderer, and an American. But once the two did meet they became the firmest of friends; and when the elderly Minor, ill from his self-mutilation, was clearly no further threat to any member of the public, Murray saw to it that he was permitted to go home to spend his final years in the America of his birth. The Home Secretary at the time, the minister ultimately responsible for the asylum, was Winston Churchill, and he signed Minor's release papers in 1910. When the ailing old soldier sailed away home—with his elderly brother, who had been at the trial where he had first been sentenced 38 years before, to escort him back—he took with him as memento the first half-dozen completed volumes of the Dictionary to which he had made so immense—but in many senses unsung—a contribution. And in his later years, which he spent in yet more asylums and later in a hospital for the elderly insane, he told visitors that he could remember almost by heart what Murray had written of him, so warmly, some years before he left:

> *The supreme position ... is certainly held by Dr. W. C. Minor of Broadmoor, who during the past two years has sent in no less [sic]*[5] *than 12,000 quots. These have nearly all been for the words with which Mr. Bradley and I were actually occupied, for Dr. Minor likes to know each month just what words we are likely to be working on during the month and to devote his whole strength to supplying quotations for those words, and thus to feel he is in touch with the making of the Dictionary.*

5   Even Homer nods.

So enormous have been Dr. Minor's contributions during the past 17 or 18 years, that we could easily illustrate the last 4 centuries from his quotations alone.

The phrase 'to feel he is in touch with the making of the Dictionary' has a kindly feel to it—an illustration, I like to think, of the little-seen compassionate side of Murray's normally rather stern nature. By then the editor had been well aware of Minor's sad condition; he thought, in a generous way (and, as it happens, with perfect correctness), that Minor would be a happier man if he could know that he was involved, however peripherally, in so grand and noble a project. Murray thought that it would give him a sense of purpose, a source of joy in his otherwise ruined life that he was doomed to spend behind the high walls and iron bars—and tortured fantasies—of his unending imprisonment.

And there were many others besides, men and women who were in their own ways just as eccentric, their stories just as strange—though generally rather more cheerful than the sagas of Hall and Minor. In all the nooks and crannies of this project there lurked learned and remarkable people—those who were paid seem at this remove to have been every bit as unusual as those who did their work as reader volunteers. Consider, for example, the kind of mind that must have been possessed by one of the most tireless of Murray's editorial assistants, Frederick Sweatman.

Sweatman was the son of a printer, and had little by way of a formal education. He joined the Bodleian Library in 1888, when he was just fifteen; and two years later, once Murray had come up from Mill Hill to the Banbury Road, joined him working in the Scriptorium. He remained as a word-slave for the following

43 years, saw the Dictionary through to its completion, and then worked on the Supplement that eventually came out in 1933. He died in 1936.

That he must have been exceedingly bright is axiomatic: no one with a less than razor-sharp mind would have survived the intellectual rigours of working under Murray and Bradley (nor under their immediate successors, William Craigie and Charles Onions, for whom Sweatman was also an assistant). But a clue to his particularly unusual imagination came in the early 1900s, when he decided to write a playful definition of the word *radium*.[6]

Pierre and Marie Curie had discovered this new radioactive element in 1898; its first mention as a linguistic entity was made in both *Nature* and *Chemistry News* the following January. By what some might think a coincidence, and others a piece of lexicographic good fortune, the newly appointed William Craigie was working on the section *R–Reactive* in 1902, within just three years of the word *radium* coming into existence. One might suppose Craigie would have swooped on the word—some volunteer reader would have uncovered the quotation ('These different reasons lead us to believe that the new radio-active substance contains a new element, to which we propose to give the name of *radium*'—because it emitted rays) and inserted it into the section, then into the part R and then the completed Volume VIII, Q–S.

But dictionaries do not respond so quickly. Craigie, like all his brother editors, was a cautious man. And James Murray, who by 1903 was sunk in a brown study pondering both *Kaiser–Kyx* and *P–Pennached*, would have agreed with his caution. Would the new

6   This is an educated conjecture. The handwriting on the slips looks very much like Sweatman's, and he was certainly in the right place at the right time for the entry to be written. But there is no absolute proof that the work is his. Some evidence suggests it might also have been an assistant named Henry Bayliss. However, the general point—that the definition of *radium* illustrates the kind of mind that was possessed by workers on the project—remains true, no matter who was the author of this particular entry.

Charles Onions, who was appointed a senior editor in 1914, was remarkably long-lived, and was still able to help with early work on the preparation of the *OED*'s later supplements in the 1960s.

William Craigie, who was senior editor at the time of the triumphant completion of the first edition in 1928, edited the final volumes from the University of Chicago, where he had been appointed Professor of English.

word last? Was it merely a scientific arcanum, jargon for a specialized priesthood? Or would it in due time enter the language proper, become a true part of the English tongue? To determine that, said Craigie, with Murray's concurrence—wait a while. And just for now, leave it out.

So *radium* is not listed in the completed first edition of the Dictionary, and makes its first appearance only in the 1933 Supplement—an 867-page volume it was found necessary to publish in order to list all the new words (such as *radium*) and all the new meanings and senses of already listed words which had appeared or had been invented during the decades that the Dictionary itself had been in preparation. It was therefore up to Craigie and Onions to write definitions for these new words and meanings—and to tackle entirely new concepts, like *radium*. Frederick Sweatman (or Henry Bayliss), it is supposed, had the first try.

First, he wrote a wondrously complex etymology, followed by the sparest of definitions:

Radium. [mod.L. *radium* (B. Balius *Add. Lex.* : not in DuCange). The orig. source is Preh.—*adamispadi*, to dig;—Antediluv. *randam* (unconnected with PanArryan *randan*.) Cognate with OH Hash, *mqdrq*; Opj. *rangtrum*; MHGug. *tsploshm*; Mubr. *dndrpq*; Baby. *daddums* and N.Pol. *rad* are unconnected.] The unknown quantity. Math. Symbol x. Cf. *Eureka*.

And then he had fun with an almost endless list of quotations and explanations, offered here in abbreviated form:

Aristotle De. P.Q. LI. xx says it may be obtained from the excrement of a squint-eyed rat that has died of a broken heart buried 50ft below the highest depths of the western ocean in a well-stopped tobacco tin, but

---

Sir T. Browne says this is a vulgar error; he also
refutes the story that it was dug in the air above
Mt. Olympus by the ancients.

[Not in *J.*, the *Court Guide*, or the *Daily Mail Year
Book* before 1510.]

1669 *Pepys Diary*, 31 June, And so to bed. Found
radium an excellent pick-me-up in the morning. **1873**
Hymns A & M 2517 Thy walls are built of *radium*.
1600 Hakluyt's *Voy.* IV.21 The kyng was attired simply in a hat of silke and *radium*-umbrella.

Probably many of the other assistants were similarly talented,
though sadly few today are remembered. One, however, is quite
unforgotten: John Ronald Reuel Tolkien, who worked under
Bradley for one year, 1919, and is known today (though by the
more formally British version of his name, J. R. R. Tolkien) by
children of all ages, for writing *The Hobbit* and *The Lord of the Rings*.
In dictionary circles he is known specifically for having laboured
mightily over words beginning with W, among them *warm*, *wasp*,
water, *wick*, *wallop*,[7] *waggle*, and *winter*. He also dealt at length with
the three very tricky W words *walnut*, *wampum*, and *walrus*, and in
lexicographical circles his struggles with *walrus* have become almost famous, since in the Bodleian library there is a ring-backed
notebook in Tolkien's distinctively neat handwriting listing a bewildering variety of its possible definitions and puzzling etymologies.

W was always in any case reckoned an interesting letter—
there are essentially no Greek or Latin derivatives that begin
with W, and its words are generally taken, as Bradley put it,
'from the oldest strata of the language'. *Walrus*, a classic example of
an extremely ancient W word,[8] is from Dutch and Low German,

---

7 Tolkien is said to have found sufficient evidence for the existence of the strange expression *the right to wallop one's own nigger* to prepare a slip for it: but his seniors at the
   Dictionary thought it too offensive (and insufficiently illustrative) and so did not use it.

8 The first quotation is from AD 893.

J. R. R. Tolkien, who worked in 1919 as an assistant editor under Henry Bradley, later became famous for his trilogy *The Lord of the Rings*: his invented word *hobbit* is in the *OED* also.

and when Tolkien finally got it right—he inserted a lengthy explanation of the etymology and of the curious word *horse-whale*, which is part of the convoluted story of *walrus*—and when he submitted his definition to the approving Bradley, what he wrote was quite masterfully precise:

> *The sea-horse, or morse (*Trichechus rosmarus*), a carnivorous pinniped marine mammal allied to the* Phocidae *(seals), and* Otariidae *(sea-lions), and chiefly distinguished by two tusks (exserted upper canine teeth). It inhabits the Arctic seas. A variety found in the N. Pacific has sometimes received the distinct specific name* obesus.[9]

Tolkien said later of the time he spent with the Dictionary that he 'learned more ... than in any other equal period of my life'.

Among the other largely unremembered notables are Sidney Herrtage, who, as already mentioned, turned out to be a kleptomaniac, and was fired for stealing; Herbert Ruthven, who was Murray's brother-in-law, a fair-to-middling lexicographer and, most importantly, the pigeon-hole-building Scriptorium carpenter; Alfred Erlebach, who was quite brilliantly supportive in the early days of the project, but vexed Murray mightily by leaving to teach at his brother's school; Charles Balk, who worked for Murray for 28 years and then wrote a lengthy meditation on life entitled *Life is Growth*; Arthur Maling, who worked from 1881 until 1927, was a wealthy Cambridge-educated mathematician and an eager Esperanto enthusiast, and who wore his distinctive green star badge in an effort to promote this most lost of causes; Wilfrid

---

9 The verb *exsert*—the use of which appears to defy the lexicographers' general rule that definitions should not include words more complex than the word being defined—means 'to protrude'. Why Tolkien decided against writing 'protruding upper canine teeth' is something requiring even closer study of the Bodleian workbook.

Lewis, the son of a college servant who managed to relieve the monotony of his 44-year stint with the slips by compiling what many still regard as the best and most comprehensive historical dictionary of the language of cricket; the magnificently named Hereward Thimbleby Price,[10] who was conscripted into the German army, captured by the Russians, and escaped overland to China—he wrote a book in 1919 called *Boche and Bolshevik: Experiences of an Englishman in the German Army and in Russian Prisons*; the equally delightful-sounding Lawrenceson Fitzroy Powell, whose father had been a trumpeter in the Charge of the Light Brigade and who himself, though without any academic qualifications, became Librarian of Oxford's Taylorian Institution and an authority on Johnson and Boswell; and the redoubtable Catholic priest and missionary Father Henry Rope, who joined the team some time before 1905 and was still working, sending in quotations at the time of his death in 1978, when the four supplements were being prepared; the archive shelves groan under the weight of Father Rope's contributions, many of them scrawled on the backs of envelopes and labels and scraps of paper.

And these were only the assistants. There were many other categories of helpers, each of which is seasoned by a number of memorable but largely unremembered characters. There were the sub-editors, for instance, those who were charged with working on specific letters; all of their names and the letters for which they were responsible, and the dates they worked—from 'W. J. Anderson, portions of M and P, 1880–1900' through to 'Mrs W. A. Craigie (Lady Craigie) revised arrangements of U, 1917–1918'—

---

10   Price, who ended up as Professor of English at the University of Michigan, was born in 1880 in a town in Madagascar that sported the equally magnificent name of Amatolakinandisamisichana. He died in Washington, DC in 1964.

were faithfully listed in the completed Volume I once the project was fully finished.[11]

Those who stand out from the dozens listed include the Sanskrit scholar and Mayor of Guildford, Philip Whittington Jacob, who worked for a while on the immense word *set*, the most complex in the entire Dictionary; William Michael Rossetti, brother of the more famous Dante Gabriel Rossetti, and the author of a letter found in the *OED* archives today that sheds an interesting light on the pronunciation of the word *Pre-Raphaelite*: 'My brother and I always pronounced the name Raphael with the sound Rahfyel ... It certainly appears to me that the other Pre-Raphaelite Brothers adopted ... the same pronunciation ... It must no doubt be true that a great number of Englishmen pronounce the raph like man, bat, &c.'; the magnificent-sounding Gustavus Adolphus Schrumpf (whose sonorous name certainly rivals that of the Bolshevik prisoner Hereward Thimbleby Price[12]), who taught, rather ordinarily, at a school near Wolverhampton, and sub-edited in A and H; an indefatigable spinster of the Cotswold village of Further Barton, near Cirencester, Janet Brown, who was an author of religio-didactic works such as *The Heart of the Servant*, which one newspaper thought should be required reading by all household staff, and to whom Murray was later to refer as 'an honoured personal friend' (she left him £1,000 in her will); and Edward Charles Hulme, who was a librarian at the Patent Office and whose

---

11   Not quite all, in fact: the editors did practise some quite harsh selectivity in deciding whom to list and whom to omit. Bradley, for example, seems not to have listed one James Bartlett, of Bramley, near Guildford, who worked on G, M, O, R, and S. Perhaps this is because of his exasperation with the man, recorded in exchanges of correspondence which still exist. Most notable among them is a discussion over the word *shake*, where Bartlett writes: 'I feel quite incompetent to tackle the formidable early forms of the word, and so leave them alone. Also the numbering off.' Bradley, with an irritable harrumph!, replies curtly: 'I move to delete all after "incompetent".'

12   As well as that of an assistant named George Washington Salisbury Friedrichsen, who was a specialist in etymology.

name was inexplicably omitted from Volume I[13]—Murray later wrote an embarrassed note in his Preface to a rather later part, apologizing and calling Hulme 'one of the best workers for the Dictionary'.

There were also plenty of linguistic advisers—towering figures of scholarship to whom Murray and Bradley would write on the finer points of their various specialities. James Platt was one such—a polymath and ghost story writer who knew scores of languages and once famously declared that the first twelve tongues were always the most difficult, but having mastered them, the following hundred should not pose too much of a problem. He helped Murray divine etymologies from obscurer languages of Africa and the Far East. Marie-Paul-Hyacinthe Meyer, who had worked on the documents relating to the Dreyfus affair, helped with medieval French and Provençal (which Murray spoke quite well anyway); the antiquarian Frederick Elworthy, a great friend of the Murray family who lived in Somerset, assisted with archaic West Country and Cornish dialect words; and Henry Yule, well known to any fan as one of the editors of the endlessly fascinating collection of Hindustani terms known as *Hobson-Jobson*,[14] assisted in matters Oriental. Professor H. R. Helwich of Vienna copied out, with barely believable assiduity, all of the *Cursor Mundi* (the most quoted work in the *OED*) and the *Destruction of Troy*. And a Mr and Mrs A. Caland, who lived in Holland, fell out with one another over the work: Mr Caland said his interest in the book was the one thing that kept him alive. His wife would only speak through gritted teeth of what she called 'that wretched dictionary'.

---

13 Alfred Erlebach made the mistake of leaving out Hulme's name, and confessed to the error in an abject letter to Murray.

14 The title is classically British Indian. It is a cockney corruption of the Shi'ite cry *Ya Hasan! Ya Hosain!* heard during the Festival of Muharram, a natural title for Yule and Burnell's splendidly enjoyable compendium.

There were many Americans, Fitzedward Hall and W. C. Minor aside. Dozens flocked to the side of Murray and his team, in part because of the energies of Francis March, whom Murray had appointed head of the American reading programme in 1879. In addition to the readers, most of whom have vanished into obscurity, there are grand figures like George Perkins Marsh, who was an environmentalist before it was fashionable to be so, the man who introduced the camel into the Wild West (to the rather limited degree that it has been introduced) and, confusingly, the first American readers' coordinator in the very early days of the project, and whose role was taken over by the so-similarly-named Francis March; Albert Matthews and C. W. Ernst of Boston, who sent in thousands of examples of peculiarly American uses and phrases, while Ernst was a diligent scholar in medieval Latin; and William Dwight Whitney, the chief editor of the enormous *Century Dictionary*, against which Murray's dictionary was constantly being measured. Job Pierson, a librarian and Presbyterian minister from Ionia, Michigan, was one of the most energetic readers: he contributed some 46,000 quotations in 1888 alone—good enough to make this chapter's epigraph, but nowhere near as productive as the man who heads it, Thomas Austin Jr. of Hornsey and Oxford, a man who also managed to edit a volume entitled *Two Fifteenth-Century Cookbooks*, and who fell ill with a nervous disorder—Victorian middle-class shorthand for madness—while doing so.

Sons of gardeners and college servants, daughters of chemists and boat-builders, ministers in all churches known to Christian (including that of Pitsligo, Banffshire) and to infidel, criminal and company and constitutional lawyers, schoolmasters from Holland and Birmingham and California and from all points between, doctors responsible for every part of body, mind, and animal, scholars of Welsh and Greek, Aramaic and Chaldean, Icelandic,

Persian, Slavonic, and English place names, elderly divines, young and muscular civil engineers, theatre critics, one ophthalmic surgeon (James Dixon, author of *Diseases of the Eye*, 1855), mathematicians, men who were antiquarians, naturalists, surgeons (and one man—Joseph Fowler of Durham—who was all three), businessmen, novelists (including Beatrice Harraden, who wrote the breathless *Ships that Pass in the Night*, became a suffragette, and went on to write *The Scholar's Daughter*, involving much derring-do among a cast of lexicographers), phoneticians, bibliographers, an iron merchant-cum-antiquarian named Richard Heslop who gave Murray advice on mining and iron-forging terms, botanists, aldermen, naval historians, geologists and geophysicists, jurists, palaeographers, Orientalists, diplomats, museum keepers, surgeons, soldiers (W. C. Minor was both, of course), climbers (John Mitchell was killed while climbing, to Murray's 'unspeakable grief'), zoologists, grammarians, patent officers, organists, runic archaeologists, fantasists, anthropologists, men of letters, bankers, medievalists, and Indian administrators—these and a thousand more professions and pastimes occupied those men and women who otherwise devoted hours, weeks, perhaps even years of their time to read for Murray and Bradley, and later for Craigie and Onions. The range of interests of these hundreds was prodigious; their knowledge was extraordinary; their determination was unequalled; and yet their legacy—aside from the book itself—remains essentially unwritten. Only their names, in long lists in the volumes, the parts, and the sections, exist to make some readers stop and wonder for a moment—*just who were these people?*

One last half-answer to the question comes from a clue that is to be found in every single part of the great book, from that which begins with *A* right through to that which finishes with *zyxt*. The clue is the existence in each one of the Prefaces of one recurring name: Thompson.

'The following readers have contributed most largely to the materials,' it says in the Appendix to the Preface of Volume I, its first part published in 1884, 'Miss E. Thompson and Miss E. P. Thompson, Wavertree, Liverpool, 15,000.' 'In the revision and improvement of the work in the proof stage [of the letter O] continuous and indefatigable help has been rendered by the Misses E. P. and Edith Thompson of Landsdown, Bath.' 'During the editorial progress of the letter W, which began in 1919, outside help has been given in the reading of proofs by the Misses Edith and E. P. Thompson.' 'The material for X, Y, Z passed through the hands of a voluntary sub-editor, the Rev. J. Smallpeice, in 1882–4,' says the Preface to the final volume, published in 1928. 'The first proofs have been read by the Misses Edith and E. P. Thompson.'

We know where these two ladies settled over the years— Liverpool, Reigate, and Bath. We know from other references that the (usually only initialled) younger sister was in fact called Elizabeth Perronet Thompson. We know that Edith Thompson was obsessively secretive and determined to remain as anonymous as possible. She seemed to shiver with excitement on occasion during her correspondence with James Murray—and when she ventured, as she very seldom did, some personal opinion, she hoped that Murray would not regard it as remiss. 'If it is, treat it as confidential.' We know that there was an interesting correspondence involving either the word *pace* or the word *gait*, with charming diagrams to illustrate the way in which horses of different breeds arrange their legs when moving. We know that the ladies were found to be so competent that they were asked to sub-edit, and did so for all the letters following C. We also know that Edith wrote a highly popular, well-regarded and long-in-print *History of England* in 1873,[15] and that young Elizabeth wrote an

15 Schoolchildren used to call the book their 'Edith'; it remained in print, continually revised, until well after the Great War. So much for anonymity.

exquisitely tame bodice-ripper of a novel set in the seventeenth century and entitled *A Dragoon's Wife*.

We know these things, but we do not really know why so many people gave so much of their time for so little apparent reward. And this is the abiding and most marvellous mystery of the enormously democratic process that was the Dictionary—that hundreds upon hundreds of people, for motives known and unknown, for reasons both stated and left unsaid, helped to chronicle the immense complexities of the language that was their own, and that they dedicated in many cases—such as the Thompson sisters did—years upon years of labour to a project of which they all, buoyed by some set of unfathomable and optimistic notions, insisted on becoming a part. The Thompson sisters of Liverpool, Reigate, and Bath, living an otherwise blameless and unremarkable (though moneyed) suburban life in three most ordinary English towns, left no greater memorial than the work they performed for the greatest literary enterprise of history. They became footnotes in eight-point Clarendon type in a preface to a volume of that enterprise. That was truly their only reward—and yet in all likelihood they, and scores of others like them, surely wanted no other.

8

From Take to Turn-down—and then, Triumphal Valediction

Clear Turtle Soup
Turbot with Lobster Sauce
Haunch of Mutton
Sweetbreads after the mode of Villeroi
Grenadines of Veal
Roast Partridge
Queen Mab Pudding
Strawberry Ice

Amontillado 1858
Champagne Pfungst, 1889
Adriatic maraschino liqueur
Chateau d'Yquem

(From the menu of the Dictionary Dinner,
The Queen's College, Oxford,
12 October 1897)

On New Year's Day of 1895, a Tuesday, a customer with half a crown in his pocket could find, at the better kind of bookshops in London and Oxford and Edinburgh and beyond—and even in Manhattan (where the cost was a dollar)—the very latest part, the twelfth, of the new Dictionary. For his money he would receive a slender, 64-page paperbacked volume—new, slimmed down, promised to be more frequently produced, a welcome change from the 352-page and endlessly awaited monsters of before—that in this case contained all the known words that lay in the lexicon between *Deceit* and *Deject* (and which naturally included long entries for the words *define, defining,* and *definition,* which some might say the entire Dictionary exercise was all about).

This volume had a signal difference about it, however, something that made it stand apart from the eleven predecessor parts and volumes that had been offered for sale or subscription. It was a change in appearance which many would say was a sign that augured well for the eventual completion of the project, which had been in more than a little doubt. It lent a new tone to the volume, gave it a certain style, and heft, and a feeling of permanence and immutability.

For printed on the outer cover—not on the inside title page, but only on the slip cover—were, for the first time, the words *Oxford English Dictionary.* The formal realization had at long last come: that while to the philologists in London this might have been begun as the *New* English Dictionary, it had for eighteen years been firmly and formally part of the majestic engine-work of Oxford—and Oxford wanted the world and his wife to know that this was so. Hence the birth, late in the day but still some cause for joy, of what we know today as the *OED,* by which initials all—including this account—would henceforward invariably refer to it.

That was the first indication of a new energy, a new mood. Before long there were others, less formal but nonetheless indicative. By the mid-1890s the Dictionary was becoming well known, its name and uncommon scope fast entering the common culture. Newspapers wrote about it. Cartoons in *Punch* featured it. Lawyers quoted it—the *OED* definition of something was frequently used as evidence presented in court, accepted by juries and judges alike as an impeccable source of lexical infallibility. On 5 December 1893, Gladstone cited the *OED* in Parliament for the meaning of the thieves' slang phrase *put-up job*; four years later Joseph Chamberlain, the great Colonial Secretary, consulted Murray over the meaning of the word *patriotism*, which he said he intended to use in his installation speech as Chancellor of Glasgow University.[1] And in 1912 the then Home Secretary, accused in the House of Commons of using un-parliamentary language by calling someone 'impertinent', opened a volume of the *OED* and displayed it to MPs to show that in early days *impertinent* meant not what the members ignorantly imagined, but 'not pertaining to the subject or matter in hand, irrelevant'. 'And I used the word', the minister said, smugly, 'in its older sense.'

The fact that the Dictionary was still incomplete, but that what had already been made was so superbly authoritative, led to some interesting complications. It was noted by an in-house Press magazine in early 1900, for example, that 'A Chinaman in Singapore, on opening up a school for his countrymen, announces that he is prepared, among other things, to teach English "up to the letter G".' And yet at the same time the book's incompleteness was, it was at long last being acknowledged, only a temporary phenomenon.

The culminating event of this long climb to assured completion came in August 1897, a time when the nation was still reverberating with the self-satisfied pleasure taken from the

---

1 The volume covering the letter P would not be ready for nearly another decade: in both cases Murray was asked to look in his notes, rather than the Dictionary itself.

Diamond Jubilee of Queen Victoria. The great ceremony itself had taken place two months earlier, on 22 June—the tiny and still much beloved monarch had pressed an electric button at eleven, to send a message from the Palace—'From my heart I thank my people. May God bless them'—to every corner of her immense Empire.

A fortnight later the University, at Murray's urging, and with the editor choosing with the greatest care every letter and syllable and courteous and courtly phrase, wrote to the Palace: 'Might Her Majesty perhaps see fit', Oxford enquired, 'to accept the Dedication of the Oxford English Dictionary to her most August Personage, by way of a mark of respect for her Sixty Glorious Years on the Throne?'

In August a private secretary replied: yes indeed, after due consideration the Queen had seen fit to accept. Oxford was duly delighted. Murray was well pleased that what was, indeed, a ploy to ensure continuance had worked. A flyleaf was hurriedly inserted into the volume just finished—it was the first volume to embrace a pair of letters: D (edited by Murray) and E (by Bradley)—and the triumphal message announcing the dedication was inscribed in extra-large type: 'To the Queen's Most Excellent Majesty this Historical Dictionary of the English language is by her gracious permission dutifully dedicated by the University of Oxford. A.D. MDCCCXCVII.'

After that, it would have been quite unthinkable to stop. The Delegates ceased all their querulous complaints about the cost—it would, after all, have been *lèse-majesté* in the extreme to indulge in pettifogging arguments over money with the Dictionary a now royally connected enterprise. Murray was suddenly given to dreamily predicting when all would be gathered in: '1908 at soonest. 1910 at latest.' The Worshipful Company of Goldsmiths—who would later give the celebratory dinner to mark the completion of

the enterprise—contributed £5,000 in 1905 to help with the production of Volume VI, which held Bradley's edit of the letters
L and M, and Craigie's of the letter N. The Goldsmiths' crest
adorns an opening title page: 'This Sixth Volume is a Memorial
of the Munificence of the Worshipful Company of Goldsmiths
who have generously Contributed Five Thousand Pounds towards
its Production'—and Oxford expressed, in private, its profoundest
thanks as well.[2]

At the same time Murray also began to notice something else
of a physical significance: for the first time since he had started
work back in Mill Hill nearly twenty years before, the number of
quotation slips that were waiting in the pigeon-holes to present
themselves for selection and inclusion was diminishing. He reported to the Philological Society (which, though it had been side-
lined as the principal producer of the Dictionary, was still
sympathetically interested) on the change:

> ... when we reached the end of A and had emptied all the A
> pigeon-holes, & packed up all the A slips used and unused in
> strong boxes, the additions to the later material were so great that
> we had more slips in the Scriptorium than when we begun ... the
> same thing happened at the end of B; and even at the end of C
> when one fifth of the material was used up, the what that remained
> occupied more space than the original whole. Now, however ... it
> begins to be apparent that the material in the Scriptorium has
> undergone considerable diminution, and we shall now be able to
> use the vacant pigeon holes ... for the materials for the letters after
> T which have hitherto ... had to be stowed away in rather in-
> accessible positions.

2   A copy of this title page found in the Oxford University Press archives has, beneath the
     words 'Five Thousand Pounds', the following neat manuscript addition: 'very little of
     which has reached the Staff.' Whoever this mutinous member was, he knew his lit-
     erature well: at the bottom of the page he adds a quotation from Shakespeare's *Comedy
     of Errors*: 'Bring me where the Goldsmith is | I long to know the truth hereof at large.'

Oxford, now fully aware that it was on the verge—still a very wide verge maybe, but a verge nonetheless—of creating a publishing epic, of making a national asset of truly historic proportions, decided to celebrate. They decided to do what Oxford was very good at: to give Murray and his now rather discreetly merry men a full-dress, all-stops-out, no-holds-barred formal dinner.

It was all the happy idea of the new Vice-Chancellor, John Magrath—a man who had first become interested in the Dictionary the year before, when during the row about the 'Webster ratio' he had been impressed by Murray's staunch refusal to bow to Gell's insistence on trimming. He was described as being 'picturesque', with a flowing beard and a kindly smile (and a fondness for swimming naked in that stretch of the River Cherwell known as Parson's Pleasure). He was also intellectually and socially a quite remarkable figure, having decided as an undergraduate to take degrees in classics and mathematics at the same time,[3] then to take holy orders and become an ordained deacon, to become President of the Union, and to row and swim for his college. He had a fellowship at—and in due course became Provost of—the Queen's College, and it was here that he decided to honour Murray. The dinner—where by tradition all are summoned by a scholar sounding a fanfare on an ancient silver trumpet—was a very grand affair indeed.

James Murray at first pooh-poohed the idea—three days' worth of carousing (for some guests planned to stay awhile) and letter-writing would take him away from work. Magrath pulled out all the stops to persuade him: 'I trust that the gathering will give you an indication that more people sympathise with you in

---

3   The result was that he won a first-class degree in classics, but only a fourth in mathematics.

your self-denying labours than perhaps in moments of depression, disappointment or annoyance you have been fully able to realise.' It worked. The editor in time came around, and in the event, enjoyed himself hugely.

Everyone of note was there, dining by candlelight on what all remarked was a glorious late autumn evening. Massed along the immense tables that glittered and glistened with the finest china, crystal, and silver were Murray and Bradley and the newly appointed Charles Onions and William Craigie, all the more junior editors and sub-editors and assistants, as many of the immense Murray family as could attend, the entire colloquium of Delegates, an entire pie of new-suited printers under their eagle-eyed Controller, most of the elderly stalwarts of the Philological Society from London, correspondents from newspapers at the better end of Fleet Street, schoolmasters from Mill Hill, the newly ennobled (as Lord Aldenham) Henry Hucks Gibbs, and a small army of the volunteer readers too—Miss Brown of Further Barton was there, a Reverend Smith of Putney too. And though W. C. Minor was unavoidably detained, and Fitzedward Hall was understandably absent also, it was whispered that the Thompson sisters might have made it from Reigate to Oxford High Street, and some say they were spied getting rather mischievously tipsy on their small glasses of amontillado.

Once Her Majesty had been toasted and her Jubilee'd status remarked upon, and once the cigars had been lit, there were fully fourteen speeches—Frederick Furnivall, irrepressible and as flirtatious as ever, made the longest, slyly attacking the universities (Cambridge included) for being so slow in their admission of women. Sir William Markby, a Delegate, a former Calcutta judge, and a fanatical supporter of temperance, responding to the toast to the Clarendon Press, made a speech that must have caused Murray some wry amusement:

We have never hesitated in the performance of what we consider a great duty which we owe to the University and to the nation, and we have never felt any doubt as to the ultimate completion of the work under the able editorship of Dr. Murray and the co-operation of those associated with him in this great work.

If Murray saw some irony—or even some mealy-mouthedness on Markby's part—he sensibly held his tongue.

He was in any case to be doubly cheered by winning yet another award that night: in this case both he and Bradley were that night made honorary members of the Netherlands Society of Arts, Science, and Literature. This was merely the latest in an immense string of honours to be added to the catalogue that Murray was busily amassing—his name on the fascicles' title pages is underpinned by an ever-enlarging paragraph that lists his collection of distinctions. Already he possessed degrees from London and Edinburgh; in the years following he was to be given honorary doctorates by the Universities of Durham, Freiburg, Glasgow, Wales, the Cape of Good Hope, Dublin, and Cambridge; he was inducted into Academies in Vienna, Ghent, Prussia, Leyden, and Uppsala and was also made, to his particular pride, a Foreign Correspondent of the Académie Française. He was a member of the Edinburgh Royal Society and the American Academy of Arts, and was on the Council of the British Academy.

He was given a knighthood in 1908: when he received the letter from Herbert Asquith—'a slight and too long delayed recognition of a great work greatly conceived and greatly executed,' the Prime Minister wrote—he rather scoffed at the idea of calling himself Sir James, 'as if I were a brewer or a local mayor'. He later said he would have preferred to have been granted the infinitely more exclusive token of state congratulation, the Order of Merit. But in the end he proved gracious: he dressed up in his court robes and fixed on his sword and his jewelled slippers with the great glee of the dandy, and went happily off to the Palace to collect his prize from the King.

Finally, but not until 1914, he got what he really wanted. He and Bradley were awarded the degree of D.Litt *honoris causa* by Oxford University itself. Ada opened the post that morning and simply said what the entire family and all of Murray's friends had been feeling ever since the great dinner of 1897: 'At last!'

And all this for a draper's son from the Borders, who left school at fourteen and went off to work in a bank.

But the dinner that night had been to honour the Dictionary, and in truth not the one figure who was already most closely associated with it. The man from *The Times* summed up the event nicely for his readers the next morning. The production of the Dictionary which the dinner had cause to celebrate was, he wrote,

> *the greatest effort which any University, it may be any printing press, has taken in hand since the invention of printing. A University Press ... might be defined as one which exists, partly at all events, for the production of unremunerative works which, however, will tend to the benefit of posterity and enrich the language and the literature of the country. An exhaustive dictionary ... was a labour which was beyond the scope of private enterprise. It will not be the least of the glories of the University of Oxford to have completed this gigantic task.*

Man proposes, but God disposes. Even with the finishing line in sight, so the runners began to fall.

Fitzedward Hall was the first of the great men to go. He had worked for twenty years, for four hours every day at least, writing from his East Anglian cottage until almost the day he died, 1 February 1901. He had not wanted to attend the great dinner; he had fallen ill fairly soon thereafter, prompting Murray to depart briefly from his usual formality: instead of ending his letter to Hall with his customary 'Yours truly', he instead wrote 'Yours very affectionately', and told Hall that he had in recent years looked upon him almost as a senior relative of his own. Hall was one of the firmest opponents of the efforts of men like Jowett and Furnivall as they tried to prompt Murray to lower his standards and to produce more pages more frequently: Hall's support to Murray was irreplaceable, and we all today owe the curiously embittered hermit as great a debt as Murray did.

Henry Hucks Gibbs, without whose solicitous influence, soothing balms—and, quite frankly, his money—the project might well have foundered, died in 1907. Fred Elworthy, who had helped Murray with West Country dialect, died a few weeks later. Walter Skeat went in 1912, Murray's friend Edward Arber was knocked down soon afterwards by a Birmingham taxi, and Robinson Ellis, a great classical scholar, translator of Catullus and a climbing friend and close adviser as well, dropped dead in 1913.

Some weeks before, Ellis had given his final lecture, on Ovid, in the Hall of Trinity College. He was lame and nearly blind, and had to be led in by a younger don who would read his lecture for him. 'How many have come?' the old man enquired. The Hall, he was told, was all but empty. 'No matter,' said Ellis. 'I just thought perhaps Dr. Murray might come.' And of course, he had. Of the seven persons present in the Hall that day, James Murray was one, constant to his friend, who many say died more happily as a consequence, just a few days later.

'Thus one by one they pass away,' Murray told an audience at the Philological Society. 'Who is to be the next?'

Of all the deaths, that of Frederick Furnivall on 2 July 1910 was perhaps the most keenly felt. Late in 1909 he had told Murray he was ill—an 'internal tumour', he called it—and thought he had six months left in him. He congratulated Murray in the same letter for his definition of the phrase *tallow ketch*,[4] but went on to mourn how 'our Dict. Men go gradually, & I am next. ... I wanted to see the Dict. before I die. But it is not to be. However, the completion of the work is certain. So that's all right.' Murray tried to cheer him up, and in a way that both men knew might work: 'Would it give you any satisfaction to see the gigantic TAKE in final, before it is too late?'

Cheered or not, Furnivall died peacefully where he had lived and worked, in Primrose Hill, and was cremated in north London. Around the catafalque, said his biographer,

> *were representatives from the many educational and learned bodies with which he had been connected, including the London Shakespeare League, the Oxford University Press, the English Association, the Board of Education, the Oxford English Dictionary, students, friends, and associates from the British Museum, the New Oxford Street A.B.C. teashop and the London Men's Working College; and a group of young people from the Furnivall Sculling Club at Hammersmith.*

He had last been seen sculling three years before: he had done fourteen miles on the day in question, and he had been 82 years old.

And then before too much longer, to universal dismay and lamentation, it was the turn of James Murray himself.

As late as 1914 he was saying publicly that he still hoped to see the Dictionary through to its completion. For most of the previous years he, Bradley, and Craigie published their monthly page

---

4   A Shakespearian term for a fat, Falstaffian man, a *catcher of tallow*.

totals, to see who was the fastest—and Murray invariably won, month after month, year after year.[5] When Furnivall died Murray was well into the letter T, and with Craigie now a full editor (he had been designated such in 1901) and with Onions similarly exalted since 1914, and with Bradley steaming away at full tilt, there seemed at least a possibility of a swift end to the enterprise: only six letters to go, and Murray not yet 80 years old. Perhaps he could manage the grand Victorian conjunction he long imagined—his golden wedding anniversary, his four-score birthday, and the finishing of the *OED*.

The Regius Professor of Medicine, Sir William Osler, once spotted the elderly Murray tricycling his way through town, his long white beard blowing in the wind, and remarked to his companion: 'The University pays me my salary to keep that old man alive until his 80th birthday in 1917, when his dictionary will be finished.'

But neither came to pass. James Murray succumbed to cancer of the prostate, and though he bore nobly the fantastic burning pain of the X-rays that in those days were used to treat the ailment, he knew he was fighting a losing battle. He continued to work on the letter T until the very end:[6] there is a photograph of him in the Scriptorium taken on 10 July 1915, his daughters Elsie and Rosfrith to his left and right, and behind him three assistants—a bearded Arthur Maling, wearing his Esperanto

5   The Delegates studied the figures very closely, a legacy of Gell's era. In October 1903 they noted with a mixture of approval and asperity that Murray had composed 18²/₃ pages, Bradley 7²/₃ and Craigie 8²/₃. One reason for Bradley's apparent tardiness was his extraordinary prolixity: while not wishing to revisit the Webster ratio crisis, it is noteworthy that while Craigie was keeping his well down, to 4.7 : 1, Bradley was preparing material that was more than 18 times as large as Webster. Murray had not managed to keep below his promised 8. In October 1903 his number was 10.7:1.

6   It is cheering to learn that Murray, despite his illness, was impish enough to enjoy including a tongue-twister among his illustrations for the verb *to thwack*, from the sixteenth century: *Thwaites thwackt him with a thwitle*.

James and Ada Murray—together with some of their eleven remarkable children—gathered in the back garden of Sunnyside, in Oxford, not long before Murray's death in 1915.

star; Frederick Sweatman of possible *radium* fame; and the little-known F. A. Yockney, a member of the team since 1905.

It was Murray's final day in the little iron room. The following Monday he contracted pleurisy, and on 26 July, he died. Popular legend has it that he was working on the word *turn-down* at the end—and certainly this is the last section (*Trink–Turn-down*) known to be edited by him. But his name also appears on the next section, *Turndun–Tzirid*, and a note from Bradley states that 'eighty-four columns of this section were already in type' at the time James Murray died.

The last word of the 84th column of this section happens to be *twentieth*. Though there is a presentiment of sleep about the word *turn-down*,[7] which some might find apposite for a dying man, I like to think that the word that defined the century in which his great work would be published was, in fact, the one for which he would most like to be have been known. He was a nineteenth-century man, and yet the author of what was to be very memorably a twentieth-century achievement.

Bradley, Craigie, and Onions then consolidated themselves in the Old Ashmolean Building, and left those at Sunnyside to suffer the peace of their bereavement. From now on, the large, many-columned building beside the Sheldonian was to be the head-quarters of the *OED*, and for the first time since 1885, the word 'Scriptorium' would cease to appear in the prefaces to the parts that still emerged, now at an ever-increasing rate. There was something of a delay in production in the aftermath of Henry

7   A turn-down bed, for example; though a turn-down is also someone who has been
    rejected for a position or a job.

Bradley's death in 1923; but the pace of dictionary-making quickened again soon after, and it did not noticeably falter when Craigie was appointed Professor of English at the University of Chicago: the preface to the letter U, indeed, is datelined Chicago, and Craigie worked happily in his office in Hyde Park until the book, no matter that it was 5,000 miles to the east of him, was finished. Craigie 'bestrode the Atlantic like a colossus', it was said.

The last sections positively tumbled out. As it happened, the alphabetically ultimate section XYZ—with its final word, *zyxt*, the last word in the entire Dictionary—was not the last to be made. Because it was so short and relatively easy it was completed seven years before the end, on 6 October 1921, under the editorship of Onions (and once again with the help, according to the Preface, of the redoubtable Thompson sisters). An earlier section, *W–Wash*, prepared by Bradley, was published on the very same day, giving subscribers a surprise bonus.

The year 1923 saw the appearance of *Wash–Wavy* and *Wh–Whisking. Unforeseeing–Unright* and *Whisky–Wilfulness* came in 1924. There was nothing—because of Bradley's passing—in 1925. The following year came *Unright–Uzzle* and *Wilga–Wise*. There was, once again, nothing published in 1927.

But on the historic afternoon of 19 April 1928, under the supervisory imprimatur of Chicago's Professor William Craigie, the final part, the 64 pages that contained the few hundreds of words that lay between *Wise* and *Wyzen*, was completed. And with the inclusion of (it has to be said) the rather disagreeable-looking and unfortunate-sounding word *wyzen*, which is an obscure Scottish form of the long obsolete and equally unattractive word *weasand*, which in some circles once meant the oesophagus or gullet, the throat or the windpipe, the work was finished.

The *OED* was finally and fully made. The English language, in what was at the time believed to be its entirety, had at long last been fixed between the hard covers of—at first ten and then, after a reprinting, a dozen—tombstone-sized volumes; and the labour of making it all, the work of the 71 years that had been taken up by this most magnificent and romantic of enterprises, was now all done. The triumphant moment that Trench and Coleridge and Furnivall and Murray—and Gell and Hart and Minor and Fitzedward Hall and the Thompson sisters besides—had all so longed for had been well and truly reached. Samuel Johnson, literature's Great Cham and the true father of English lexicography, had once remarked on the human creation of words, compared with the divine creation of the things they described. He had put it more elegantly: that words were the daughters of earth, while things were the sons of heaven. With the finishing of the *OED*, it could now fairly be said that all of earth's daughters, so very long sought, had now been brought safely to their home.

What happened next—in the weeks after completion in April, and before Stanley Baldwin's great celebration dinner on Derby Day in June—was all down to the obsessions of one of those curious and eccentric figures who lurk in the woodwork of England and Oxford, and of whose strange endeavours we are all mightily delighted to learn. This particular figure was named R. M. Leonard, and for the previous many years he had been carefully watching the growth of the Dictionary, keeping silent track of its progress and noting down, most significantly, all of the numbers.

Leonard was a newspaperman, who until 1896 had worked on the *Pall Mall Gazette*. He was also a first-class composer of occasional verse, rather better than the poetasters of the day; he was an anthologist; and he was an active and prominent member of the Anti-Bribery and Corruption League. Henry Frowde, the august

The first nine volumes of the Dictionary—published here under the project's original title—together with unbound fascicles for the tenth, shortly before completion in 1928.

Publisher to the University, had spotted him as an interesting kind of cove, and had hired him to edit, from London, a brand-new sixteen-page quarterly journal about the doings of the Press, which Frowde thought, in a flash of what now would be called public relations genius, ought to be called *The Periodical*.

The paper was duly made and sent out free of charge and postage paid—'With Mr. Henry Frowde's Compliments'—to anyone who expressed an interest. And as a small sign of the beneficence of the Press there was a charming rubric sentence on the front of every issue: '*The Periodical* is printed on one side of the paper only, for the convenience of those who may care to take extracts from its pages.'

And within, a perpetual gallimaufry of delights. We learn, for instance, about Oxford India Paper, used for Bibles and prayer books. It was first made in the Potteries, from rope, and was used in the factories for wrapping up china. The Oxford paper mill at Wolvercote then started making it, and soon astonished Press men were proudly showing off its extraordinary strength—a three-inch-wide strip could support a load of a quarter of a hundredweight, one sheet could support an entire volume of 1,500 pages, and when rubbed hard it turned into something like chamois leather and could be used for cleaning windows. One blesses Mr Leonard for telling us such things.

As we bless him most relevantly here for painstakingly working out and then telling us, in a 1900 issue of *The Periodical*, some of the *OED*'s early statistics. Back then the Dictionary had only reached *I* (though it lacked the words between *Graded* and *Gyzzarn*, which had not then been published). And yet, if all the columns thus far made were piled on top of one another they would be four times as high as Snowdon, the Welsh mountain, fourteen times the height of the Eiffel Tower, and would reach around the Reading Room of the British Museum almost 100 times. Moreover, the *OED* was very cheap indeed: for one penny piece the purchaser receives '1 yard 1 foot and 8 odd inches of solid printed matter, 2½ inches wide, on unexceptionable paper, turned out in the best manner of the University Press'.

In 1928 R. M. Leonard was still there, eagle-eyed and eager to celebrate. By then Henry Frowde had long retired,[8] and the triumphal issue of *The Periodical* came 'With Mr. Humphrey Milford's Compliments' instead. From its pages we learn that what Arnold Bennett had called 'the longest sensational serial ever written' contained, as mentioned in the Prologue, no fewer than 414,825 headwords and 1,827,306 illustrative quotations; Mr. Leonard had calculated that, even when leaving out every full stop and colon and comma, there were 227,779,589 letters and numbers in the finished work. The total amount of type used would stretch 178 miles, the distance from London to the suburbs of Manchester.

The man who printed this magisterial work, the man fortunate enough to enjoy the practical side of the lexicographical triumph, was John deMonins Johnson, the then 44-year-old former papyrologist with the Egyptian Civil Service, who had been Printer to the University since 1925. Together with the famous *Oxford Lectern Bible*, designed by the legendary Bruce Rogers, the *OED* was the most signal achievement in the career of a man who, like so many in this story, was remarkable in myriad ways.

Johnson, for example, was a great collector of printed ephemera: there is a Johnson Room in the Bodleian Library today which houses a million items rescued from the waste-paper baskets of the last 300 years. The *DNB* hints at the scale: early seventeenth-century book proposals and prospectuses, title pages, specimen

---

8 Among Frowde's achievements were to preside over what many still regard as the best of all best-sellers—the distribution of one million copies of the Revised New Testament on one day, 17 May 1881. He did not live to see the finishing of the *OED*, but died the year before.

pages, material illustrating the history of printing, including copy-right, spelling, and design, specialized collections of banknotes, postage stamps, political pamphlets, Christmas cards, valentines, and cigarette cards. There are tourist brochures from Albania to Zanzibar, directions for making cocoa, advertisements for corselettes—in short, 'the richest collection of jobbing printing in existence'.

John Johnson calculated the costs and, come April 1928, he advertised the price—once the Delegates and Publisher Milford had agreed upon it. The work, emblazoned with the names of the editors—Sir James A. H. Murray, Henry Bradley, W. A. Craigie, C. T. Onions—was now available, according to a special flyer, at the price of '50 guineas for 10 volumes bound as 12 [for as 10 two would have been too bulky] in half-morocco; 50 guineas for 20 half-volumes in quarter persian; and 55 guineas for 20 half-volumes in half-morocco'.[9] Then follows the odd phrase '*OF* ALL BOOKSELLERS'—which suggests a prepositional error, though heaven forfend that John deMonins Johnson could ever perpetrate such a thing.[10] The phrase appears in much later flyers too, sug-gesting unusual style rather than careless mistake.

Praise for the book was, in the months after first publication, well-nigh universal, perhaps taking itself to a point that, since this story is not supposed to be overtly hagiographical, becomes almost tedious to relate. To my mind two quotations sum up,

9 Mr Leonard worked out that this amounted to eight-tenths of a penny per page—a bargain, he said.

10 There are, however, oddities in the Dictionary itself, which look like errors. James Murray favoured such spelling as *ax*, *Shakspere*, *tire* (of motor cars), and *rime*—eccentricities abound, both in the book and in its advertisements. But in the book the alternative spellings are included as well, which is not true of the ad. There are discovered errors, too: the word *syllabus*, for example, is a ghost-word, coming from a mistransliteration by Cicero, who wrote the word instead of what he wanted, *sittybas* (which means a label), by mistake. The word *syllabus* should by rights not be in the English language at all.

deftly and rather more lightly than most, the delight in the admixture of excellence and the pride that dominated the weeks and months in the aftermath of the appearance of the completed work.

The first, by now well known, came from the acerbic Baltimore wit and sometime lexicographer H. L. Mencken. He wrote in his newspaper column that 'his spies had told him' that the appearance of the finished Dictionary would be celebrated in Oxford with 'military exercises, boxing matches between the dons, orations in Latin, Greek, English and the Oxford dialect, yelling contests between the different Colleges and a series of medieval drinking bouts'.

The second harks back to the man who started it all, Richard Chenevix Trench, who, it will be remembered, made his caustic speech of November 1857 attacking the deficiencies of the English dictionaries of the day. What had now been created, all its makers hoped, was a monument that would turn out to be quite wanting in deficiencies of any kind. To illustrate the point, Craigie—newly made Sir William Craigie at the Derby Day dinner, and given an Honorary LL D by Oxford the day before—quoted an obviously deficient but nonetheless memorable definition that he winkled out of Falconer's not widely known *Dictionary of Marine*.

It was the definition of the simple word *retreat*. As Falconer has it: 'Retreat is the order in which a French fleet retires before an enemy. As it is not properly a term of the British marine, any fuller account would be out of place.'

Incorrect, and facetious. Very Johnsonian, one might say. Moderately witty of course, if in an unspeakably chauvinistic and these days politically incorrect way. But its existence, however shocking to the lexicographic purist, made a point. It was important for everyone to know, declaimed Professor Sir William Craigie, LL D, D.Litt, the fifth editor: no such definition—in fact nothing of the kind—would ever be allowed to occur, except inadvertently, within the pages of the *Oxford English Dictionary*.

No sir! In this dictionary there would be no oats to feed those Scottish peasants. No definition would list unreadable complications involving decussated and reticulated networks. No guesses would be made of gymnastically unattainable positions for the mating of elephants. And there would be no sly cross-Channel sniping suggesting that only Frenchmen knew properly how to retreat. The work that he had made, the magisterial creation of all his distinguished forefathers that he was now so proud to offer, was, as near as could be made, the perfect dictionary, and so it would ever remain.

Epilogue:
And Always Beginning Again

A work of such magnificent proportions may perhaps not find access to many private houses except those of the rich; but it should be the most coveted possession of all public libraries in the United Kingdom, in the Colonies, and at least at the headquarters of every District in India and at her principal Colleges.

(*Asiatic Quarterly Review*, 1898)

B ut of course, it wasn't really finished. It never could be, it never would be, and it never will be. One of the infuriating marvels of the slippery fluidity of the English language is that for all of its 1,500 years of history it has been changing, enlarging, evolving: it would continue to do so long after the 1928 publication date, even as Herbert Coleridge had anticipated it would, when he undertook the beginnings of the task back in 1860.

What was essentially finished, though, was the new Dictionary's structure. In creating it, James Murray had made something that was so good in all its essentials that, no matter how many editions and evolutions the *OED* would subsequently undergo, Murray's basic plan remained intact. Sir William Craigie, when he came to be Senior Editor on the death of Henry Bradley, remarked, generously, that Murray's form and methods and design 'proved to be adequate to the end, standing the test of fifty years without requiring any essential modification'.

The Murray methods would still be firmly entrenched when the first Supplement emerged, five years later, in 1933. There was no doubt but that a Supplement would be made. Those who had bought the complete edition in 1928 were told of it, and advised it would be supplied to them gratis, so long as they had already paid in full. Someone in the Press—possibly it was Craigie, though that is doubtful, since the editors themselves tended to adopt in public a rather modest pose—made a suitably Grandisonian announcement:

> *The superiority of the Dictionary to all other English Dictionaries, in accuracy and completeness, is everywhere admitted. The Oxford Dictionary is the supreme authority, and without a rival. It is perhaps less generally appreciated that what makes the Dictionary unique is its historical method; it is a Dictionary not of our English, but of all English; the English of Chaucer, of the Bible, of Shakespeare is unfolded in it with the same wealth of illustration as is devoted to the most modern authors. When considered in this light, the fact that the first part of the Dictionary was published in 1884 is seen to be relatively unimportant; 44 years is a small period in the life of a language. It is, however, obviously desirable that* aeroplane *and* appendicitis *should receive due recognition. A supplement is accordingly in preparation, the main object of which will be to include words which were born too late for inclusion. Copies of the Supplement will be offered free to all holders of the complete Dictionary.*[1]

---

1   Oddly enough, it would be far less expensive for the customer who waited: those induced to buy in 1928 had to fork out 50 guineas for a ten-volume set bound as twelve. In 1933 one could obtain—'*of* all booksellers' once again—the thirteen volumes bound in cloth for 20 guineas, or only £21.

mechanicall, ⎱ (g) handie
mechanick, ⎰ craft.

Robert Cawdrey: *Table Alphabeticall* (1604)

MECHA'NICAL. ⎱ *adj.* [*mechanicus*, Lat. *mechanique*, French;
MECHA'NICK. ⎰ from μηχανη.]

1. Mean; fervile; of mean occupation.

Know you not, being *mechanical*, you ought not walk upon a labouring day, without the fign of your profeffion? *Shak.*

Hang him, *mechanical* falt-butter rogue; I will ftare him out of his wits; I will hew him with my cudgel. *Shakefp.*

Mechanick flaves,

With greafy aprons, rules, and hammers, fhall
Uplift us to the view. *Shakefp. Ant. and Cleopatra.*

To make a god, a hero, or a king,
Defcend to a *mechanick* dialect. *Rofcommon.*

Samuel Johnson: *Dictionary of the English Language* (1755)

MECHAN'IC, ⎱ *a.* [L. *mechanicus*; Fr.
MECHAN'ICAL, ⎰ *mechanique*; Gr. μη-
χανικος, from μηχαν, a machine.]

1. Pertaining to machines, or to the art of constructing machines; pertaining to the art of making wares, goods, instruments, furniture, &c. We say, a man is employed in *mechanical* labor; he lives by *mechanical* occupation.

2. Constructed or performed by the rules or laws of mechanics. The work is not *mechanical*.

3. Skilled in the art of making machines; bred to manual labor. *Johnson.*

4. Pertaining to artisans or mechanics; vulgar.

To make a god, a hero or a king,
Descend to a *mechanic* dialect. *Roscommon.*

5. Pertaining to the principles of mechanics, in philosophy; as, *mechanical* powers or forces; a *mechanical* principle.

Noah Webster: *American Dictionary of the English Language* (1828)

Mechanical (mĭkœ′nikăl), *a.* and *sb.* [I. late 1.. *mĕchanic-us*: see prec. and -ICAL.] A. *adj.*
1. Of arts, trades, occupations : Concerned with machines or tools. Hence,
a. Concerned with the contrivance and construction of machines or mechanism.
1432-50 tr. *Higden* (Rolls) VII. 73 Certeyne instrumentis of his makynge made by arte mechanicalle, and specially organes. **1626** BACON *New Att.* 36 Wee haue also diuerse Mechanicall Arts, which you haue not; and Stuffes made iry them; as Papers, Linnen [etc.]. **1756-7** tr. *Keysler's Trav.* (1760) IV. 395 Those who are fond of mechanical arts, manufactures, &c. **1815** J. SMITH *Panorama Sci. & Art* I. 124 To make any useful proficiency in mechanical pursuits. **1872** YEATS *Techn. Hist. Comm.* 367 Machinemaking..belongs to a high order of mechanical art.
b. Concerned with manual operations ; of the nature of handicraft.

8. Pertaining to mechanics as a science.
1648 Bp. WILKINS *Math. Magick* I. i. 3 Art may be said.. to overcome, and advance nature, as in these Mechanicall disciplines. **1827** JAMIESON (*title*) A Dictionary of Mechanical Science. **1861** W. FAIRBAIRN *Pres. Addr. to Brit. Assoc.* p. lviii, The mechanical sciences..may be divided into Theoretical Mechanics and Dynamics..and Applied Mechanics.
b. Having to do with machinery.
1793 SMEATON *Edystone L.* § 122 Subjects of mechanical invention and investigation. **1863** FAWCETT *Pol. Econ.* I. iv. (1876) 33 The foremost mechanical genius of this mechanical age is devoted to the production of weapons of death. **1881** *Instr. Census Clerks* (1885) 42 Mechanical Engineer, Inventor, Draughtsman, Student. **1897** MARY KINGSLEY *W. Africa* 669 The great inferiority of the African to the European lies in the matter of mechanical idea.

Oxford English Dictionary (1928)

mechanical, *a.* and *n.*

A. *adj.*   **I. Senses relating to manual or practical work.**

1. Of an art, trade, or occupation: concerned with manual work; of the nature of or relating to handicraft, craftsmanship, or artisanship. Now *rare*.

*c*1450 *Contin. Lydgate's Secrees* (Sloane 2464) 2097 Whoom his ffadir for worldly avauntage..dysposyd to crafft mechanycalle. *a*1550 (*c*1477) T. NORTON *Ordinal of Alchemy* (Bodl. e Mus.) 49 Handcrafte, called arte mechanicall. **1592** A. DAY *Eng. Secretorie* II. sig. Q2ᵛ, A seruaunt, meanely trained in some Mechanicall science. **1605** BACON *Of Aduancem. Learning* II. sig. Bb1ᵛ, Arts Mechanicall contract Brotherhoods in communalties. **1706** *Phillips's New World of Words* (ed. 6) (title-page), The Arts and Sciences, either Liberal or Mechanical. **1753** W. HOGARTH *Anal. Beauty* 4 Many other little circumstances belonging to the mechanical part of the art. **1834** MACAULAY *William Pitt* in *Ess.* (1899) 288 Almost every mechanical employment..has a tendency to injure some one or other of the bodily organs of the artisan. **1837** DR. WARTON in H. Hallam *Introd. Lit. Europe* I. I. v. 479 Most of the youth..betook themselves to mechanical or other illiberal employments. **1841** R. W. EMERSON *Method Nature* in *Wks.* (1881) II. 220, I look on trade and every mechanical craft as education also.

OED third edition, draft entry (December 2001)

Four centuries of definitions, from Robert Cawdrey's single-word attempt of 1604, to the draft prepared in 2001 for the *OED*'s third edition. The small and subtle differences between the two *OED* entries, written about a century apart, indicate powerfully just how English, and our employment of it, is subject to ceaseless change—and thus why dictionary-making is an endless task.

And so in due course all these modern words were included, and the histories of both these and scores of words which deserved more amplification or explication—or which had evolved new meaning in the years between—were duly inscribed. Most related to technologies that had not even been imagined when Coleridge and Furnivall sat down to work, as Craigie wrote—words connected to biochemistry, wireless telegraphy and telephony, mechanical transport, aerial locomotion, psycho-analysis, the cinema. In the end, 867 pages accommodated them all. The inclusions began with the use of the letter *A* to denote the highest attainable mark given in American schools (the phrase *straight A* is there as well: 1897 for the first use of *A*, 1926 for *straight A*). And they ended with the word *zooming*, defined as 'making or accompanied by a humming or buzzing sound', and first noted in a July edition of *Blackwood's Magazine* in 1923.

The word *pacifist* is in the Supplement too. Some critics had earlier written of their disappointment in discovering that 'though of decent parentage and respectable antiquity' it was a word that for some mysterious and perhaps politically sinister reason 'found no place in the *OED*'. But the truth was far simpler: the word had simply not been quoted in any published material until the year 1906—even though *pacify* had been around since the fifteenth century and *pacific* since the sixteenth. The notion that Murray had overlooked it because quotations that included *pacifist* were destroyed with the other Pa slips in the southern Irish barn does not stand up: lexicographers have scoured the literature ever since, and it is an Edwardian neologism, pure and simple.

African was in the Supplement, now that Murray had taken his hostility to the word with him to the grave. The forlornly misplaced *bondmaid* was there, its slips having been found lurking under a pile of books in the Scriptorium long after the B volume had gone to press. *Television* was there (in the 1928 edition it was too, but with the caveat 'not yet perfected'). *Radio* was fleshed out (earlier there had been merely a passing reference, taken from *Tit-Bits*, to a Mr Marconi and 'his radio or coherer', which transmitted wireless telegraphy). And *radium* was properly included too—'a rare metallic element ... Curie ... 1898 ... atomic number 88'. Nary a mention of tobacco tins or squint-eyed rats; nothing untoward had crept into the definition.

The only notable omission is not a word, but a listing in the Preface: for the first time since 1884 there is no mention anywhere of either Miss Edith or Miss E. P. Thompson, of Liverpool, Reigate, and Bath. The Dictionary had outlived them, as it would eventually outlive all who helped to make it. And as it always will.

And so there, with its thirteen majestic, gold-blocked dark blue cloth and clotted-cream-coloured paper-covered volumes, the *Oxford English Dictionary* duly stood guard over the tongue for the next 40 years. It had taken 76 years and had cost £375,000 to get to this point—though nobody at Oxford had a real idea of what the monetary figures really meant: overheads had never been included, and the value of money had changed beyond all reason. The Dictionary was no money-spinner, that was for sure—the coincidence of the Supplement's publication with the Great Depression limited still further any sales which might optimistically have been predicted.

The new Delegates' wonderfully old-fashioned Secretary, R. W. Chapman—a man who never rode in a car nor ever used a typewriter or a fountain pen—ordered up 10,000 sets of the complete Dictionary in 1935. It was supposed they would endure for all time, and there would never be the need to print again. At the outbreak of the war in 1939 there were 6,000 of them left, and it was thought that if the worst came to the worst they could be used as some kind of air raid shelter, at least as efficacious as sandbags and, for Oxford people, rather more suitable.

Once the debris of war had been cleared away and the dreaming leisure of peace began to settle back onto Oxford, the single admitted deficiency of the *OED*, one common to any dictionary of English—the fact that it was always bound to be out of date— was addressed once more. A further clutch of supplements were planned, this time under the editorship of a genially energetic New Zealander, Robert Burchfield, who took a suite of nondescript offices in a house near to the Press, in Walton Crescent, and eventually installed eighteen staff members there. One formal picture of the team, taken in the same style and the same place (the main quadrangle of the Press) as all the formal pictures of Murray's and Bradley's and Craigie's teams before—shows, in the front row, one 'Mr. J. P. Barnes'. Rarely does an *OED* man become a celebrity beyond his own rather crabbed field of endeavour: but, as Julian Barnes, this particular young editorial assistant was soon to emerge from the harmless drudgery of lexicography to become one of Britain's most celebrated essayists and novelists.

Burchfield's four-volume Supplement, assembled from the vast hoard of words that scattered members of the Dictionary team had been gathering all the while[2]—and which tried to make sense of the vocabulary havoc that was being played by some authors, James Joyce most notable among them—came out at four-year intervals, the first in 1972, the last, dedicated to Queen Elizabeth II, in 1986. Charles Onions[3] was still alive, and helped Burchfield until the mid-1960s. In the end, 50,000 words were added— including (as Burchfield wrote in his final Preface to Volume IV) several which their creators helped to define: Anthony Powell, for

2   With the prescience of the historically aware, Oxford had set up a skeleton office in 1955, under the superintendence of a deputy publisher named R. C. Goffin: his instructions were simply to await the arrival of an editorial team. Burchfield was eventually appointed editor in 1957.

3   Who stammered.

Robert Burchfield, the New Zealand-born lexicographer who created the four-volume supplement to the completed *OED*, which appeared between 1972 and 1986. He added a further 50,000 words to the amassment of the tongue.

example, helped with *acceptance world*, A. J. Ayer with *drogulus*, Buckminster Fuller with *Dymaxion*, J. R. R. Tolkien—a former assistant and walrus expert—with *hobbit*, and the cosmologist Murray Gell-Mann with *quark*. *Psychedelic*, coined in 1957, but popular at the time that Volume III was being printed, made it, just in time.

The books that resulted, superficially identical in design and layout to their predecessors, were composed on machines, printed lithographically and bound, not by hand as before, but on a wondrous contraption known as a No. 3 Smyth-Horne Casing-In Machine. Whole quires were sent to Tokyo and New York to be similarly assembled there. And at the same time as Oxford's printing passed from letterpress to lithography, so all the steel-and-antimony printing plates that served the *OED* for decades past were dumped, eventually to be tossed away. A few survive: I still have, mounted in a frame, the plate for page 452 of Volume V, which encompasses the words *Humoral* to *Humour*. It was made in 1933. I would like to think that it might have been made in perhaps June 1899 and used to print sheets for the following 70 years.

In 1971, just before the publication of the first of the Supplement volumes, and to help OUP make money out of this enormous enterprise and inject some cash into Burchfield's endeavours, the entire first edition was 'micrographically reproduced', its print made near-invisibly tiny so that all thirteen volumes could be compressed into two. The entire *OED* was thus able to be sold in one big blue box, along with a handsome magnifying glass in a nifty little drawer at the top—and it sold like hot cakes, particularly in America, where book clubs bought it at massive discounts and used it as a free gift to induce readers to join.

One major task lay ahead, however. In 1986 the language as corralled by Oxford was now arranged into not one but three parallel alphabetical lists: the main *OED*, the 1933 Supplement, and the four-volume Burchfield Supplement. Anyone looking for a word had of necessity to look in three different places. The *OED* was, in short, a mess. To make some sort of sense, all of the words, no matter how young or how old they might be, had now to be alphabetically integrated with one another, and one complete list had to be created in place of the existing three. The only way to do this—and to ensure that later expansions could take place with ease and without the need to unpick and rewrite all over again— was to take all of the original material and to recast it, from *A* to *Zyxt*, by using what in those days was a giant computer.

And so in the mid-1980s, with an enormously generous donation from IBM of computers and staff, with the work of a number of specialists at Canada's University of Waterloo in Ontario, by employing the keyboarding labours of hundreds of men and women who, in a vast warehouse in Florida, had hitherto been accustomed to the assembling of telephone directories,[4] and under the editorial supervision of two brand new co-editors, John Simpson and Edmund Weiner, the entire *OED* was ripped asunder, retyped, turned into binary code, and then reprinted. It came out on time in 1989 as an immense twenty-volume second edition, which defined a total of 615,100 words, and illustrated those definitions with 2,436,600 quotations. To do so took 59,000,000 words and 21,730 pages, and consumed almost 140 pounds of paper, for every single set of books.

And though that final number might seem merely a facetiously introduced piece of trivia, it does in fact concern John Simpson, who currently edits (with Edmund Weiner as his Deputy Chief Editor) what is being called the Revised Edition. For this will truly be a monster—an *OED* so massive as perhaps only to be amenable to use on-line. Just as in Murray's time, no-one is precisely certain

---

4   And by happy coincidence, Webster's dictionaries too.

John Simpson, the current editor of the *OED*, with some of his staff and their electronic versions of Murray's pigeon-hole filing systems. The third edition of the Dictionary, on which Simpson and his colleagues have been working since the 1990s, is due out some time in the early 21st century.

when it will be finished. It may include a million defined words. It could run to as many as forty volumes. It could weigh in at nearly a sixth of a ton, for each and every set. Each printing would consume a sizeable acreage of woodland. The environment would be affected, significantly. Would it be worthwhile? Would everyone like the comfort of knowing there was a beautiful 40-volume book out there? Or would all the world prefer the wisdom of the Dictionary to be purveyed electronically, with no physical harm to anyone or anything at all, and only the intellectual benefits deriving from all those decades of scholarship?

Such are the concerns of those who superintend the cataloguing and describing of our language today—concerns that go beyond the plain demands of learning, that so entirely consumed the lives of all those editors, sub-editors, and assistants who went before.

The pictures of those who began the *OED* haunt us still: legions of elderly, usually bearded men, formally dressed in tweeds and gabardine, sitting at high desks, pens in hand, volumes open beside them, sheaves of paper in racks and shelves and pigeon-holes behind them, a heavy, cloistered atmosphere of academic rigour and polymathic knowledge enveloping and embracing them like the very air itself. Today's images are very different: the men and women are younger, they come to work dressed as they please, they spend their times in brightly lit offices, computer screens are everywhere, telephones warble, modems blink, files are transmitted across oceans in microseconds, queries of all kinds are asked and answered in an instant. And yet the sepia pictures of the times before are still around, high on the walls, talked about, pointed at, revered. It is as if they offer to the editors of today some reassurance that the task upon which they are bent is not much different in its essence from how it was when Herbert Coleridge sat down in Regent's Park, all those years before.

So different now—and yet so very much the same. 'The circle of the English language has a well-defined centre,' James Murray wrote in his famous Introduction, 'but no discernible circumference.' Those who worked before in London and Mill Hill, in the Scriptorium on Banbury Road and in the Old Ashmolean and on Walton Crescent, indeed found and defined the well-defined centre of the English language. That is all now safely gathered in, and for this all must be eternally grateful. Those who work today, building on these undeniable triumphs of the past, are trying now to catch and snare the indiscernible, ever outward-spreading ripples of idiom and neologism and slang and linguistic invention by which the English language expands and changes, year by year, decade by decade, century by century.

We cannot tell what the editors will be like, will look like, how their working places will be designed or defined, in another 50 years, in another century, or in the next millennium. But the English language will be there for sure. Its centre will remain static and well defined. The circumferential ripples of new-formed English words will become ever larger, ever wider, and ever less well defined: that much is certain. And what is certain too is that humans, being humans, will be on hand as well, in some way or another, as they have been for so long, to catch all these words, to list them all, and to record and fix them all in time, for always.

Bibliography and Further Reading

Benzie, William, *Dr. F. J. Furnivall: Victorian Scholar Adventurer*. Norman, Okla.: Pilgrim Books, 1983.

Berg, Donna Lee, *A Guide to the Oxford English Dictionary*. Oxford: Oxford University Press, 1993.

Bridges, R. (ed.), *The Collected Papers of Henry Bradley*. Oxford: Clarendon Press, 1928.

Brock, M. G., and Curthoys, M. C. (eds.), *The History of the University of Oxford*, vols. vi and vii: *Nineteenth-Century Oxford*. Oxford: Clarendon Press, 1997.

Bryson, Bill, *Mother Tongue: The English Language*. London: Longman, 1990.

Burchfield, R. W., *Supplement to the Oxford English Dictionary*. 4 vols., Oxford: Oxford University Press, 1972–86. Prefaces.

—— *The English Language*. Oxford: Oxford University Press, 1985. Reissued 2002 with afterword by John Simpson.

—— *Unlocking the English Language*. London: Faber & Faber, 1989.

—— **and Aarsleff, Hans**, *The Oxford English Dictionary and the State of the Language*. Washington, DC: Library of Congress, 1988.

Coleridge, Herbert, *A Dictionary of the First, or Oldest Words in the English Language*. London: John Camden Hotten, 1863.

Craigie, W. A., 'New Dictionary Schemes Presented to the Philological Society, 4th April 1919', *Transactions of the Philological Society 1925–1930* (1931), 8.

Crystal, David, *The Cambridge Encyclopaedia of the English Language*. Cambridge: Cambridge University Press, 1995.

Furnivall, F. J., *A Volume of Personal Record*. Oxford: Oxford University Press, 1911.

Gowers, Sir Ernest, *Plain Words*. London: HM Stationery Office, 1951.

Green, Jonathon, *Chasing the Sun. Dictionary Makers and the Dictionaries They Made*. London: Cape, 1996.

Landau, Sidney I., *Dictionaries: The Art and Craft of Lexicography*, 2nd edn. Cambridge: Cambridge University Press, 2001.

McAdam, E. L., and Milne, G., *Johnson's Dictionary: A Modern Selection*. New York: Pantheon, 1963.

McArthur, T. (ed.), *The Oxford Companion to the English Language*. Oxford: Oxford University Press, 1992.

—— *The Oxford Guide to World English*. Oxford: Oxford University Press, 2002.

McMorris, Jenny, *The Warden of English: The Life of H. W. Fowler*. Oxford: Oxford University Press, 2002.

McCrum, R., Cran, W., and MacNeil, R., *The Story of English*. London: Faber & Faber, 1986.

Mathews, M. M., *A Survey of English Dictionaries*. London: Oxford University Press, 1933.

Middlemas, K., and Barnes, J., *Baldwin: A Biography*. London: Weidenfeld & Nicolson, 1969.

Moore, John, *You English Words*. London: Collins, 1961.

Mugglestone, Lynda (ed.), *Lexicography and the OED*. Oxford: Oxford University Press, 2000.

Murray, K. M. Elisabeth, *Caught in the Web of Words: James A. H. Murray and the Oxford English Dictionary*. New Haven, Conn.: Yale University Press, 1977.

Murray, Wilfrid G. R., *Murray the Dictionary-Maker*. Cape Town: Rustica Press, 1943.

Raymond, Darrell R. (ed.), *Dispatches from the Front: The Prefaces to the Oxford English Dictionary*. Waterloo, Ontario: University of Waterloo, 1987.

Shenker, Israel, *Harmless Drudges: Wizards of Language—Ancient, Medieval and Modern*. Bronxville: Barnhardt, 1979.

Simpson, John, and Weiner, Edmund, *The Oxford English Dictionary*, 2nd edn. Oxford: Oxford University Press, 1989. Prefatory material in vol. i: 'The History of the Oxford English Dictionary'.

Sutcliffe, Peter, *The Oxford University Press: An Informal History*. Oxford: Oxford University Press, 1978.

Trench, Richard Chenevix, *A Select Glossary of Words Used Formerly in Senses Different from their Present*. London: Kegan, Paul, Trench, 1887.

Weiner, E. S. C., 'The Federation of English', in C. Ricks and L. Michaels (eds.), *The State of the Language*. London: Faber & Faber, 1990.

Wells, John, *Rude Words: A Discursive History of the London Library*. London: Macmillan, 1991.

Willinsky, John, *Empire of Words: The Reign of the OED*. Princeton, NJ: Princeton University Press, 1994.

Winchester, Simon, *The Professor and the Madman*. New York: HarperCollins, 1998. Also published as *The Surgeon of Crowthorne*. London: Viking, 1998.

The Oxford English Dictionary. Oxford, 1933 and 1989. With Supplements.

The Dictionary of National Biography. Oxford, 1917–

The Periodical

Notes and Queries

Index

Sub-entries are in chronological order. Italic numbers denote references to illustrations. JM = James Murray.

254

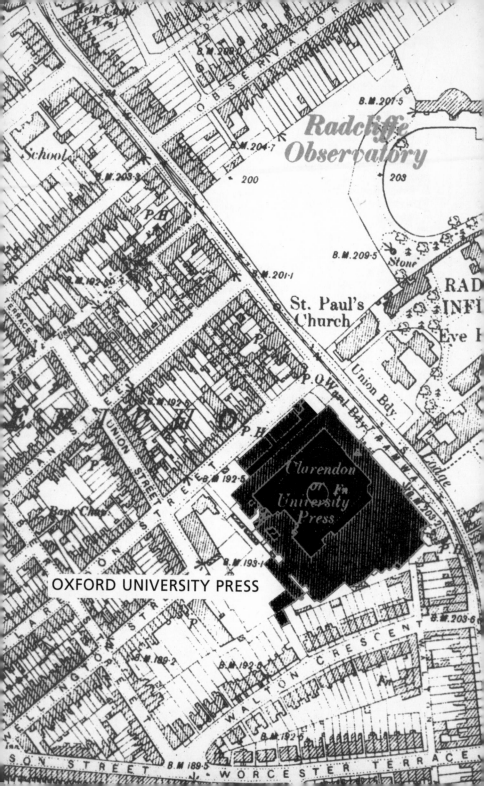